Science Topics for Infants

Redvers Brandling

SIMON & SCHUSTER
EDUCATION

Acknowledgements

I am, as always, grateful to the staff and children of Dewhurst St Mary School, Cheshunt.

I am grateful to Denise Reed, Education Liaison Officer, Pedigree Petfoods, for her help and encouragement in so much work to do with animals, pets and science. The 'problem page' in 'Living Things – Animals and Birds' is adapted from material which I wrote for *Pets in the Eighties* published by Pedigree Petfoods. In 'Festive Occasions' I have also adapted and enlarged upon material which first appeared in *Festive Occasions in the Primary School*.

Much of the material in this book has been used, re-used and re-adapted in topic work with children. If original sources of ideas have been used in a way which has unwittingly caused the infringement of copyright, the author apologises and will correct the omission in future editions, if notified.

Text © Redvers Brandling 1992
Design and artwork © Simon and Schuster Education 1992

All rights reserved

First published in 1992 in Great Britian by
Simon & Schuster Education
Campus 400, Maylands Avenue
Hemel Hempstead, Herts HP2 7EZ

A catalogue record for this book is available from the British Library

ISBN 0 7501 0190 3

Typeset in 10/12pt Times
by VAP Publishing Services, Langford Lane, Kidlington
Printed in Great Britain by Bell & Bain Ltd., Glasgow

Introduction

The aim of this book is to provide infant teachers who are not science specialists with as many ideas and suggestions for science work as possible. All the ideas are linked very carefully to the Attainment Targets relevant to National Curriculum infant assessment.

A recent DES booklet (*National Curriculum Assessment – Speeches on Education*) stressed the need for material which is not 'frighteningly novel but a confirmation and distillation of best practice'. This has been a yardstick in the selection of work for this book. Another DES comment is also relevant: 'our proposals will only be effective if the traditional freedom which teachers have enjoyed to plan and organise the curriculum can be protected.' (National Curriculum – Science). This is unarguable and this book is intended as a further resource which can be adapted and used throughout the infant age group.

Some practical points

This book contains a wide variety of activities appropriate for different levels of ability. Whether the teacher decides to try some of the more difficult activities will depend both on the age and ability of the children, and on the number of adults available for supervision. Similarly, when taking children out of school, LEA rules on the ratio of adults to children should always be followed.

Recording of activities and experiments may either be done by the children themselves, or by the teacher, after discussion with the children.

The RSPCA provides rules which should be followed when animals/pets are kept or brought in to school.

1 Provide adequate food and water.
2 Ensure there is no thermal or physical discomfort.
3 Ensure animals are free from illness or injury.
4 Avoid any treatment or activity which could cause the animal fear or distress.
5 Do not suppress normal behaviour in animals.

'Animals need time, care and understanding. Try and see it their way.' (RSPCA)

Organisation of the book

Contents
The *Contents chart* on pages vi–vii lists topic titles, page numbers, coverage of main and subsidiary ATs, and indicates when each topic may best be done in the school year. A further section looks at coverage of AT1.

Planning and record keeping
The *Individual Record Sheet* on page viii records the individual child's progress. The sheet can be filled in as and when a child completes the various components in the topics. This could be entered by topic number and component letter, ie 16c, 14a, 20a, etc. 'Revisiting' could be noted by adding a tick to the original entry, ie 16c ✓ , 14a ✓✓ etc. Assessing the work done in these topics requires current record keeping on both this sheet and the *Record of a Topic* sheet.

The *Record of a Topic* on page x shows more broadly what has been accomplished at class or group level. It also notes details of 'How children's work was recorded'. The *Record of a Topic* could be used for an appraisal by the teacher of how well the topic succeeded. It could also be used in whole-school discussion, in establishing a 'bank' of suitable topics and a source of information for teachers who wish to re-visit areas that have been covered.

The *Anatomy of a Topic* on page ix is intended as an aid to planning and preparation.

Finally, there is a list of *Popular Infant Topics* (page xii) which shows how the science work described here can be linked with other aspects of infant school work.

The topics
There are 20 topics in the book. They are organised as follows:

- Anatomy of a topic – a short introduction which highlights special features of the work, suggests timescale and lists equipment, resources and links with other topics.
- 'Components' containing ideas and detailed instructions for practical work and experiments. Each component includes a note on NC coverage.
- A section on cross-curricular links which shows how work in this topic connects with other subject areas.

18 of the topics are directly related to specific issues: two are more general. Topic 19: *Special Occasions* gives a spread of science-based material which covers Diwali, Easter and May 1st – one topic for each school term. The last topic in the book, 20 *Calling Earth*, provides material which can be referred to throughout the year.

At the end of the book is a list of Useful Addresses, which provides information about the suppliers, publishers etc mentioned in the Resources sections.

Topics related to Attainment Target 1

All the topics in this book have AT1 as one of their main areas of coverage. This could be summarised as requiring:

- observing at first hand
- communicating observations
- asking relevant questions
- identifying differences
- measuring
- listing observations
- interpreting findings
- recording in various ways
- formulating hypotheses
- identifying change
- using instruments

These aspects form the basic ingredients of every topic; the work throughout is constantly related to them, and interwoven between the various components.

With their limited experience, infants are likely to arrive at any sort of hypothesis only after discussion and observation. Hypothesising could then feature before practical work in the context of prediction, and after practical work in connection with conclusions reached.

The teacher on the spot is, of course, the best judge of how information and results may be recorded. This judgement will be based on ability of the children, structure of the class, materials available, variation within groups, and the need to present a balanced selection of recording methods (spoken, written, drawn, acted, individual, group etc). Many suggestions are included but these can be adapted and adjusted as appropriate.

Contents

(This chart shows main and subsidiary coverage of ATs and time of school year

		Page	Attainment Target Coverage
1	Sound and music	1	1, 4 (1c, 3d)
2	Light, colour and shade	8	1, 2 (1a), 3 (2a, 2b), 4 (1c, 2d,
3	Energy	17	1, 2 (1a), 3 (1a), 4 (1b, 2c, 3c)
4	Electricity and magnetism	24	1, 4 (1a, 2a, 2d, 3a)
5	Ourselves	32	1, 2 (1a, 1b, 2b, 3a, 3b)
6	Living things – Animals and birds	42	1, 2 (1b, 2a, 2b, 2c, 3a, 3b)
7	Living things – Plants	50	1, 2 (1a, 1b, 2a, 2b, 2c, 3c)
8	Cold	56	1, 3 (2a, 2b, 3a), 4 (1d, 2b, 2e,
9	Heat	65	1, 2 (3a), 3 (1a, 2b, 3a), 4 (2b)
10	Buildings	73	1, 3 (1a, 2a, 3a, 3b), 4 (2d)
11	Sending messages	81	1, 3 (3a), 4 (1a, 1c, 3a, 3d)
12	Looking after our environment	87	1, 2 (2d, 3b), 3 (3c), 4 (1c)
13	Water	95	1, 2 (2a, 2b, 2c, 3a, 3b), 3 (1a,
14	Hygiene and health	105	1, 2 (1a, 2a, 3a)
15	Now and then	117	1, 2 (1a, 1b, 2a, 2b, 2d)
16	Moving	123	1, 2 (1b, 2c), 3 (1a, 2a), 4 (1b,
17	More about materials	134	1, 3 (1a, 2a, 2b, 3a, 3b, 3c)
18	Home and school	143	1, 2 (2a, 2b, 2c, 2d), 3 (1a, 2a,
19	Festive occasions	155	1, 2 (1a, 1b, 2a, 2c, 2d, 3b),
20	Calling Earth	170	1, 3 (2a, 3c), 4 (1d, 2b, 2d, 2e,

appropriate for the topic.)

	Time of school year
	ANY TIME
3d)	FIRST HALF AUTUMN TERM
	ANY
	AUTUMN TERM PRIOR TO AND INCLUDING CHRISTMAS
	BEGINNING OF AUTUMN TERM OR END OF SUMMER TERM
	SUMMER TERM
	EARLY AUTUMN OR VERY EARLY SUMMER TERM
3b, 3e)	SPRING TERM
	SUMMER TERM
	ANY
	ANY
	ANY BUT THERE IS A NEED FOR MUCH OUTSIDE WORK
2a)	ANY
	ANY
	ANY
2c, 3c)	ANY
	ANY
b, 3a, b), 4 (1c, 3d)	SUMMER TERM
3 (1a, 2a, b, 3a, b), 4 (2d, 3c, 3d)	DIWALI, EASTER, MAY 1ST
3c, 3e)	THROUGHOUT THE SCHOOL YEAR

Individual Assessment Record Sheet Name:

	LEVEL 1		LEVEL 2				LEVEL 3		
AT2	a	b	a	b	c	d	a	b	c

	LEVEL 1	LEVEL 2		LEVEL 3		
AT3	a	a	b	a	b	c

	LEVEL 1				LEVEL 2					LEVEL 3				
AT4	a	b	c	d	a	b	c	d	e	a	b	c	d	e

AT1 Scientific Investigation.   Observing
Level 1a
Questioning, relating, concluding
Level 2a   2b   2c
Suggesting, communicating, predicting, measuring, testing, identifying change
Level 3a   3b   3c   3d
Teacher's Comments:

© Redvers Brandling/Simon & Schuster Ltd 1992

Anatomy of a topic

1 What teaching planning requirements are there to achieve objectives?

2 Is the equipment adequate? Has the resources section been checked/followed up?

3 Have visitors, or outside visits, been arranged where required?

4 What gain is sought in increased knowledge, understanding, and awareness of child thinking?

7 Could the topic be recommended to other teachers? Has it been a success? Could it fit into a 'whole school' plan?

6 Have the recording processes been varied enough? Were they successful in noting progress? Is there scope for amending/improving for future use?

5 Are the objectives being realised? ATs covered?

(N.B. The above is an on-going document. When the topic has been completed a retrospective record would also be useful for further whole-school planning. A specimen record sheet is shown on the next page.)

Record of a topic

Resources used
Those recommended in the equipment and resources section were easy to obtain.

Topic title
Festive occasions (Diwali).

Teacher expertise used
No other teacher was required. Some parental help was very useful in cutting out masks and making lamps. Hindu parents were invited in to tell traditional Diwali stories.

Subject ATs and levels
Attainment Targets covered were 1, 2 (L2a) 3 (Ls 2b, 3a, 3c, 3d) 4 (L2d)

Time required
A fairly intensive two weeks – not counting the teacher's preparation time.

Working arrangements (individual, groups, whole class)
In the main the work was done in groups; individual results stemmed from work on masks. Whole class activity was mainly involved with pre-group work, discussion and consideration of each group's work.

How children's achievements recorded
There was written recording of some activities (bridges/cleanliness); decorated masks were a 'physical record' of work done. Much recording was done by talking about the tasks completed and conclusions drawn from these.

Further comments of teacher who instigated topic
The amount of science work derived from this topic was not surprising once the possibilities had been carefully examined. The same components could be done again with different methods of recording, eg drama work following the making of masks.

Science curriculum guide

	Autumn	**Spring**	**Summer**
Reception:	Ourselves Sound and music	Cold Moving	Home and school Heat
Year 1	Light, colour, shade More about materials	Now and then Buildings	Water Living things (Animals)
Year 2	Living things (Plants) Electricity and magnetism	Hygiene and health Sending messages	Energy Spoiling our environment

Festive occasions: Autumn (Diwali)
 Spring (Easter)
 Summer (May 1st)
Calling earth: components adapted/integrated throughout the year as needed.

I do not think any book can adequately prescribe a three year KS1 Science Curriculum for a school. Obstacles to this are changing staff and staff expertise, local knowledge and circumstances, the need to be flexible, unexpected opportunities for topicality which arise, class structuring.

Having said this, it is possible to suggest a framework which can offer quite comprehensive coverage of a science curriculum. The pattern above is based on the following essentials:

a The need to offer varied topics throughout the year.
b The awareness that, as the children develop, they should have opportunities to 're-visit' areas previously covered.
c The 'placing' of topics which require special circumstances – outside work, visits which require detailed preparation, specific visitors etc.
d The long-term location of topics so that there is adequate time for material and equipment to be collected from whatever source.
e The availability of substantial material, which is not pinned down to a specific time or age group, and which can be adapted and integrated where and when necessary.

Popular infant topics

A list of popular infant topics to which work in this book can be related.

Topic title	Suggested helpful material references
Animals	1f, 6a/b/c, 8a, 12a, 13d, 15a/d, 16e
Beginnings	5a/e, 6e, 12e, 14a, 15b, 19 (Easter)
Caring for others	6a, 8a, 12a/b/c/d/e, 14e, 18g
Christmas	4e, 8a, 16b
Easter	19 (complete section on this topic)
Families	4a/e, 5b/e, 11c, 12a, 13b, 15a/b
Food	2b, 5d, 7a/b, 9a, 12c, 14e, 17c, 19c (Easter)
Friends	2a, 3a, 4e, 5b, 8a, 15a, 16a
Growth	1c, 3a, 6b, 7a/b, 8b, 13b, 14a/b/c/d, 15b
Holidays	9b, 12a, 13d, 19 (May 1st)
Homes	2a, 4a, 6c, 7d, 10a/b, 12a, 13d, 17/a/b, 18a/b/c/d/e/f/g/h
Journeys	1b, 3d, 6c, 7c, 9c, 11b, 12a, 13a, 15d, 16c/d, 18f
Joy	3e, 4e, 7c, 12e, 19 (Easter)
Living together	4a, 6a, 9b, 12a/b/c/d, 14a, 18g
Machines	1f/g, 2d, 3e, 4a/b, 9a, 10b, 11a/b/c/d/e, 16c/f, 18e
Names	2d, 5d, 6a, 7a/c, 10a
Neighbours	12a/b/d, 18g/h
Rules	2b, 3e, 4a, 4b, 10d, 14a/e
Seasons:	
Spring	7a/c, 12a/b/c/d/e, 19a/b/c/d (Easter), 19a/b/c/d (May 1st), 20a
Summer	7c, 9a/b/c/d, 12a/b/c/d/e, 13d, 20a
Autumn	7a, 12a/b/c/d/e, 20a
Winter	8a/b/c, 12a/b/c/d/e, 20a
Time	8a, 9a, 11a, 15b/c/d, 19 (Easter), 20a/b/c
Those who help us	6a, 10d, 11a, 11b, 14e, 16c/d, 18g
Treasure	4e, 7c, 12e, 16b, 18a/b/c/d

1 Sound and Music

a) **Starting with sound**
b) **Travelling sound**
c) **Increasing and decreasing sound**
d) **Bouncing back**
e) **Making musical sounds**
f) **Making sounds (experimental and simulated)**
g) **Listening in**

Anatomy of a topic

Sound and music is one of the most exciting topics to do with young children. The components which follow encourage children to listen, to question, to experiment with sounds and to record their findings and impressions. Although the components build on each other, there is no 'set' order: the teacher can select and adapt as necessary. A suggested duration is about four weeks.

By the time the topic is completed, the children should be aware (at an appropriate level for infants) that:

- sounds are detected by our ears
- vibrations result in sounds
- energy is needed to produce sound
- sounds travel better through some things than others
- pitch varies
- sounds can be increased and decreased
- sounds can be communicated in a number of ways
- sounds can be pleasant or unpleasant.

'Noise pollution' is a feature of Topic 12: *Looking after our environment*.

Equipment

elastic bands	string	dried peas, beans
paper	sellotape	record player
length of wood	bottles	records/tapes
model cars	radio	tuning fork
cylinders of card	whistle	clock
yoghurt pots	horn	nail/hammer
tape recorder	tin lids (to spin)	material

bicycle bell   length of hose   water
rulers   two empty cans   computer
card   cotton wool   telephone

a variety of musical instruments and photographs of old instruments.

Resources
- Harbutt's Educational Services produce 'Case Study' boxes related to the National Science Curriculum. The *'Sound'* case study contains a great deal of useful equipment.
- A computer software package called *Rhythm and Pitch* (BBC 40/80 track disc) is available from Rickitt Educational Media.
- A video called *How the telephone works* is available on free loan from British Telecom Education Service.

Pattern of a topic

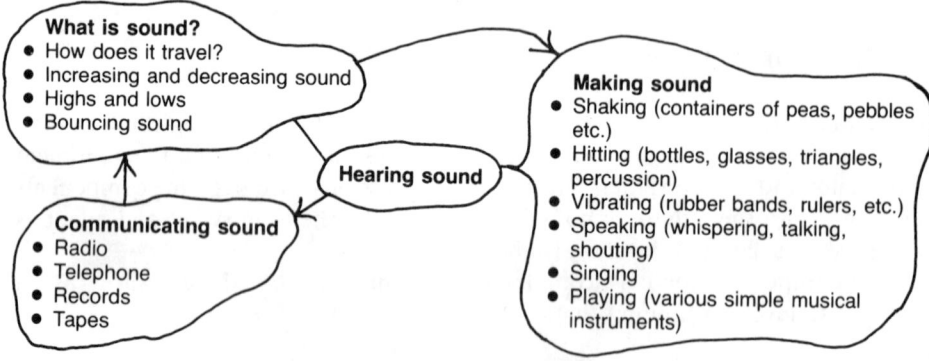

a) Starting with sound

Begin with some basic introductory discussion, guided by the teacher: *What parts of the body do we hear with? What sounds do we hear every day? Do we hear some at different times of day? Are some sounds louder than others? What sounds do we enjoy hearing? What sounds are frightening/warning/telling us something/pleasing/exciting?*

This leads on to the first experiment in making sounds, based on 'vibration'.

Vibrations
Get the children to hold elastic bands between their teeth, pulling and twanging them as they do so. As they feel the vibration they could describe what they feel, see and hear. Encourage the children to lengthen and shorten the bands and note the different sounds this produces.

Follow this with more 'vibrating' experiments: a ruler held on a desk top and 'plucked'; spinning a round tray or tin lid on a hard surface (then on a soft surface to note the difference); hitting and 'sounding' a tuning fork.

Musical paper
Give out sheets of thin but stiff paper. Show the children how to hold the paper between thumb and forefinger, so that the top sheet covers the top lip and the lower sheet the bottom lip. Then blow – and the papers will vibrate with a loud noise. (It's a good idea for the teacher to practise this in advance!)

NC coverage
AT4 Level 1c: *know about the simple properties of sound and light*

b) Travelling sound

The process of sending sound from one place to another is called 'transmission'. Before practical work on this component begins, there could again be discussion around questions such as: *How does sound travel? Does it travel through some things better than others? Does it travel at the same speed all the time?*

Hose-pipe speaking tube
Get a length of clean hose-pipe, about 15 m long. Position a child at each end of the pipe – one speaking into it, the other holding it to their ear. The sound travels clearly through the enclosed air in the pipe. Discuss how and why this happens. Another interesting theme might be 'speaking tubes' in past times.

Hear the clock
Place a clock (the sort that ticks!) on a bare table. Get the children to listen to it in a variety of ways, eg at the other side of the room; with an ear pressed to the opposite end of the table. *What happens if we place the clock on a piece of wood overlapping the table and 'listen' to the other end of the wood?* Discuss their findings with the children.

Tin-can telephone
Prepare two clean, empty tins and a 15 m length of string. Make a 'telephone' as shown:

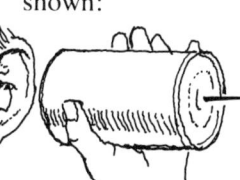

Invite volunteers to phone each other. Make sure the string is taut and not touching anything.
When one tin is spoken into, the tight string carries the vibrations from it and makes the other tin vibrate. This, in turn, makes the ear drum of the listener vibrate. Make sure all the children have a turn and get them to comment on what they heard and felt.

I hear thunder!
Make the most of a thunderstorm for some science work. Get the children to time – by counting aloud – the gap between when they see a flash of lightning and when

they hear the sound of thunder. This gives an idea of how far away the storm is (roughly, 5 seconds = 1 mile). It can also be a starting point for discussion about how sound travels.

NC coverage
AT4 Level 1c: *know about the simple properties of sound and light*

c) Increasing and decreasing sound

Write two words on the board/a large sheet of paper, as follows:

LOUDER softer

What do these words mean? Think of some loud sounds. Think of some soft sounds. How can we make sounds louder or softer?

Getting louder
Make a simple 'megaphone' as follows:

a Cut out a circle of paper.
b Cut across the radius of the circle.
c Fold the paper into a cone-shape and sellotape into place. Invite the children to experiment with the 'megaphone', comparing normal speech and projected speech, seeing how far their voices will carry with and without the device, etc.

A further activity might be to strike a tuning fork, then place it on to a hollow box, noting how this increases the volume of sound.

Getting softer
Provide as wide a range as possible of sound-making items. Draw up a chart like this and ask the children to work in groups to fill it in:

Sounds I can hear	How far away is it?	How clearly can I hear it?	What is it like (eg ticking/ banging/ringing)
1 Clock 2 3 4	5 m	very	ticking

Having experimented with sounds/distances, the children can go on to try out various ways of diminishing/blocking their hearing of the sound by devising different 'ear muffs', eg hands over ears, paper, cloth, manufactured ear muffs, headphones from a personal stereo. . . Which is the most effective method? Is it the same for all the sounds, or does it vary for different sounds?

An alternative might be to try different ways of muffling the sound source itself.
From this, the teacher could go on to talk about high, low, constant and intermittent sounds.

NC coverage
AT4 Level 1c: *know about the simple properties of sound and light*

d) Bouncing back

Echoes fascinate children of all ages. Begin by discussing children's own experiences of echoes. *Where have you heard an echo?* (eg in an empty church or hall, in a valley, under a railway bridge). *Where do you think the echo comes from?*

This simple experiment shows that vibrations 'bounce off' objects. Put a clock on a deadened surface on a desk. (The 'deadening' material could be fabric or other suitable padding.) Place two hollow rolls of card adjacent to the clock, as follows:

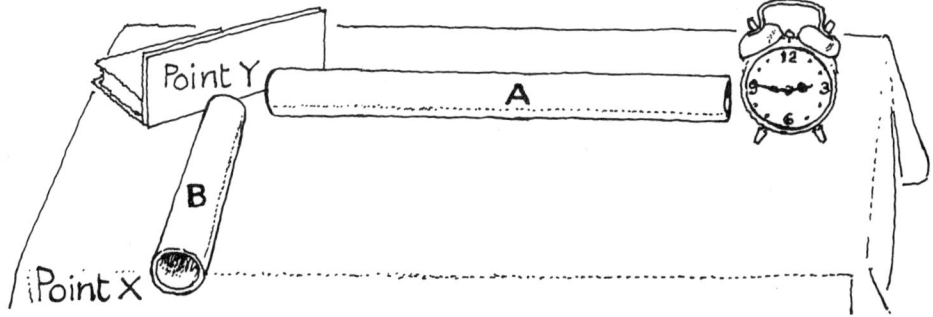

Invite the children to take turns to listen at Point X. They should be able to hear the clock faintly. Now place a piece of card at Point Y and repeat the experiment. This time the tick will seem much louder. This is because the vibrations going through tube A bounce off the card and travel up tube B.

NC coverage
AT4 Level 3d: *know that light and sound can be reflected*

e) Making musical sounds

Sorting sounds
Provide as many different musical instruments as you can. Encourage children to experiment with making different sounds with the instruments. Then help them sort the instruments according to the different sounds/ways of making sounds, eg

Things we hit	*Things we pluck*	*Things we blow*	*Things we shake*
drum	guitar	recorder	tambourine
glockenspiel	banjo	trumpet	maracas

6 *Science Topics for Infants*

chime bars   zither   flute   shaker pole
claves
triangles
cymbals

Alternative groupings could be high and low, loud and soft... This exercise is very good for developing descriptive vocabulary.

Home-made instruments
Children also enjoy making and using their own 'musical instruments', especially if they can produce a recognisable tune from them.

An effective tuned instrument can be made easily from bottles and water. Prepare the following arrangement:

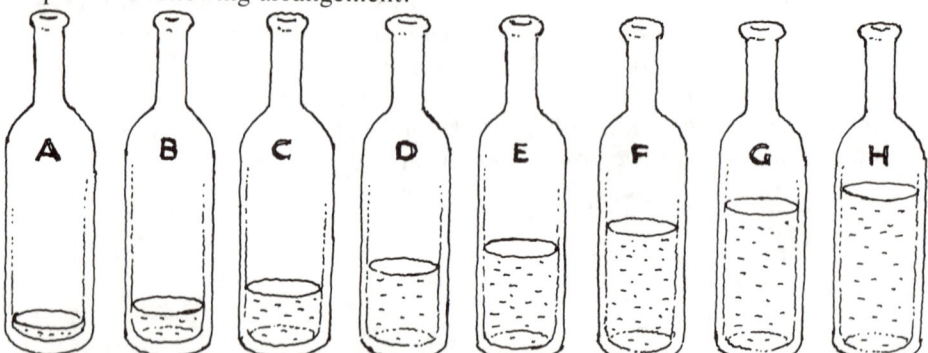

All the bottles should be identical in size and shape. They should be labelled as shown and filled with the shown amounts of water. Before involving the children, perfect the 'tuning' by playing the following:

        FF   EE   D   C   B   C   D
        EE   FF   GG   H

Everyone will recognise the tune!

NC coverage
AT4 Level 1c: *know about the simple properties of sound and light*

f) Making sounds (experimental and simulated)

Encourage the children to experiment with a variety of 'instruments', eg plucking elastic bands stretched over open-topped containers, tapping drums covered with small objects...

An exciting area to explore is how our voices, and collections of everyday objects, can be used to simulate other sounds. A dramatic demonstration of, for example, 'galloping horses' produced by clashing two empty yoghurt pots, opens the way to lots of imaginative work. Interesting sounds to simulate include: falling rain, footsteps, running feet, creaking doors, fire (crumpling paper produces a highly realistic effect), hammering nails, police sirens and so on.

Sound and Music 7

g) Listening in

Collect some devices which transmit sound, eg radios, record players, tape recorders etc. Encourage the children to manipulate the devices (switching on, turning off, increasing volume, tuning etc). They could also listen to a telephone in the school office (with adult supervision). Discuss what happens.

NC coverage
AT4 Level 1c: *know about the simple properties of sound and light*
　　　Level 3d: *know that light and sound can be reflected*

Cross-curricular links

Work on this topic offers an ideal opportunity to develop children's appreciation of **music**. Short extracts from evocative pieces could be introduced throughout the topic. Most teachers will have their own favourites, but the following have proved successful: passages from *Carnival of the Animals* by Saint-Saens; the 'can-can' from Offenbach's *Tales of Hoffman; Flight of the Bumble-bee* by Rimsky-Korsakov; *The Dam Busters' March* by Eric Coates and *Chattanooga Choo-Choo* by Glenn Miller.

　　The musical interpretation of a broom in Dukas' *The Sorcerer's Apprentice* and of a Viennese Clock in Kodaly's *Hary Janos* offer tremendous potential for work combining **music** and **drama/mime**. The stories behind the music can be found in *The Sorcerer's Apprentice and Other Stories* by John Hosier, published by Oxford University Press.

　　Related work in **English** might focus on words that can be associated with sound: sad, happy, slow, fast, exciting, loud, soft etc. Children could explore expressions/ tone of voice, eg the voices used to ask a favour, to give an order, to shout a warning, to whisper secrets. . . It is interesting to compare phrases from different languages – children are intrigued to hear what a familiar phrase like 'Merry Christmas' can sound like in another tongue. Here are some versions: *Vesele Vanoch* (Czechoslovakian); *Gelukkig Kerstfeest* (Dutch); *Joyeux Noel* (French); *Frohliche Weinachten* (German); *Buone Feste Natalizie* (Italian); *Glad Jul* (Swedish). Teacher and children will probably be able to contribute many more.

　　Discussion of 'alarm' sounds – fire bell, whistle, bicycle bell, car horn, fog horn etc might lead to simple **technology**, with investigations into how they work.

　　Photographs of old-fashioned instruments (with perhaps some recordings of the sounds they made) offer links with **history**.

　　Geography can be introduced through the study of ethnic music and instruments – with recordings and even perhaps some live performance.

　　Sounds linked with **RE** could include music (hymns, sung prayers, spirituals etc), bells, the organ etc.

　　PE could include movement to music/rhythm and different sounds.

2 Light, Colour and Shade

a) Start with a colour
b) Working with colours
c) We need light
d) Mirror work
e) Rounding up

Anatomy of a topic

Work in this section includes activities in the playground, and further afield (if this is necessary to see a good showing of autumn colour). The school hall is also required, and parental help would be an asset, particularly if the cooking aspect is developed.

The ideal location in the school year would be the first half of the Autumn Term. The sun is lower in the sky by this time, but is still good for shadow work, and this season offers very rich colours.

For more work on the sun and shadows see Topic 20 *Calling Earth*. There is an experiment on making stained-glass windows in Topic 19 *Festive Occasions: Easter*.

Equipment

Personal and classroom items which are coloured	paint brushes	sellotape
Coloured card, paints, pencils, materials, flowers, sweets...	variety of mirrors	kettle
	strong artificial lights/lamps	make-up mirror
	white sheet	strip of wood
	curtaining	string
water	shiny and dull materials	hessian
water dish	bottle for 'bending' light	glue

Resources
- The Macdonald/Schools Council publication *Science 5/13 – Coloured Things – Stages 1 and 2* is a useful book to have on hand for this topic.
- Harbutt's Educational Services produce a 'Case Study' (box of equipment to aid 'developing a knowledge and understanding of the effects of colour mixing and separation', teacher's notes and activity sheets.)
- Two photo-packs from Philip Green Educational Ltd are A13 *Colours* (which contains poems as well as twelve A4 photographs) and P50 *Colours 2* (which contains twelve more A4 photographs).

Light, Colour and Shade 9

Pattern of a topic

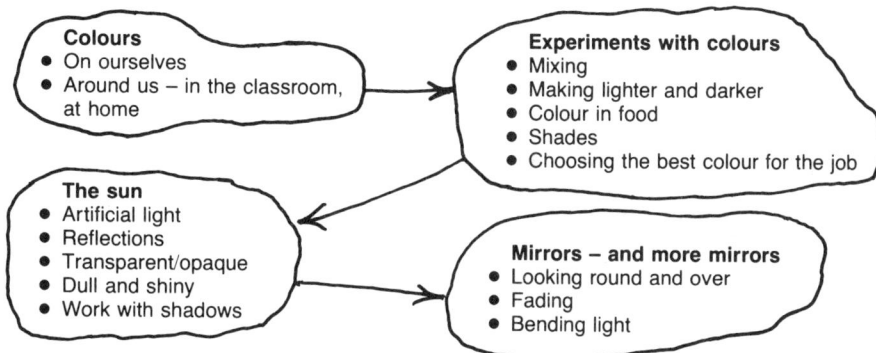

a) Start with a colour

Begin with some direct observation. The simple question, *What colours can we see now?* could start things off.

Looking at each other and each other's possessions, the children could note the colour of eyes, hair, teeth, clothes, shoes, hair ribbons, lunch boxes etc. Extend this to the classroom and talk about the colours of doors, walls, chairs, books, pictures, music trolley, paint corner and so on. *What colours can we see outside the window?*

Moving on to remembered observation, invite the children to tell of the colours in their bedrooms – door, duvet, wallpaper, carpet, favourite toys. Extend this to other home features – front door, window frames, front gate, car etc.

This questioning, discussing and observation offers plenty of scope for the children to record and display some of their findings. Some ideas are:

1 A *classroom colour chart*, like this:

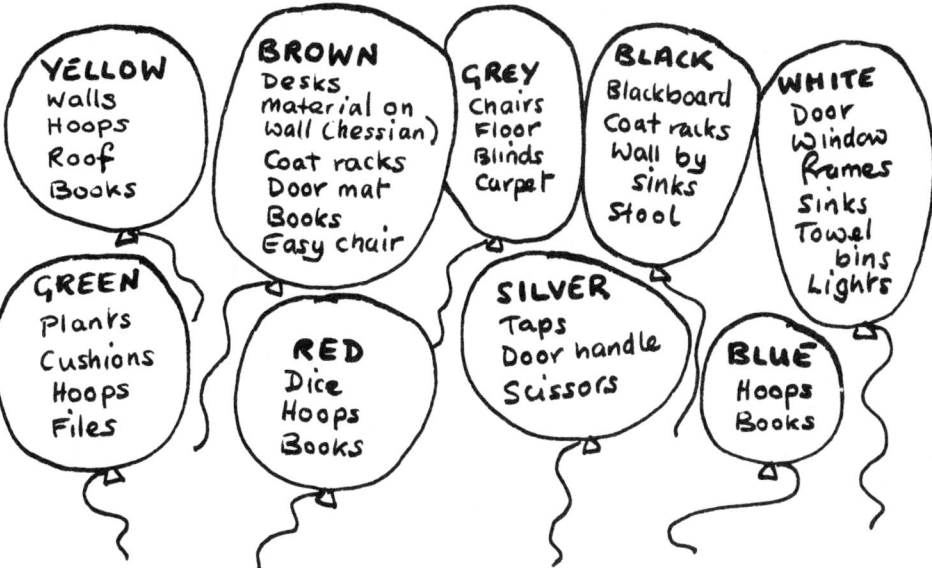

10 *Science Topics for Infants*

2 The same information could then be used for a *simple bar chart*

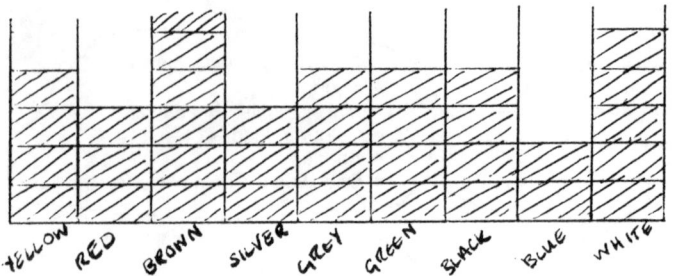

3 If the school has a uniform, what colour(s) is it? If not the children could survey their T shirts, blouses, pullovers etc and record their findings in a *picture chart*, eg

RED 👕 👕 👕 👕

BLUE 👕 👕

GREEN

GREY

MIXED

4 A group of children might enjoy making a **colour profile** of the teacher – another useful exercise in observing and recording. The end product might look something like this:

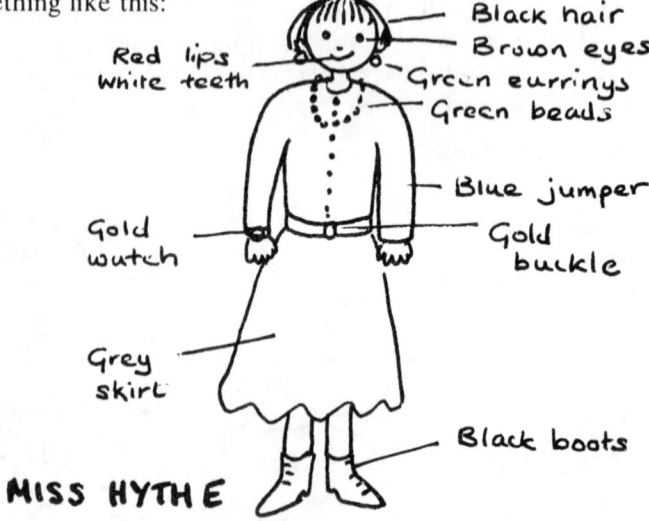

5 Children could gather and display collections of items: different items in the same colour range; similar items in a wide spectrum of colours, eg paper, crayons, flowers, sweets (Smarties are ideal!).
6 Groups could create displays focusing on some imaginative colour combinations: happy/sad colours; hot/cold; friendly/hostile; spring/summer/autumn/winter; indoor/outdoor.

NC coverage
AT2 Level 1a: *be able to name the external parts of the human body*
AT3 Level 2a: *be able to group materials according to observable features*
AT4 Level 1c: *know about simple properties of sound and light*

b) Working with colours

Children could build on their work for *Start with a colour* by testing and experimenting with colours.

Making colours

Encourage children to experiment with water colours, paper and brushes. Raise questions like: *How do we make the colours darker? How do we make them lighter? What does 'a different shade of green' mean? Can we make different shades of green? What do we need to use? What happens when we mix different colours?*

The results of this problem solving could be a display of papers on which the children have painted, which represent deep colours, diluted colours, 'shading', and colours derived from mixing. The children could then take turns to explain how the results were achieved.

Using colours

The next combination of 'question – problem – experiment – solution' could centre round the effective use of colours. *Which colour is best for a simple block diagram in the classroom? Which is best to use for a written message to be held up in the hall in assembly? Which is best to mark out the playground? Which is the best colour for someone to wear so that they can easily be seen on the other side of the school field?*

Experimenting to find answers to these questions helps the children appreciate the usefulness of colours in many different situations, eg red for danger, yellow for visibility, black and white for ease of reading. They could make simple posters to show their findings.

Another interesting use of colour is for camouflage, especially by animals and insects.

Colouring foods

Start off with more questions: *Why are sweets coloured? Why is jelly different colours? Why do cakes have coloured icing? Can we colour foods?*

Various tests could take place with jars of hot and cold water and different food colourings. *What happens to the colouring when it is put in hot/cold water? Can we change the colour of icing sugar with colourings?*

Smarties are a popular taste test! *Does a brown Smartie taste different from an orange one? Or a blue one?* In pairs, children could take turns to close their eyes and taste a Smartie, then guess its colour.

Children could experiment with subtle ranges of colour by diluting orange squash to different strengths.

12 *Science Topics for Infants*

NC coverage
AT3 Level 2a: *be able to group materials according to observable features*
    Level 2b: *know that heating and cooling everyday materials can cause them to melt or solidify or change permanently*
AT4 Level 1c: *know about the simple properties of sound and light*

c) We need light

Discuss with the children the idea that to see colours we need light, either from the sun or from an artificial source.

Colours of the rainbow
(NB this experiment only works if the sun is shining!)
  Put a flat dish with water in it beside a window through which the sun is shining. At the end of the dish place a small mirror, to catch the rays of the sun. Hold a piece of paper above the mirror so that it catches the reflection of the sun's rays through the water and the mirror. The colours of the rainbow will appear on the paper.

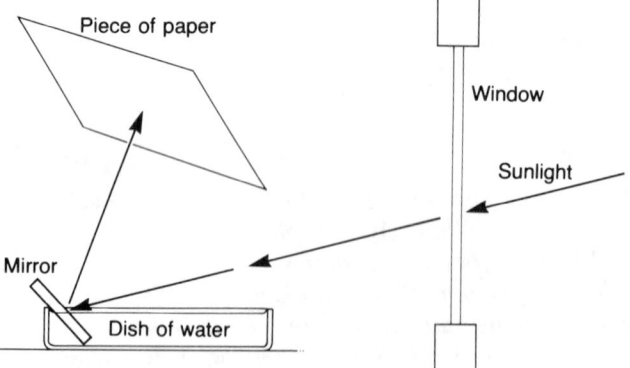

Shadow play
An artificial light source gives the best results here. The basic set-up is:

light source ⟶ opaque object ⟶ shadow

Encourage the children to experiment with this. Here are some ideas:

a *How does changing the angle of light affect the shape and size of the shadow? When is the shadow longest/smallest? At which point is the shadow sharpest?*
b *Whose silhouette?* Can children recognise each other's silhouette 'portraits'?
c Hand puppets – interesting and amusing 'animated' figures can be created simply by using the hands to form shadow shapes, eg a bird in flight, a duck's head...
d Puppet plays – simple card shapes can be mounted on sticks to create characters for a shadow puppet drama.

The same set-up could be used to investigate differences between opaque and transparent materials.

Light, Colour and Shade 13

Shiny surfaces
Taking this activity of light shining on shapes a step further could provoke more questions: *What happens when the sun shines on the school playground after rain? What happens when the sun shines through the hall windows onto the polished floor? What other things 'shine' when the sun is on them?*

The children could experiment with a wide variety of things here, working both inside and outdoors. They could list the things which shine and those which don't. They could find ways of stopping things shining. Encourage them to observe reflections – of light, of the sky, of themselves!

NC coverage
AT4 Level 1c: *know about the simple properties of sound and light*
      Level 2d: *know that light passes through some materials and that when it does not shadows may be formed*
      Level 3d: *know that light and sound can be reflected*

d) Mirror work

Experiments showing that shiny surfaces offer reflections lead naturally on to work with mirrors.

1 *What happens when you put two mirrors close together?*
Position the mirrors like this:

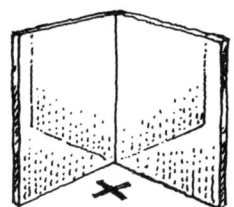

Discuss with the children what they can see. Now place an object at point X. What happens?

2 *How can we use two mirrors to see the back of our heads?*
Allow the children time to experiment with placing the mirrors. The answer is as follows:

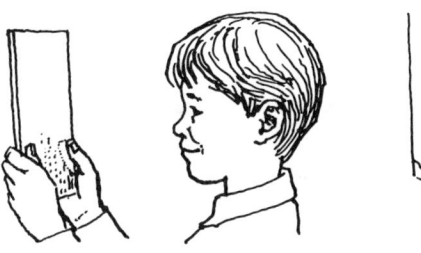

14 *Science Topics for Infants*

3 *How can mirrors help you see round a corner, or over the top of something?*
The children could experiment with hand mirrors. After this, the teacher could construct a more substantial periscope, as follows:

a Mark off a long sheet of stiff card in four sections of equal width, running lengthways:

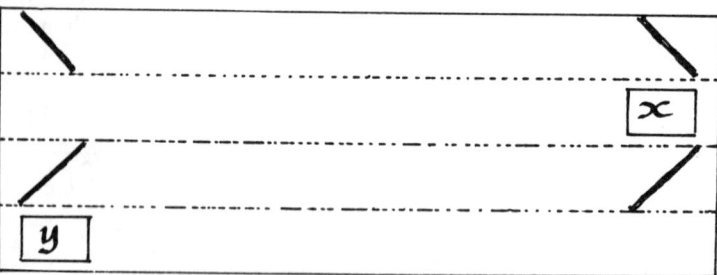

b Score the lines and fold the card.
c Cut out viewing holes at X and Y, and make slots at A and B to hold a mirror at 45°.
d Fold the card into a square tube and sellotape down the join. Insert two small mirrors in the slots so that they face out through the viewing holes.
e Invite the children to experiment with the periscope, eg to help them look out of a high-up window.

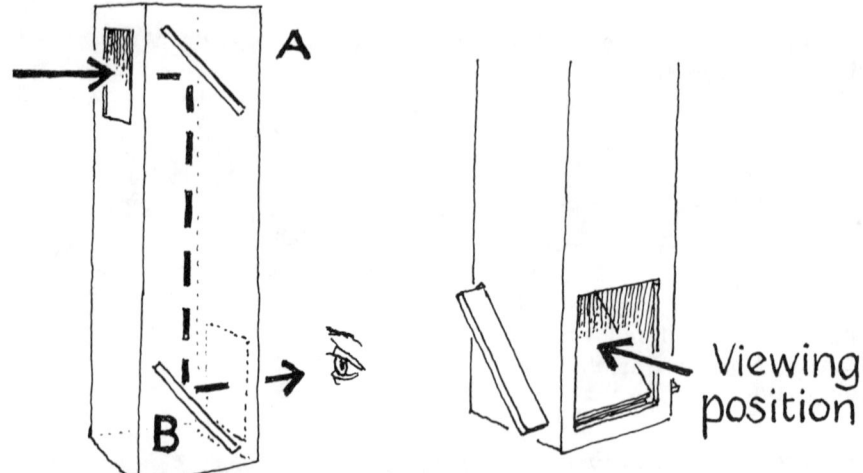

4 *How can we solve problems with mirrors?*
Give the children cards with their names printed clearly on them. *What happens if you stand in front of a mirror?* ie

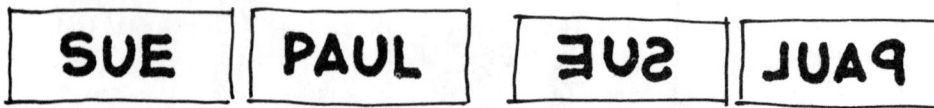

The children could give each other cards with 'backwards' writing to 'solve' by placing them in front of a mirror.

Light, Colour and Shade 15

5 *Make a kaleidoscope*
A simple kaleidoscope can be constructed as follows:

a Tape three mirrors together in a tube, facing inwards.
b Cut out a triangle of card to fit the bottom of the tube and stick it in place.
c Scatter coloured pieces of paper on to the card and look down into the kaleidoscope.

As the children gently shake the apparatus, the coloured pictures will change.

NC coverage
AT4 Level 3d: *know that light and sound can be reflected*

e) Rounding up

Round up with some activities that build on and link the themes of colour and light.

1 Groups could collect objects which are shiny/dull, translucent/opaque.
2 Experiment to discover the effects of sunlight on colour. Cover half a sheet of coloured paper and leave it in sunlight for a day or two. Observe how much it has faded. This could lead on to investigations with different colours. *Which colour fades most? Which fades most quickly? Does the paper still fade in cloudy weather?*
3 Give the children different-coloured pieces of cellophane to look through. *What happens to the colours they see?*
4 Demonstrate how light 'bends'. Place a straw in a glass of water. The object will appear to bend at the surface of the water, because light bends when it passes from one substance to another. Placing a bottle on its side in a path of light also demonstrates how light 'bends'.

NC coverage
AT4 Level 1c: *know about the simple properties of sound and light*
　　　Level 2d: *know that light passes through some materials and that when it does not shadows may be formed*
　　　Level 3d: *know that light and sound can be reflected*

Cross-curricular links

This topic involves a lot of specialised or technical words which could be explored in **English**, eg reflection, shadow, periscope, kaleidoscope, camouflage, transparent, opaque. These should be pointed out to the children, although of course, infants will find it difficult to remember them.

Colours are an excellent stimulus for **creative writing**. Children could write their own poems, or listen to others' poems on colours or the seasons. If you have access to coloured lights and filters, there is scope for some imaginative **drama** work.

The links with **art** are obvious. One idea is to make a simple mobile of hessian-covered card, to which the children can attach coloured items, eg leaves, feathers etc found outside, or items of one colour. Other ideas for display work have been explored in the text.

Maths is involved in the food experiments and in measuring of shadows. **Technology** is involved in the construction of different models.

Light/darkness has symbolic uses in many religious faiths and this could be explored in **RE** work.

There are clear links with **environmental studies/geography** in looking at seasonal colours (particularly in spring and autumn), light and colour in the built environment . . .

3 Energy

a) Power!
b) More about power
c) Movement
d) More about movement
e) Teacher demonstration

Anatomy of a topic

Energy is 'the power of doing work' and the activities which follow give the children opportunities to find out about how things move; the power needed to make this movement; how speed can be increased, decreased and stopped; how shape is changed by powered movement.

Nearly all of this work is practical; it provides the children with many opportunities to ask – and answer – questions; to find out what happens in given situations; to speculate on what *might* happen and to experiment accordingly; to survey various activities; to record findings. The topic could last about four weeks. There is more work on pulleys in Topic 10 *Buildings*.

Equipment

hall PE apparatus
various pieces of classroom furniture
a variety of balls
card
paper
pencils
plasticine
a sand tray
balloon
wood (for a simple boat)
handkerchief
material
paper clips (for parachute weighting)
model cars and vehicles (free wheel, wind up, battery powered)
wood (for ramp)
various materials to cover ramp – cloth, sandpaper, corrugated card, carpet
rulers
bulldog clips
cardboard box
infant building bricks
paint tin lid
marbles
elastic bands
cotton reels
candles
pieces of thin stick
sellotape
hard-boiled egg
toilet roll
card
glass of water

Resources

- Visitors and visits would be valuable to this topic. The former might include a police officer, a car mechanic, a road safety officer. Visits might be made to a garage.

- *How a car is made* and *How a car is designed* are free fact sheets available from Ford Motor Company.
- BP Educational Service issues a pack of booklets and worksheets entitled: *Making Work Easier* (pulleys and inclined planes are included).

Energy – pattern of a topic

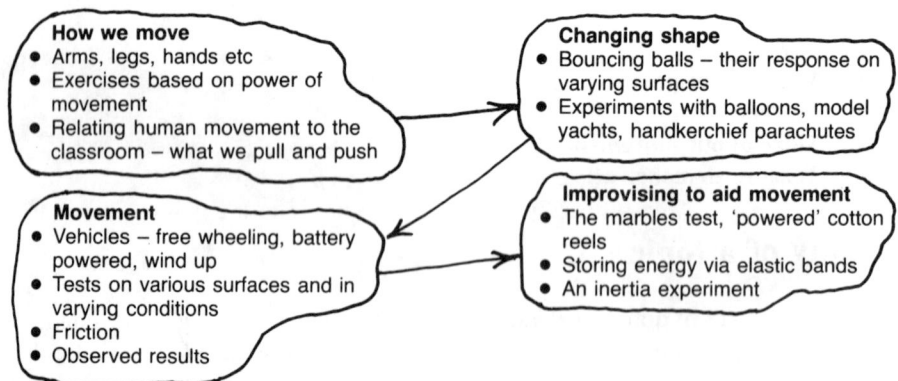

a) Power!

This component is mainly concerned with making the children aware of the power needed to move things. A good starting point might be a consideration of the children's muscles: *Let's look at our arms, legs, hands – how do we make them look strong?*

Exercises
After clenching and feeling their muscles the children could do some paired practical work – doing push ups and counting them; facing each other, joining hands and doing pushing and pulling exercises; bending and stretching legs to get from a squatting position to standing and vice-versa. These activities could be recorded in simple graphs:

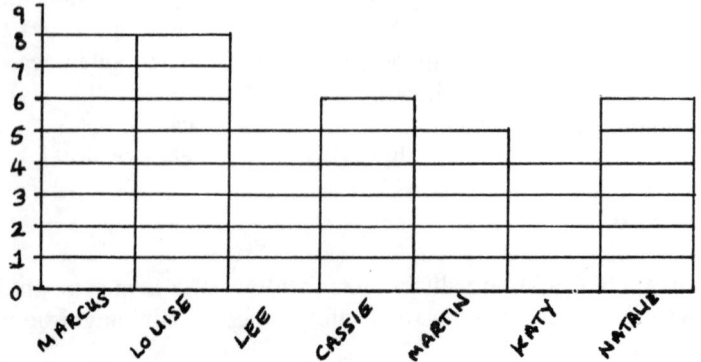

Energy 19

These exercises and observations could be extended in the hall, with PE equipment. Actions required to drag PE mats into place, to lower the ropes, to climb them, to pull out the climbing frame, to climb it, could all be noted and recorded in graph form.

The next step is to relate this 'human power' to everyday tasks in the classroom. Through discussion and observation, the children can investigate what actions require pushing and pulling movements, eg pushing and pulling windows and doors open and closed; opening and closing drawers; pressing on handles and taps; pulling toilet chains; pushing in drawing pins etc. Again these could be recorded in a list or table.

Bring the discussion back to muscles/power and make the point that the human body is like a machine. The 'fuel' needed to make it work is food.

This component could end by posing the question: *What do we do when our muscles don't have enough power to do a job?* This could lead on to how human brains thought of ways to help human bodies – by inventing machines, by using power sources like water and wind.

NC coverage
AT2 Level 1a: *be able to name the main external parts of the human body and a flowering plant*
     Level 3a: *know the basic life processes common to humans and other animals*
AT4 Level 2c: *understand that pushes and pulls can make things start moving, speed up, slow down, or stop*

b) More about power

Leaning heavily on practical work this component should again provoke plenty of questions, observations, experiments and attempts to solve problems.

Bouncing balls
a Drop a series of balls on a hard floor. Record how far they bounce back up. For fair testing the children should realise that all balls have to be dropped from the same height onto the same type of surface. This could be measured in various ways, eg 'hand spans'.

Recording the results requires some skill because one person will have to do the dropping while another marks the rise of the ball on paper pinned to the wall.

Questions which follow might be: *Why do the balls bounce back? Why do they bounce to different heights? Does what they bounce on make a difference to how high they come? Do they change shape at all?*

b The last question could promote another interesting test. From the same height drop a ball of plasticine on to the hard floor. Ask the children to observe what happens. First, it obviously doesn't bounce back, second, they'll notice that the plasticine has 'flattened' where it hit the floor.

This time the energy has been used to dent the plasticine. If neither balls nor floor dent, this means that both have kept their shape and the energy has caused the balls to bounce back.

c   The next step could be to drop the balls from the same height – but this time into a tray of levelled-off sand. This time, because this surface is soft, it changes shape. The energy is used in making dents in the sand.

The apparent complexity of all this when written down indicates the absolute necessity of practical experience for the children, along with lots of guidance and support from the teacher.

More experiments with shape/energy

a   How does a balloon change shape when we blow in it? What happens when we then let go?
b   Construct a simple boat with a material sail. Place it in a bowl or sink of water. What happens when we blow on the sail? What does the sail do? What does the boat do?
c   Make a simple parachute out of a handkerchief. Weight it with a collection of paper clips. Drop it from various heights. Record the findings.

NC coverage
AT4 Level 3c: *understand that forces can affect the position, movement and shape of an object*

c) Movement

What makes things move?
Collect an army of model vehicles. (These could range from free-wheeling 'Dinky' type models to clockwork or battery-powered toys.)

Start off by experimenting with these vehicles on a hard, bare floor. Ask the children to predict, estimate and then measure distances travelled. Some of the following questions will probably arise: *How do we make a free-wheeling car go as far as possible?* (a strong push) *What causes wind-up vehicles to stop so soon?* (not enough turns on the key) *What determines the distances the battery-powered car travels?* (strength of the battery) *Why do all vehicles stop in the end?*

Trying out surfaces
Now more variables can be brought into play in considering how things move.

a   Try the vehicles on a carpeted surface. What happens? Why don't they travel as far?
b   Help the children to construct a simple ramp from a piece of wood and some books. Ask them to note the effects of travelling up or downhill on speed and distance travelled. *Does varying the height of the ramp make any difference?*
c   This could lead on to more sophisticated work with ramps. The surface of the ramp could be changed by adding various materials (sandpaper, carpet, slightly corrugated paper etc). These should be cut to the same size as the ramp and held in place with narrow strips of wood (or rulers) at the side – all firmly secured by bulldog clips. The ramp can then be propped up on books for trials. The children could also experiment with wheel-less objects.

These experiments introduce – at a very simple level – the concept of friction: 'a force acting in the tangent plane of two bodies when opposite to that of the movement'.

d Observations on which surfaces offered the best grip could form the starting point for a discussion on road safety. Which sorts of roads are most dangerous to drive on? Which are best to drive on? Why do tyres need grips? etc

NC coverage
AT3 Level 1a: *be able to describe the simple properties of familiar materials*
AT4 Level 1b: *understand that things can be moved by pushing or pulling them*
    Level 2c: *understand that pushes and pulls can make things start moving, speed up, slow down or stop*

d More about moving

Inventing the wheel
Begin by posing a question: *How would you move a solid object more easily than simply pushing or pulling it?* Allow plenty of time for discussion and experiment, and eventually they will probably work out that using some sort of wheel or roller will make things much easier.

See what initiatives develop when the children start working with a range of materials, eg
a small cardboard box containing classroom bricks
a paint-tin lid
a box of marbles

After some experiment, the children may come up with the following solution:

a Put some marbles on the floor.
b Place the paint-tin lid over the marbles so that the rim (facing downwards) holds them together and stops them running out.
c Put the box of bricks on top of the lid and marbles.
d Try moving the whole contraption. *What is the best way to move it? What movements should be avoided? How far/how long can it travel? What difficulties might be encountered in pushing it a long way. . . etc.*

Powered movement
A very simple form of powered movement is the well-known 'cotton reel tank'. To make the tank:

a Push an elastic band through an empty cotton reel. Insert a piece of matchstick through the loop at one end and sellotape it in place. (The matchstick should be shorter than the diameter of the reel.)

b Cut a small piece of candle and make a hole in it. Thread the free end of the elastic band through the hole. Insert a thin stick through the loop at that end.

c Use the stick to wind up the band.

d Place the 'tank' on the floor and it will move away, powered by the elastic band.

22 *Science Topics for Infants*

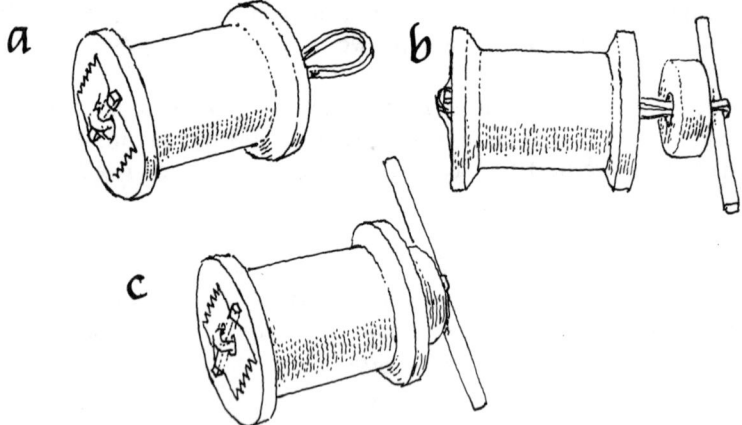

In discussion with the children, draw out the idea that the movement of the 'tank' is an example of storing energy.

NC coverage
AT4 Level 1b: *understand that things can be moved by pushing or pulling them*
     Level 2c: *understand that pushes and pulls can make things start moving, speed up, slow down or stop*
     Level 3c: *understand that forces can affect the position, movement, shape of an object*

e) Teacher demonstration

Although primary school science is mainly about 'finding out for themselves' there is still a place for teacher demonstration. A striking and lively demonstration will remain in the children's minds for a long time. They will go on thinking about it and, perhaps later, want to try it themselves.

The following demonstration may at first appear to the children as 'magic' or a trick. However it is a genuinely scientific demonstration. The equipment consists of a hard-boiled egg, a glass of water, a toilet roll and a piece of card. These should be set up as follows:

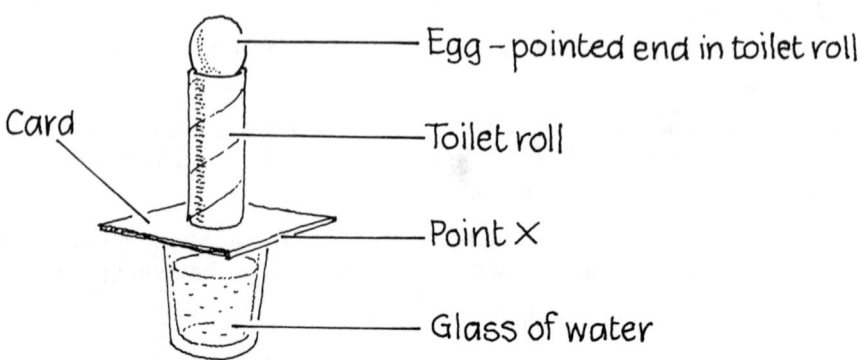

When everything has been set up and the children are ready, take hold of the card at point X, using thumb and forefinger. Then, with a sudden, level pull, quickly jerk the card out from between the toilet roll and the glass. The roll should topple away and the egg fall into the glass. (It's advisable to practice this in advance!)

The scientific purpose of the demonstration is to show (in simple terms) that a motionless object remains standing still until it is acted upon by an outside force. In this demonstration involving inertia, the egg falls under gravitational pull.

NC coverage
AT4 Level 3c: *understand that forces can effect the position, movement and shape of an object*

Cross-curricular links

Work with toy vehicles could lead to studies of the real thing and links with **maths/ technology/environmental studies**:

- Children could do a survey of traffic passing the school gates and present their findings in graph form.
- Children could visit a garage and learn, in particular, about safety aspects such as brakes, tyre grips etc.
- A police or road safety officer could be invited in to talk about road safety.

There are numerous stimuli for **creative writing** and **art**, focusing on movement, energy, cars. . . A visit to a toy shop would provide a useful and enjoyable stimulus.

Children enjoy making their own sounds and **music** on the theme of energy. Evocative music such as 'Anitra's Dance' from Grieg's *Peer Gynt* Suite, or the overture from Wagner's *Flying Dutchman* could form the starting point for **music/ drama** activities. These pieces emphasise different kinds of energy and have contrasting slow and fast movements.

In **history**, some 'then and now' work could look at the development of cars, ships and machines, as well as early forms of power and energy.

In **RE** the use of energy for 'doing good' could be explored.

4 Electricity and Magnetism

a) **Know and be safe**
b) **Lighting up**
c) **Models**
d) **What about magnets?**
e) **It's Christmas**

Anatomy of a topic

The best positioning of this topic would be the last few weeks of the Autumn Term, leading up to Christmas. Several aspects of the topic could feature specifically in Christmas activities.

Equipment

plugs	bulbs	sand tray
drawing pins	wrapping paper from	wires
scissors	Lucozade bottle	small block of wood
pencils	Christmas tree lights	silver paper
varied paper	metal strips	card
various magnets	batteries	paper clips
screwdrivers	cardboard boxes	

various metallic objects to go in sand tray and for use in magnetic experiments
assorted materials for circuit 'joining up' testing

Resources
- The Electricity Council Film and Video Library produces a wide range of free materials. One film at the time of writing is *Safe as Houses* – which deals with electrical safety in the home.
- The Electricity Council offers an extensive range of teaching aids. These are detailed in the catalogue: *Understanding Electricity*.
- Teachers who have access to the two volumes: *Early Experiences* and *Science from Toys* in the Macdonald/Schools Council Science 5/13 series will find them very helpful for this topic.
- A very useful catalogue for anything from a wire stripper 'that really works' to a wide selection of magnets, metal strips, bulbs, bulb holders etc is provided by Technology Teaching Systems Ltd.

Electricity and Magnetism 25

'Thinking cards'

Before work on this topic begins, prepare a few 'thinking cards' like the ones below. Place these cards around the room, without comment, so that the children can reflect upon and talk about them as the topic progresses. This would be particularly valuable with older infants.

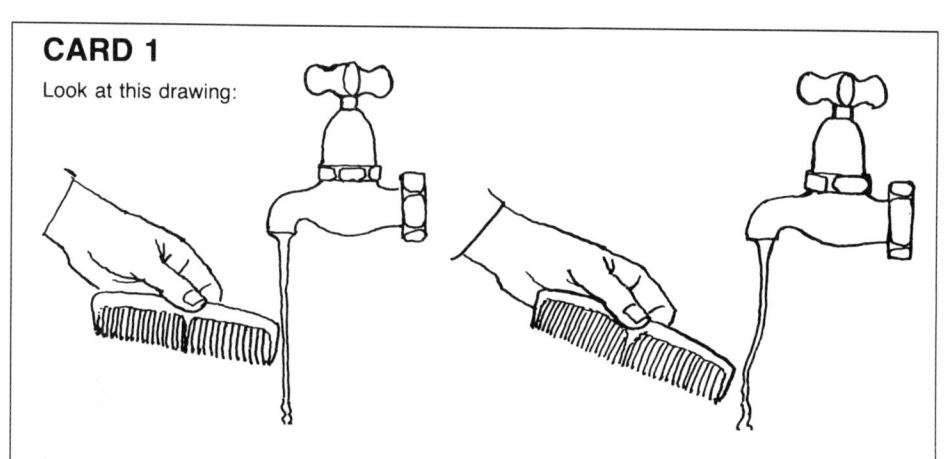

CARD 1

Look at this drawing:

In A a plastic comb is held near a very thin stream of water. In B, the same comb, which has just been rubbed hard on a woollen jersey, is held in exactly the same position.
What happens to the water in drawing B?
What is different about the comb in drawing B?
What has caused the comb to change?
Put in the missing letters in this word: .L.C.R.C.T.

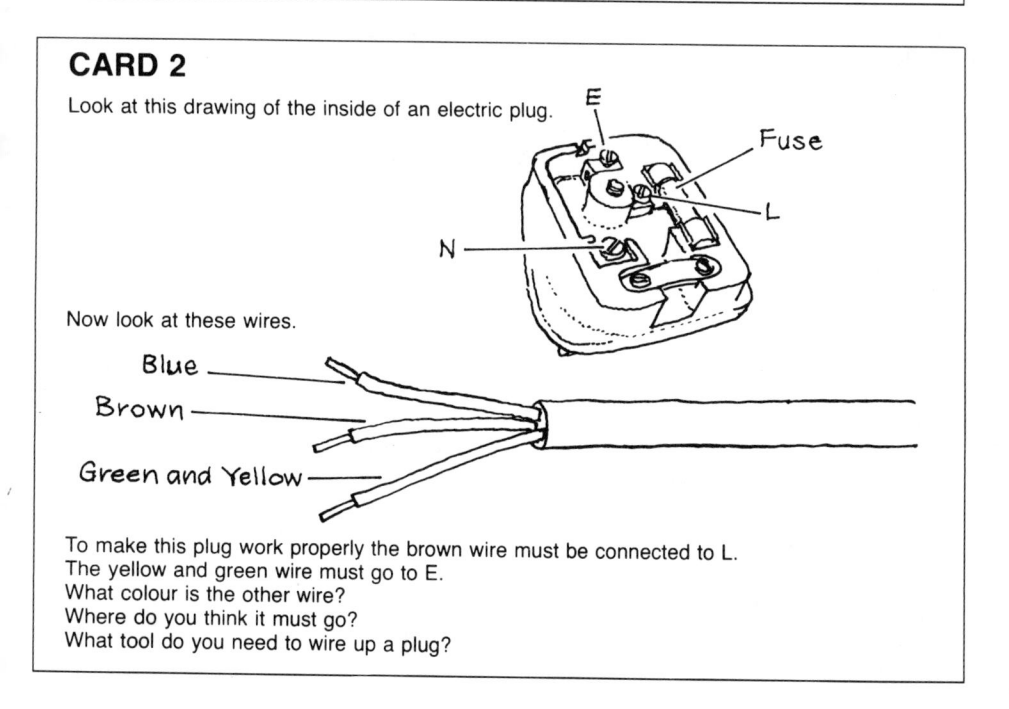

CARD 2

Look at this drawing of the inside of an electric plug.

Now look at these wires.

Blue
Brown
Green and Yellow

To make this plug work properly the brown wire must be connected to L.
The yellow and green wire must go to E.
What colour is the other wire?
Where do you think it must go?
What tool do you need to wire up a plug?

26 *Science Topics for Infants*

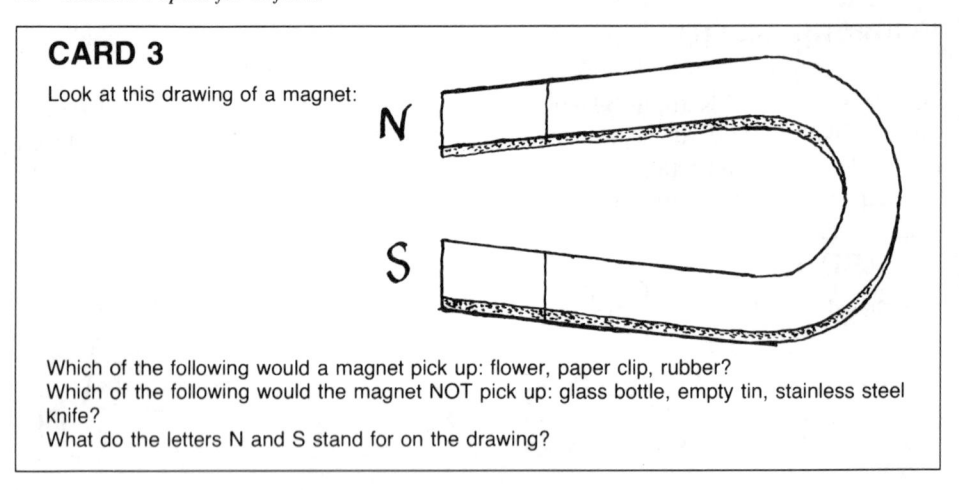

CARD 3

Look at this drawing of a magnet:

N

S

Which of the following would a magnet pick up: flower, paper clip, rubber?
Which of the following would the magnet NOT pick up: glass bottle, empty tin, stainless steel knife?
What do the letters N and S stand for on the drawing?

a) Know and be safe

Perhaps the first and most important fact to get across to young children is that mains electricity is *dangerous*; and that water and electricity don't mix. These safety factors should be emphasised right at the start of the project and throughout.

After this a good starting point is to look at what is worked by electricity in the school and at home.

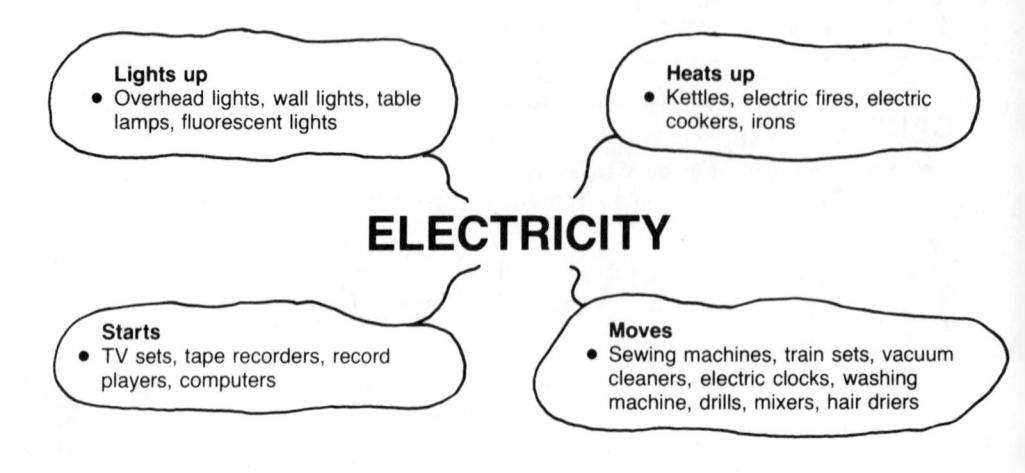

Lights up
- Overhead lights, wall lights, table lamps, fluorescent lights

Heats up
- Kettles, electric fires, electric cookers, irons

ELECTRICITY

Starts
- TV sets, tape recorders, record players, computers

Moves
- Sewing machines, train sets, vacuum cleaners, electric clocks, washing machine, drills, mixers, hair driers

This is likely to lead to a lot of 'How?' questions. One way this could be developed is to look at the path:

mains ⟶ sockets ⟶ plugs ⟶ wires ⟶ appliances

Look inside a plug
(NB stress that children should NEVER try this at home or without adult supervision.)

Electricity and Magnetism

The children should be given the opportunity to look at the inside of plugs; note wire colourings and become aware of how to use a screwdriver to connect things up. Practice in wiring plugs could then take place (using unconnected wires of course!) This would provide valuable practical skills and also demand careful recording. The latter might be composed of writing and drawing, perhaps guided by questions/comments such as: 1 *How do we take the back off a plug?* 2 *What does the plug look like inside?* 3 *What tool is needed to work on a plug?* 4 *What is a terminal?* 5 *How do we fasten a wire to a terminal?* 6 *What coloured wires go where?* 7 *How do we put the plug back together?*

Danger!
Having done this practical work, and talked at length about electricity in the home and school, the children could complete a *Never* chart or poster. The finished product might look something like this:

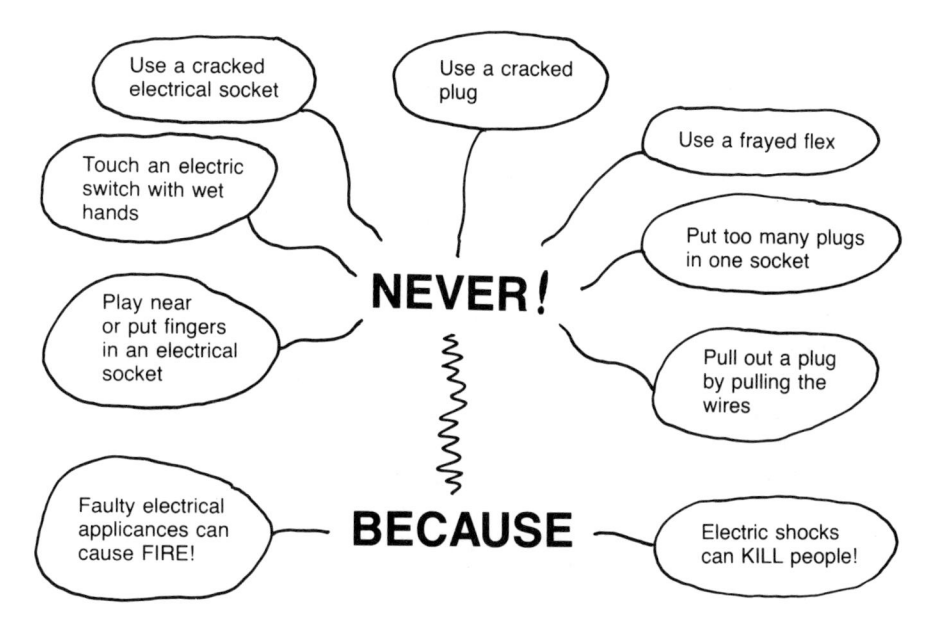

NEVER!
- Use a cracked electrical socket
- Use a cracked plug
- Use a frayed flex
- Touch an electric switch with wet hands
- Put too many plugs in one socket
- Play near or put fingers in an electrical socket
- Pull out a plug by pulling the wires

BECAUSE
- Faulty electrical appliances can cause FIRE!
- Electric shocks can KILL people!

NC coverage
AT4 Level 1a: *know that many household appliances use electricity but that misuse is dangerous*

b) Lighting up

Battery power
First of all, focus on a few everyday things: torches, alarm clocks, electrical school clocks. Talk about the use of batteries as power sources. (There is a carbon rod in

the centre of a battery which is surrounded by a paste. The metal casing on the outside of the battery is made of zinc. The carbon and zinc are linked by wires to produce electricity.) This could lead on to the children making a simple circuit.

The children should work in pairs or small groups. They will need a battery, two pieces of wire, a bulb and a bulb holder. Help them to set up the equipment as follows:

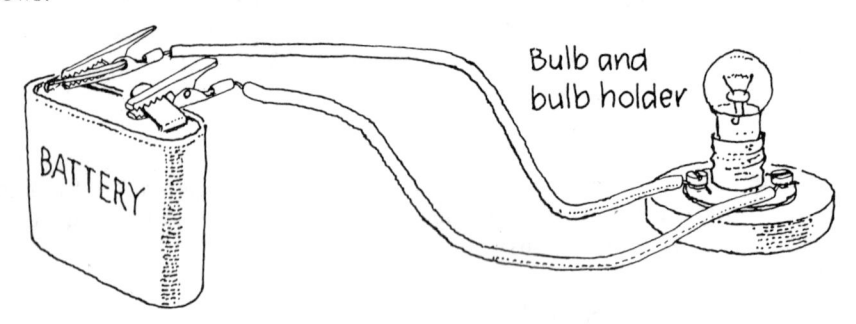

What happens when you connect the last piece of wire? What happens if you disconnect the wire again?

The children could then practise dismantling a torch, clock etc, then reassembling them. They will soon find out that the batteries have to go in opposite directions for the apparatus to work. In discussion, link this with the circuit experiment they have just done.

Conductors

The previous experiment focuses on 'connections'. This problem-solving exercise investigates what electricity will/will not flow through. ('Conduct' is a key word to use here.) Return to the simple circuit (see above). Now part and bare one of the connecting wires to create a break in the circuit.

Give the children a range of materials to place in the gap. *Which materials complete the circuit and make the bulb light up?* Ask the children to note the different materials before they start, and predict for each one whether they think it will make the bulb light up. When they try the experiment, the results can be noted alongside, in a chart like this:

Material used	Does the bulb light up?	
	Guess (Yes or No)	Result (Yes or No)
Another piece of wire Silver paper A pencil A paper clip		

NC coverage
AT4 Level 3a: *know that a complete circuit is needed for electrical devices to work*

c) Models

Following the work in 'Lighting-up' children can be introduced to the idea of a simple switch. They can use this to make simple, but very satisfying 'light-up' models.

The switch is made as follows:

a Take a springy metal strip and make a hole in it at one end.
b Fasten a copper wire round a drawing pin. Push the pin through the hole and into a piece of wood.
c Attach another piece of wire to the other end of the block of wood with a drawing pin – so that the connecting point is under the end of the metal strip.

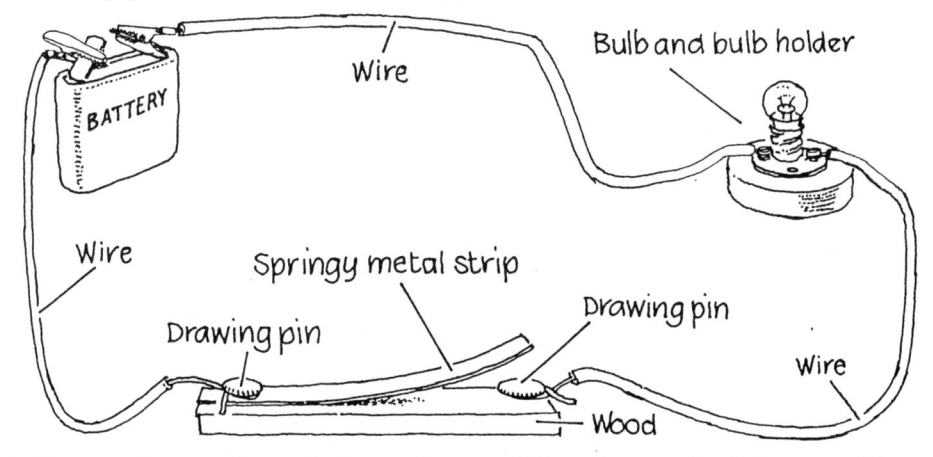

d Connect the two pieces of wire to a battery. When the metal strip is pressed down it will complete the circuit.
e Connect a light bulb into part of the circuit. When the 'switch' is pressed down, the bulb will light up.

The children can make all sorts of imaginative models based around a box into which the light-bulb is inserted (making sure, of course, that it is well clear of the sides). Ideas include: a decorated 'mask' with cellophane eye-holes which light up when the switch is pressed; a doll's house with illuminated windows; a model car with a warning light on top...

NC coverage
AT4 Level 2d: *know that light passes through some materials and when it does not shadows may be formed*
AT4 Level 3a: *know that a complete circuit is needed for electrical devices to work*

d) What about magnets?

The link with magnets can be brought into this topic as an example of some of the other 'powers' of electricity.

Wire up a battery as above, this time connecting the other ends of wire to a nail.

30 *Science Topics for Infants*

Experiments to see what the nail would pick up could then take place. Paper clips are one obvious choice here. *What happens to the paper clips when the nail has been disconnected?*

Teachers will be aware that this is an electro-magnet, and more work with other kinds of magnet could follow on. A framework for this activity might look like:

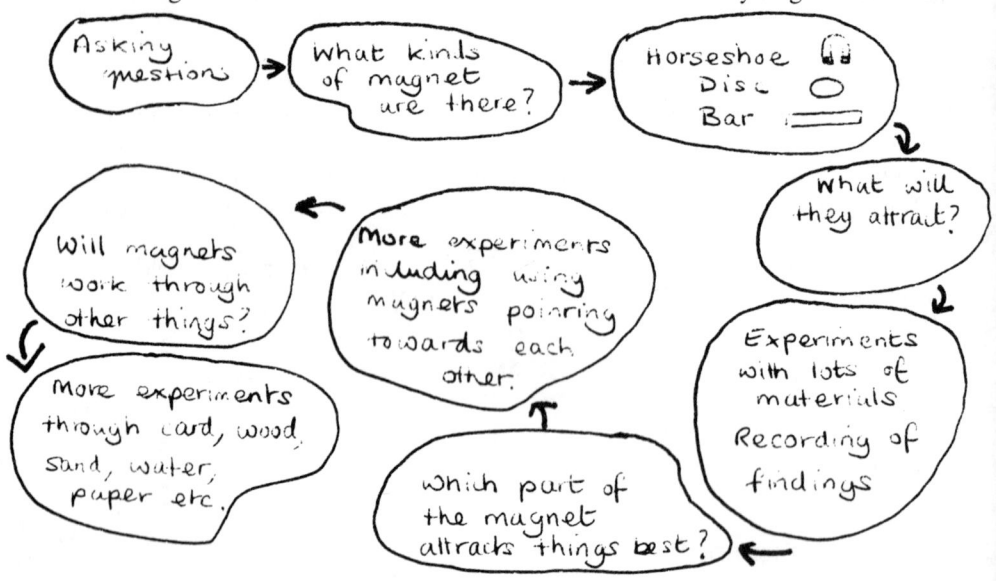

- Asking questions
- What kinds of magnet are there?
- Horseshoe, Disc, Bar
- What will they attract?
- Experiments with lots of materials
- Recording of findings
- Which part of the magnet attracts things best?
- More experiments including using magnets pointing towards each other.
- Will magnets work through other things?
- More experiments through card, wood, sand, water, paper etc.

NC coverage
AT4 Level 2a: *know that magnets attract some materials and not others and can repel each other*

e) It's Christmas

The work in this component is linked with Christmas, but the activities would be equally appropriate for many other celebrations, eg Diwali.

A Christmas crib with a difference
The simple battery/bulb/switch circuit can be used to add interest to scenes or tableaux, such as a Christmas crib:

a Take the lid off a cardboard box. Cut a 'viewing hole' in one end of the box.
b Paint the inside of the box and position Nativity figures at the other end.
c Paint the inside of the lid to match.
d Discuss where the light bulb should be positioned. *Where will it give the best light?* Place the bulb/holder inside the box (well clear of the sides). Cut a small hole in the side to pass the wires through:
e Connect the wires to a simple switch circuit as described above.
f As the viewer approaches the peep hole, they press on the switch and the scene is illuminated.

Magnetic Santa Claus
A lively Christmas activity could be based on a 'Can Santa Claus find our school?' game. Draw a plan of the area around the school on thick paper. Locate the school in one corner of the paper, the starting point at another. The streets should connect up so that Santa Claus can go from start to finish – his conveyance could be a paper clip! Players have to guide the 'sleigh' from the start to the school, by means of a magnet underneath the paper, without touching any of the lines of the streets.

Lucky dip!
A magnetised 'lucky dip' could feature at the Christmas party. Bury a selection of paper clips, screws, nuts etc in the sand tray (not too deep). Invite the children to take turns to 'detect' the objects with a magnet. Once found, the objects could be exchanged for a sweet or small gift.

NC coverage
AT4 Level 2a: *know that magnets attract some materials and not others and can repel each other*

Cross-curricular links

English work could range from factual descriptions of how to make circuits and simple switches to the sort of message which should feature on a poster as a warning of the dangers of electricity. There is also plenty of opportunity for specific vocabulary development – shock, danger, flashing, illumination etc and again this could be used in descriptive writing about shops at Christmas, towns at night, the school play, and so on.

  Art work could be closely linked with this, and there are many possibilities for poster work here.

  Technology would be served by making models linked with light circuits, and **maths** would be involved with any measuring needed.

  Links with **geography** could look at electrical storms and compasses. **History** might involve the development of electricity and the changes it has brought.

5 Ourselves

a) Finding out about our bodies
b) We are different!
c) Seeing, hearing, smelling, tasting, touching
d) Feeding, breathing, moving, behaving
e) Our family

Anatomy of a topic

Work on this topic offers enormous scope for activities of the 'Do. . . Describe which. . . Find a way to' type, identified in *Science in the National Curriculum*.

This would be a good topic to start a school year in the Autumn Term, or to end a school year in the Summer Term. Some playground work for the children would be advantageous. The topic could occupy four weeks to half a term. There is more work on 'food' in Topic 9: *Heat* and Topic 14 *Hygiene and Health*. Listening, smelling and tasting are also covered in Topic 18 *Home and School*.

Equipment

newspaper	perfume	onion
yoghurt pots	coloured paper	Marmite
tape recorder	lemons	card
ball	carrot	bananas
pencils	jar	paint blocks
oranges	sellotape	cheese
apple	beans	potatoes
bucket	crisps	peas
clock	selected 'memory'	TCP
plasticine	objects	trays
rubber hose	water	bread
large sheets of paper	talcum powder	

Resources

- One or two wall charts would be helpful. *Health and the Human Body* (about breathing) and *Early Years* about moving and 'the variety of life' are available from: Pictorial Charts Educational Trust.

Pattern of a topic

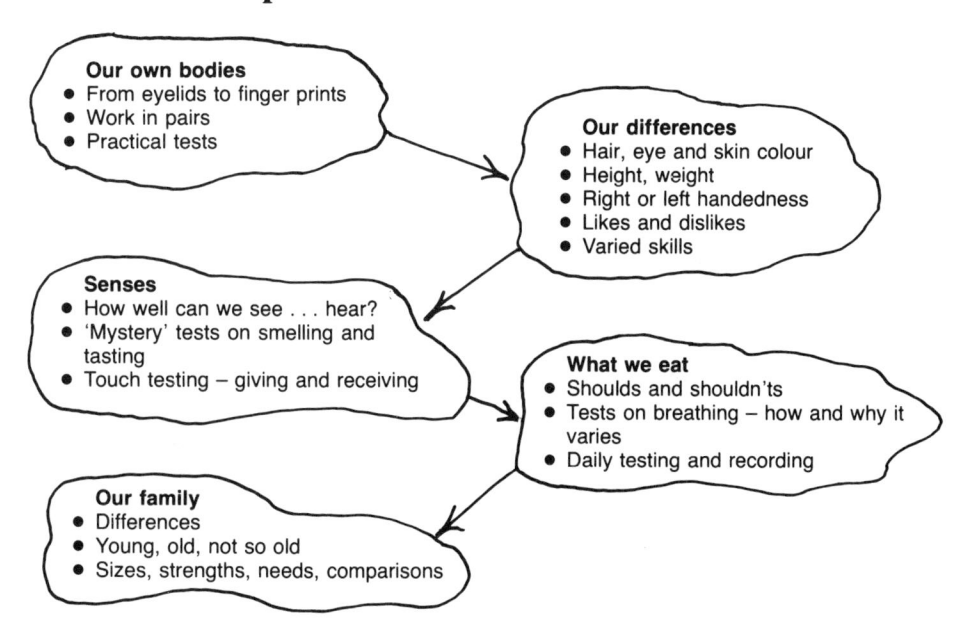

Our own bodies
- From eyelids to finger prints
- Work in pairs
- Practical tests

Our differences
- Hair, eye and skin colour
- Height, weight
- Right or left handedness
- Likes and dislikes
- Varied skills

Senses
- How well can we see... hear?
- 'Mystery' tests on smelling and tasting
- Touch testing – giving and receiving

What we eat
- Shoulds and shouldn'ts
- Tests on breathing – how and why it varies
- Daily testing and recording

Our family
- Differences
- Young, old, not so old
- Sizes, strengths, needs, comparisons

Children are fascinated by their own and others' bodies. The following components will need to be linked by plenty of discussion, questioning, speculating, testing, experimenting and recording. This topic lends itself particularly to paired work. (NB Clearly a topic such as 'ourselves' which involves individual differences, will need sensitive handling by the teacher to ensure that all the children view 'difference' in a positive way.) For the initial activities it's probably best to concentrate on discussion and verbal observations; later in the project the children will use charts and diagrams to record their findings.

a) Finding out about our bodies

Introduce the topic in general terms. Then begin to focus attention on parts of the body. Ask for ideas about where to start, or suggest that, since we use our eyes to see each other, 'the eyes' make a good place to start.

Eyes
Encourage the children to feel gently around their own eyes. *What feels hard? What is soft? What are the things which protect our eyes? What do our eyelids do? What are eyelashes for?* The children could then feel around their partner's eyes and compare their findings.

Skin
Next focus on the skin. We are all covered in skin, but it varies from person to person. The children could observe colour, texture, feel – even smell! (These investigations will need sensitive handling by the teacher.)

How much skin have we got? Provide a pile of old newspapers and get the children to wrap paper around each other's bodies, arms, legs, heads. . . Then the paper is laid out on the floor to show approximately how much skin the child has.

Other skin qualities that could be investigated include waterproofing, resilience, temperature. . .

Hands and feet

Explain that each person's fingerprints are unique. Get the children to take each other's fingerprints to see for themselves that this is so. Two ways of doing this are:

a Press each finger onto a damp paint block and then onto white paper.
b Dust each finger with talcum powder and press the fingertips onto a strip of sellotape.

Get the children to draw round each other's naked feet on large sheets of paper and compare 'footprints'. An interesting follow-up might be for pairs to draw around their shoes, then cut out their original footprint and place it inside the shoe outline. *Is the shoe a good fit? Do the shoe shapes match their owner's feet?*

Muscles

Encourage the children to work in pairs and observe – by feeling – the movement of different muscles, eg *What happens to the arm muscles when we clench a fist? How do the cheek muscles move when the jaw is tensed?*

NC coverage
AT2 Level 1a: *be able to name the main external parts of the human body and a flowering plant*

b) We are different!

Moving on from 'ourselves' to 'each other', encourage the children to concentrate on differences.

Class surveys
A survey of eye colour in the class could be recorded as a block graph:

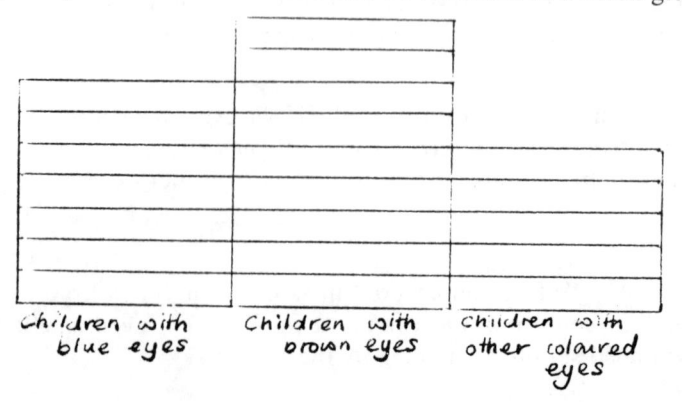

| Children with blue eyes | Children with brown eyes | Children with other coloured eyes |

A comparison of hair colour might be next. The results could be displayed on large circles of coloured paper, ie

Black paper for black hair	Brown paper for brown hair	Yellow paper for blond hair	Red paper for red hair
John, Mario, Marcus, Wayne, Jayne, Surinda	Emily, Carla, Hilary, Janet, Bobbie, Michael, Lee	Lucy, Natalie, Kassie, Jodie, Adam, Karen	Mark, Scott, Kevin, Louise

Other differences that might be observed, measured and compared include height, weight, left or right-handedness. Again it's important to stress that there is nothing wrong with being different (for example, some children might be self-conscious about weight, or feel that being left-handed is 'odd').

Likes and skills

The children could go on to survey classmates' 'likes' and skills. They could then explore different ways of recording and presenting their findings. 'Favourite colours' for example, might be a tick chart.

FAVOURITE COLOURS

	BLUE	GREEN	YELLOW	RED	BLACK	BROWN	WHITE
John				✓			
Mario				✓			
Surinda		✓					
Emily							✓
Wayne					✓		
Carla		✓					
Jayne	✓						
Natalie							
Lee			✓				

'Favourite foods' might be displayed like this:

FAVOURITE FOODS

HAMBURGERS — Emily, Carla, Hilary
CHIPS — Janet, Bobbie, Michael
APPLES — Lee
ICE CREAM — Lucy, Natalie, Kassie, Adam
RICE PUDDING — Kevin

36   *Science Topics for Infants*

A survey of skills might be recorded in a simple Venn diagram:

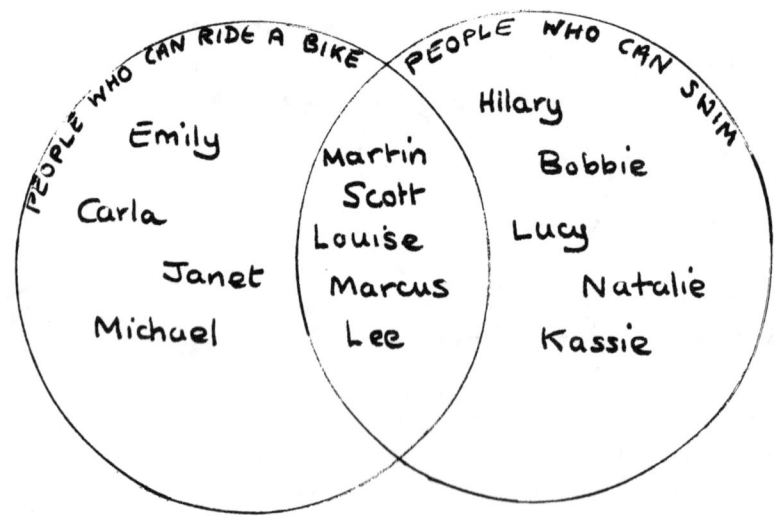

PEOPLE WHO CAN RIDE A BIKE / PEOPLE WHO CAN SWIM

- Emily
- Carla
- Janet
- Michael

(intersection)
- Martin
- Scott
- Louise
- Marcus
- Lee

- Hilary
- Bobbie
- Lucy
- Natalie
- Kassie

Profiles
The end product of all this research could be the creation of a simple profile card for each child. To give added interest, the children might work in pairs and record and write up their partner's card:

NAME	L. OR R. HANDED
DATE OF BIRTH	FAVOURITE FOOD
EYE COLOUR	FAVOURITE DRINK
HAIR COLOUR	FAVOURITE TV PROGRAMME
HEIGHT	FAVOURITE TOY
WEIGHT	FAVOURITE SKILL OR HOBBY

NC coverage

AT2 Level 1a: *be able to name the main external parts of the human body and a flowering plant*
  Level 1b: *know that there is a wide variety of living things, which includes humans*
  Level 2b: *be able to sort familiar living things into broad groups according to easily observable features*

c) Seeing, hearing, smelling, tasting, touching

This component could again be started by paired or group work in a memory/sight game. Prepare some trays with a few simple objects on them. Allow the children to study them for a short period, then remove the trays, *How many of the items can the children then remember seeing, and name?*

Hearing could be emphasised by comparing different people's ability to hear a clock, and at what range. The teacher could make a tape of everyday 'mystery' sounds and then ask the children to identify what these are.

Smelling
A simple 'smelling test' can be devised as follows:

a Thoroughly cleanse six yoghurt pots. Label them from A to F.
b In each pot, place a different, strong-smelling substance.
  Suggestions might be:
  A – cheese; B – onion; C – hot water and Marmite;
  D – perfume or after-shave; E – antiseptic (eg TCP);
  F – bacon-flavoured crisps
c Seal each pot with kitchen foil/clingfilm etc, leaving a small hole as the 'smelling position'.
d Arrange the pots in a row on a desk or table.
e Give each child a check sheet. As they sniff the pots, they tick off their responses on the sheet. Older children could be asked to speculate on what the product was.

Overall results could be presented in a variety of forms.

Tasting
This investigation focuses on the link between smell and taste. Children work in pairs. One partner is blindfolded and holds their nose between thumb and forefinger, thus blocking out both sight and smell.

The other child feeds their partner small pieces of different foods: apple, bread, carrot etc. The blindfolded child has to guess the food, working on taste alone. After a few tries, the partners swap roles. (The variety of foods available is likely to be quite limited, so it is important that both partners get an equal chance.)

Touching
The sense of touch can be explored in a number of ways.

1 Link touch with sight – or rather, the lack of it. A discussion on blindness will bring home to the children just how important touch is to a blind person. Children could be blindfolded and 'guided' around the room by a partner, negotiating their way by touch. The Braille alphabet could be introduced, and children could construct Braille letters and words out of Plasticine.
2 Show the children how to feel and time each other's pulse and heartbeat. Pulse rate could be recorded before and after exercise. *How is it different? Why?* (Obviously, this could open up a very wide field for further investigation.)
3 The nerve endings below the surface of the skin sense different things. Some record pain, others cold, others touch... and so on. However, these nerve endings are not distributed evenly throughout the body, as this experiment illustrates.

a One partner is blindfolded and sits with palm upwards.
b The other partner lightly presses a sharpened pencil onto the blindfolded child's hand.
c Repeat this with two pencils, slightly apart. *Can the 'feeler' guess whether one or two pencils are being pressed?*
d Repeat several times, increasing the distance between the pencils.
e The 'feeler's' responses should be recorded. *How many times were they right?*

Next try the experiment again, this time pressing the pencils at the nape of the neck. *What are the results? Is the 'feeler' right more or less often?*

NC coverage
AT2 Level 2a: *be able to sort familiar living things into broad groups according to easily observable features*
Level 3b: *know that human activity may produce changes in the environment that can affect plants and animals*

d) Feeding, breathing, moving, behaving

Food is an easy starting point with young children. Early topics of discussion might include: favourite food; school dinners; *What I've got in my sandwiches*; ethnic food; *What I have for tea*; foods that are 'good' or 'bad' for us.

Sorting food
Bring in a variety of different foods and ask the children to sort them into groups, eg vegetables/fruit; sweet/salty; juicy/dry. Children could do 'taste tests' as described above to help them group 'mystery' foods.

How we eat
The children could carefully note 'how' some familiar foods are eaten (again this could have practical applications!). They could record their findings like this:

Biscuits — Nuts — (CRUNCH) — Crisps

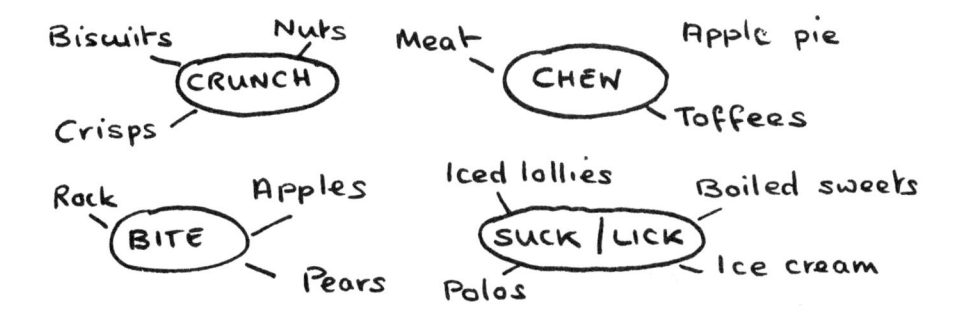

Meat — (CHEW) — Apple pie — Toffees

Rock — Apples — (BITE) — Pears

Iced lollies — (SUCK/LICK) — Boiled sweets — Ice cream — Polos

The children could add to the categories as their testing/knowledge increases. Some more sophisticated recording might follow, eg:

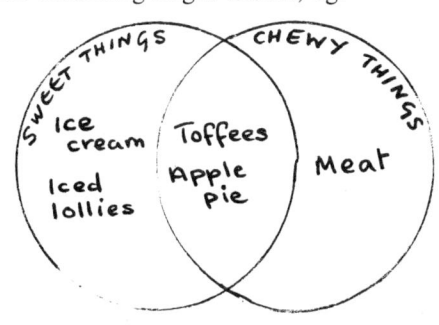

Venn diagram: SWEET THINGS (Ice cream, Iced lollies) ∩ CHEWY THINGS (Meat), intersection: Toffees, Apple pie

How we breathe

If a wall chart is available (see Resources on pages 179–80) children could look at the size/shape/position of the lungs. This could lead on to some simple investigations:

a Partners take turns to feel each other's chests as they take a very deep breath, then comment on what they saw and felt.

b One partner holds a hand slightly in front of the other's mouth and observes what happens as they exhale.

c Teachers of older children could try a more sophisticated experiment to illustrate air in the lungs. Lightly tilt a glass jar in a bucket of water and insert one end of a rubber tube into it.

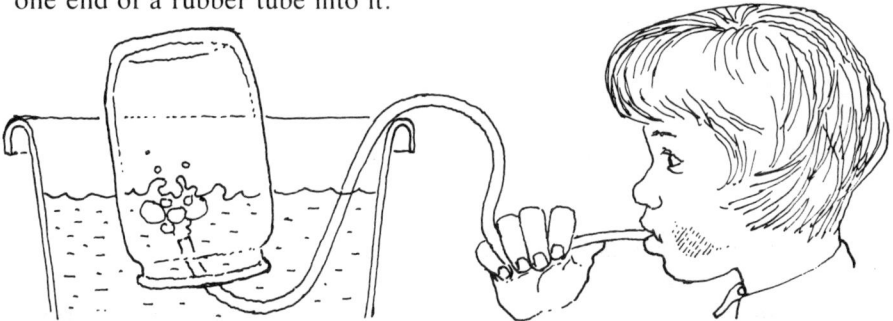

Ask a child to blow into the tube as hard as possible. The amount of water forced out of the jar indicates the amount of air in the lungs.

How fast?

Young children are always interested in superlatives – quickest, slowest etc and this interest could be utilised to focus attention on movements. In groups, suggest they find out who is the fastest in certain kinds of movement, eg running, climbing ropes in the hall, standing up from a lying position (then reversing the procedure). It is a good idea to test a few reaction times at this point, too.

One way of doing this is for one child to hold a ball at arm's length, and drop it without warning. Their partner must then try to catch the ball before it hits the ground. Simple charts could be made of the success rate of this and the exercise could be practised when the children are fresh (am) and tired (pm), with the significance of this being noted.

Invite the children to try moving slowly as opposed to as quickly as possible. This could be practised by some slow marching to suitable music, and in miming action in slow motion.

How we behave

Behaving is included in this section because it is another feature which conveys to children how we are different. Compile some class lists of 'people who make us laugh; people or things we like to watch; favourite sounds' etc. This could lead on naturally to an examination of how we ourselves behave in different situations. To get responses here a wide range of questions could be asked: *What would you do if: somebody gave you a present; you were frightened; you were angry with someone. . .?*

Within the classroom the children themselves will be aware of who is the best at telling jokes, being kind and so on. (If negative behaviour is discussed, ensure that comments are not made about individuals in the class.)

NC coverage

AT2 Level 3a: *know the basic life processes common to humans and other animals*
    Level 3b: *know that human activity may produce changes in the environment that can affect plants and animals*

e) Our family

This component focuses on children's awareness of the main stages of the life cycle, through a closer look at families. Simple drawings might represent a 'symbolic' family of Grandad, Grandma, Mum, Dad, big brother, baby sister. (In doing this work, it is important to point out that there are all sorts of family arrangements – two parents and two children are by no means the 'norm'. The teacher needs to be sensitive to children in the class who may have experienced family break-up.)

This simple visual stimulus should prompt children to talk about their own families and home situations. Talking points might include size of family and family members, ages, strength, ability to run, jump, climb etc, the progress a baby makes through its early stages. . . Questions arising from this discussion might be: *How do people's bodies change as they get older? What is important for a baby's development? How long does it take a baby to start to walk, talk, run? What are the differences between a young person's movements and an old person's movements? Who sits down most in the family? Who runs around most?*

Children's growing awareness of the life cycle could be reinforced by asking the children to enact movements in different ways: *Pretend you're a baby, a seven-year-old, an old lady. . .* and taping observations. A class 'birthday chart' would show how members have begun their journey through life at different times, and could include other significant events.

NC coverage
AT2 Level 2b: *be able to sort familiar living things into broad groups according to easily observable features*

Cross-curricular links

Maths is involved in measuring and estimating, looking at dates for the birthday chart, looking at calendars.

English work could range from factual descriptions based on observation: *I know an old lady who walks down our street. She has a stick in each hand. She walks slow and hunched up. She has glasses. She is old.* (Elizabeth, aged 7) to creative writing and poems. *Families and Friends* by John Foster and Rod Hunt (Macmillan) is a useful junior book which can be adapted for use with younger children. For **drama** work, children could enact 'my most exciting/scary/funny . . . situation'.

In **art**, children could paint portraits or make papier mache models of themselves and other family members. A class mural could be created, with 3D cut-outs of every member and/or finger and thumb prints.

RE could focus on themes such as: helping – with our hands, our voices; people who help us; good behaviour. . .

In **music**, children could try rhythmic clapping of names: ELIZ-A-BETH, JON-A-THON etc. There are many tunes linked to names and ages, eg *Sweet Polly Oliver, Don't bring Lulu, Dinah, Old Macdonald, When I'm 64*. A number of infant song books include items on this theme.

6 Living Things – Animals and Birds

a) **Pets and looking after them**
b) **Shape**
c) **Keeping track**
d) **Bird watch**
e) **Rounding up**

Anatomy of a topic

This topic greatly appeals to children. For teachers who wish to start things with a light touch, AT2 Level 1b: *know that there is a wide variety of living things . . .* can be brought into focus straightaway with the following jingle:

> *Way down South where bananas grow,*
> *A grasshopper stood on an elephant's toe.*
> *The elephant said, with tears in his eyes,*
> *'Pick on somebody your own size.'*

This topic has the potential to be one of the longer ones in the book. There is sufficient material for it to last for half a term and its location would seem well suited to May, June, July. There is further work on animals and animal homes in Topic 18 *Home and School*. For information on animals in the classroom, see the *Introduction*.

Equipment

card	chalk	food for pets
paper	tracing paper	an incubator and chick's
pencils	animal comb	eggs (if possible)
rulers	magnifying glass	binoculars (preferably of
school pets (hamsters,	balsa wood	the tough, unbreakable
gerbils etc)	glue	kind for children's use)
pets brought from home	scissors	bird table
(under proper	piece of glass	wool
supervision)	photographs of animals	feathers
cotton wool		

various materials if animal habitats are to be constructed (cardboard box, straw, water container etc for tortoise; wood, glass, for wormery; more substantial materials for larger school pets).

Resources
- The Pedigree Petfoods Education Centre is a wonderful source of material and advice.
- Other useful organisations in connection with this topic are: Animal Information Bureau; British Rabbit Council; Dogs' Home, Battersea; The National Dog Owners' Association; RSPCA Education Department; RSPB Head of Education; Cat Action Trust.
- Philip Green Educational Ltd. produce the following useful material: *British wild animals* (F54); *Birds* (F45); *Pets* (F29); *Small Creatures* (F23). All are 56 half-frame filmstrips with Teachers' Notes.
- Books which would be useful for this topic include: *The Guinness Book of Pet Records* by Gerald L Wood, published by Guinness. *The Illustrated Book of Birds* Octopus. *The Easy Way to Bird Recognition* J Kilbracken, Kingfisher Books. *Your obedient servant – the story of man's best friend*, by Angela Patmore, published by Hutchinson.

Human resources could include visits from a vet, a farmer, a zoo keeper, an RSPCA inspector, or any other useful contact in this area. Similarly visits to a farm, a zoo, a field studies centre or a local park would all be of value.

Pattern of a topic

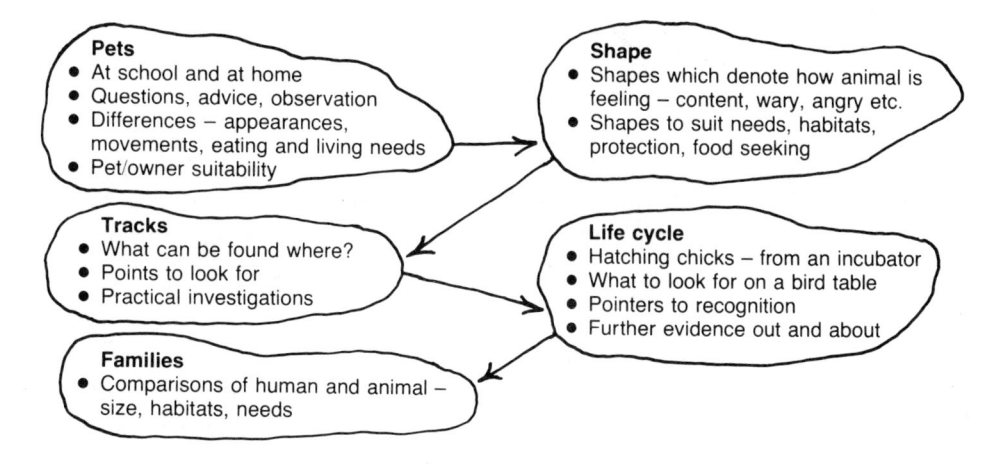

Pets
- At school and at home
- Questions, advice, observation
- Differences – appearances, movements, eating and living needs
- Pet/owner suitability

Shape
- Shapes which denote how animal is feeling – content, wary, angry etc.
- Shapes to suit needs, habitats, protection, food seeking

Tracks
- What can be found where?
- Points to look for
- Practical investigations

Life cycle
- Hatching chicks – from an incubator
- What to look for on a bird table
- Pointers to recognition
- Further evidence out and about

Families
- Comparisons of human and animal – size, habitats, needs

a) Pets, and looking after them

Class pets
During all of the work on this component it is necessary to keep reminding children of some basic rules:

1. Always wash your hands after touching pets.
2. Treat bites and scratches immediately.
3. Handle pets gently and never force them to do things they do not want to do.

Teachers will also need to be aware of children's allergies when bringing pets into the classroom.

Begin with discussion around questions like: *What pets do we have at home? In school? Can we bring a home pet to school? Do all pets look alike? How do they differ in appearance, in what they eat, in where they live? Can they all be looked after in the same way? Are some pets better suited to some people than others? Why is this?*

The first step might be to record what pets the children have, as a bar graph.

Some of the children had more than one pet, so another graph could be drawn to give this information.

'Look alikes'

Once ownership has been discussed then 'look alikes' could be talked about and illustrated; that is, features which the pets have in common (number of legs/wings etc).

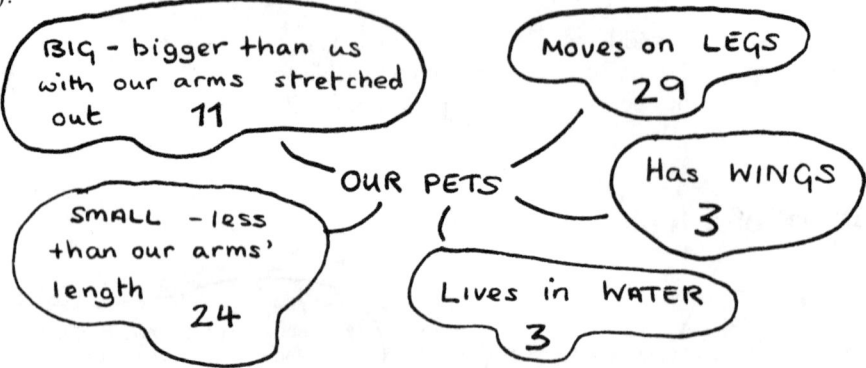

OUR PETS
- BIG – bigger than us with our arms stretched out 11
- SMALL – less than our arms' length 24
- Moves on LEGS 29
- Has WINGS 3
- Lives in WATER 3

Next the 'outside' of pets could be discussed: *Are coats hairy or smooth? Do they stay the same all the year? Which have feathers and which have scales?*

Following this a survey of how each pet moves might be considered and recorded.

More about dogs

This information-gathering is likely to raise a lot of questions – *What dogs move differently – how and why? How are cats' movements different from dogs? Which is the slowest moving of these creatures? Which one jumps? Which needs the most protection?*

In considering movement practical work could include a simple way of taking a dog's footprints. Wet the dog's feet with damp cotton wool and encourage it to walk on a hard, dry surface. The wet footprints could then be drawn around with chalk, covered with thin paper and traced.

Investigating a dog's coat is interesting. Get the dog to stand on a sheet of paper and groom it thoroughly. Help the children to examine what is on the paper with a magnifying glass.

Other recording could show the different colours of various pets' eyes, and note whether these are linked to body colours. A closer look at mouths and teeth is also informative and with teacher guidance, can provoke interesting discussion.

Who owns what?
Give the children a series of facts related to pets and owners and ask them to work out the most likely owner for each pet. For older children, this could take the form of a 'problem page' as follows:

Mrs Benn. Aged 70. Home - small flat. Can't walk far.

Mr Wedge. Farmer. Owns lots of land. Has very big house.

Marcus. Lives in small house with big garden. He has lots of energy.

Pauline. Aged 20 has small house and garden. Likes walking and grooming dogs.

Now match these people with the following dogs. Think about your choice.

Rip. Large Alsation. Strong, good protector. Eats a lot. Needs lots of room.

Lulu - a tiny dog gentle and loving. Very quiet.

Pete - a mongrel likes running and jumping. At his best with young people.

Julie - very smart. An Afghan. Quiet nature, likes walking.

The final activity would involve a class/school pet—hamster, mouse or guinea pig. Preparatory work for this could include some discussion about food and how to care for pets.

Construct a simple 'maze' of balsa wood and glue. Make sure that it is quite big enough for the animal, and cover it with a piece of glass. The pet should be allowed to find its way through the maze. Then put some food at Point X and observe the pet's actions again when it is in the maze.

46   Science Topics for Infants

NC coverage
AT2 Level 1b: *know that there is a wide variety of living things, which includes humans*
   Level 2a: *know that plants and animals need certain conditions to sustain life*
   Level 2b: *be able to sort familiar living things into broad groups according to easily observable features*

b) Shape
This work links animals with which children are familiar on an everyday basis, to those which they know via zoos, TV, photographs, and books.

The different shapes of animals can provoke a great deal of thought. As a starting point, look at the shapes cats and dogs take up for different reasons and on different occasions:

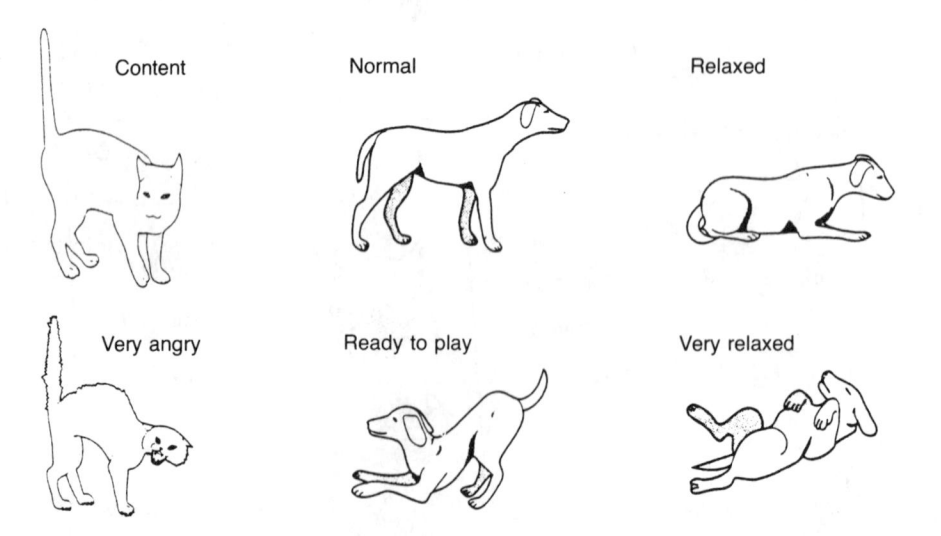

Content   Normal   Relaxed

Very angry   Ready to play   Very relaxed

As well as noting the different body shapes, look at particular details, for example in the cat's case, the significance of ears and mouth. Observation of other animals' body shapes might begin with a 'who knows what this is?' quiz. Some silhouettes could start things off:

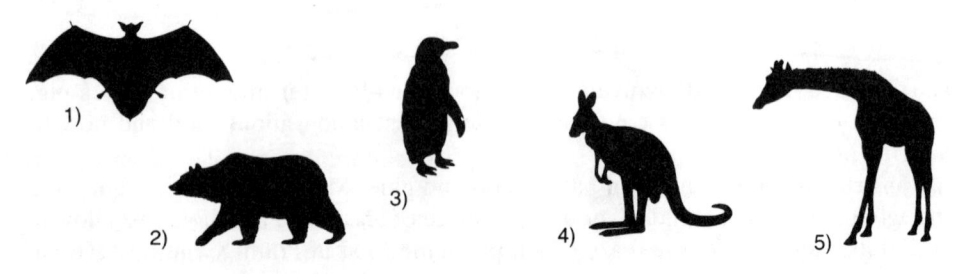

1)
2)
3)
4)
5)

One question arising from this might be *'Why do different animals have such strange shapes?'* This could lead to considerations of how animals' shapes help them to survive in their particular habitat, catch their food, protect themselves and so on. Some animals are very small and can hide easily, some are armoured or spiked for protection, others are equipped to burrow holes, others such as the camel (the hump contains food stored in the form of fat), are shaped for durability. Findings can be recorded, perhaps by drawings and tape-recorded comment.

NC coverage
AT2 Level 2b: *be able to sort familiar living things into broad groups according to easily observable features*
   Level 2c: *know that different kinds of living things are found in different localities*

c) Keeping track

In any work on animals it will obviously be desirable to consider some habitats and a trip out of school could be very rewarding. Rabbits, squirrels and sometimes deer can be found in parks; hedgehogs, and often foxes, are found on the outskirts of towns.

Habitats
Young children like 'detective work' and the following guidelines might help their observation in a 'habitat search':

1 Tracks might be found in mud, sand, snow or on wet ground.
2 Worm trails can sometimes be seen which lead to an animal's home.
3 Watch out for dropped 'bedding' and flattened undergrowth.
4 Look for hair and droppings on the ground.
5 Scatterings of half-eaten nuts and cones often show an animal has been nearby.

Perhaps the easiest animals for young children to track are squirrels and rabbits. A good identification guide, particularly one which illustrates animal tracks, will be a useful resource here.

NC coverage
AT2 Level 2c: *know that different kinds of living things are found in different localities*

d) Bird watch

Birds have already featured in the context of children's pets. This component widens the study to look at wild birds.

Schools with an incubator could hatch out some chicks. The children could record a time scale of events from first placing the eggs in the heat until the fully developed chick breaks through the shell.

If the school has a bird table the children could watch it and compile a log of information about what birds use it, when they come, their different appearances, seasonal and regular visitors and so on.

For young children a very basic level of observation could be introduced: *How big was the bird? What was its shape?* (long, thin, short, plump) *What colour was it? What sort of beak did it have? Did it have any markings?* (spotted breast, strip of colour). *Do more birds come at any one particular time?* A good identification guide (see *Resources*) and some colour pictures will be invaluable.

Nesting

If the topic overlaps with the nesting season (spring/summer) the children could hang nesting materials like wool and feathers on a 'watchable' tree and make notes of when birds take them away. They could also look out for birds flying with nesting materials in their mouths.

There are many books on bird watching. A particularly useful and colourful one for use with young children is *The Nature Trail Book of Birdwatching* by Malcolm Hart, published by Usborne.

NC coverage

AT2 Level 2b: *be able to sort familiar living things into broad groups according to easily observable features*

Level 3a: *know the basic life processes common to humans and other animals*

e) Rounding up

The 'family' idea of human beings and animals could be taken a little further here. This might start with a chart of the children's family sizes:

Living Things – Animals and Birds 49

This could then be compared with pet families:

```
Number of
babies       Martin's dog   🐾 🐾 🐾 🐾 🐾    5
class pets   Katy's cat     🐾 🐾 🐾 🐾 🐾    5
had          Lee's fish     = = = = = = =    too many to count
```

From families discussion could move on to the homes they live in – and the fact that animals need homes too.

With the teacher's help, the children might make some ideal habitats for pets/animals. Points to consider here would be: *How big is the animal? How much exercise does it need? What about safety, comfort, warmth, hygiene?* Work here could range from wormeries, fish tanks and cardboard boxes for tortoises, to more substantial habitats.

Another 'round up' possibility could be to focus on specific differences – numbers of legs of different creatures; type of teeth; differing feet of birds. Visits to a farm, a zoo, a park, a bird hide etc would be a useful way of consolidating the experience.

NC coverage
AT2 Level 3a: *know the basic life processes common to humans and other animals*
Level 3b: *know that human activity may produce changes in the environment that can affect plants and animals*

Cross-curricular links

Maths work is included: estimating, weighing, measuring, working out costs of food and materials, noting time in the sense of daily and seasonal changes. **Technology** is involved in the construction of habitats.

English could involve talk about pictures, actual pets and animals, visits; there could also be factual writing – *my pet, a day in the life of the classroom pet, my diary of our animal topic* etc. Creative work could result in poems and narrative work, eg *I am Billy the tortoise and one day . . . A story of a hamster called Joker.* In both spoken and written forms, 'technical' vocabulary could be introduced. **Drama** could involve miming animal movements; miming to tape recordings of various animal noises; creative drama about the adventures of pets.

In **art and craft**, children could make animals out of scrap materials such as wool, fabric, string, feathers, stick, boxes etc. They could also make a mural of birds and animals seen on the school premises, and some simple bird mobiles might be made.

Animals in **RE** could focus on animals which help us – guide dogs for the blind, search and rescue dogs, sheepdogs etc.

There are plenty of **musical** extracts and songs about animals, eg Saint-Saens' *Carnival of the Animals, Peter and the Wolf* and popular songs like *The Hippopotamus Song, Yellow Bird, La Golandrina. . .*

7 Living Things – Plants

    a) **Starters**
    b) **Let's look at seeds**
    c) **Looking at flowers**
    d) **Rounding up**

Anatomy of a topic

Plants are not instantly of riveting interest to young children, so this topic needs careful planning, plenty of variety and a relatively short time span. It is best at a time of year when the plant world outside is at its most spectacular – spring or autumn. It is important to take the children out and about in the local environment (parks, fields, field studies centre, garden centre) and visitors such as a local park keeper or keen gardener who could 'enthuse' the children are a valuable asset.

Equipment

selections of fruit and vegetables; pips, seeds, fruit, leaves	card	plastic bags
	glue	pebbles
	pencils	stones
soil	water	bulbs
peat	water containers	plastic sheeting
compost	paper	large tray
yoghurt pots	jam jars	
boxes	cotton wool	
saucers	magnifying glasses	
old cutlery to serve as gardening tools	clipboards	
	tape recorder	

Resources
- Human resources in the form of 'green-fingered' visitors are the best way to enthuse the children. The Countryside Commission publish leaflets of country parks, and there may be one near enough to visit.
- A piece of useful software for BBC computers is *Wildflowers* (GTV 26BD), available from GSN Software Ltd. This is an identikit type of program, in which identification is aided by colour, number of petals and shape. Used selectively, it can be a valuable resource.
- One of the problems of work with plants is that it cannot be hurried – or can it? The SAPS (Science and Plants for Schools) organisation believes that 'fast plants'

Living Things – Plants 51

can be developed by using a light bank of fluorescent tubes.
- *Fruit and vegetables* (F14) and *Plants in a house* (F15) in the Ginn 'First Interest' series are excellent for infants.
- *The bulb* by Pamela Nash (Macmillan) has large pictures and extremely simple text which detail the growth of a daffodil bulb.
- Two useful identification guides are *The Oxford Book of Wild Flowers* by Nicholson, Amy and Gregory, and *The Children's Book of the Countryside* (Usborne).

Pattern of a topic

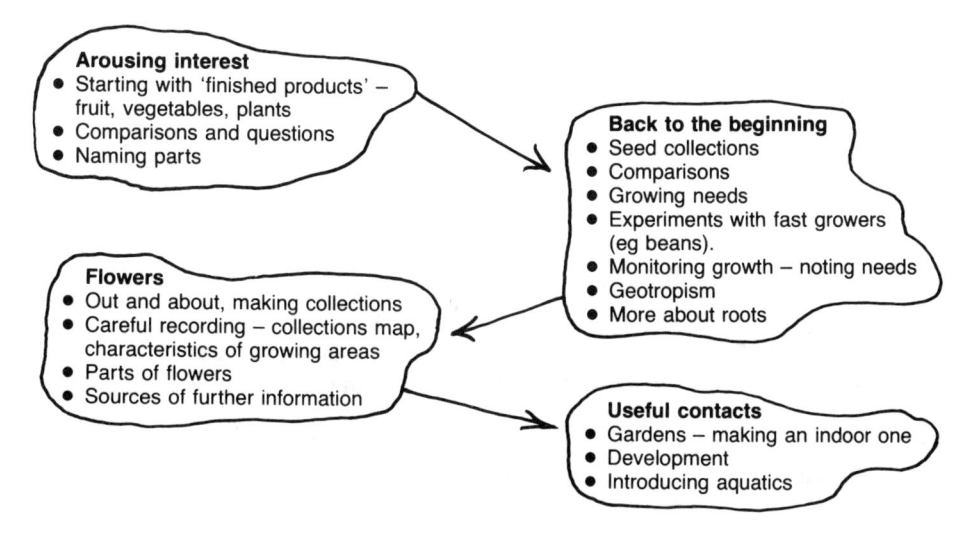

Arousing interest
- Starting with 'finished products' – fruit, vegetables, plants
- Comparisons and questions
- Naming parts

Back to the beginning
- Seed collections
- Comparisons
- Growing needs
- Experiments with fast growers (eg beans).
- Monitoring growth – noting needs
- Geotropism
- More about roots

Flowers
- Out and about, making collections
- Careful recording – collections map, characteristics of growing areas
- Parts of flowers
- Sources of further information

Useful contacts
- Gardens – making an indoor one
- Development
- Introducing aquatics

a) Starters

One of the best ways to start things off is for the teacher and children to make collections. These could be used to stimulate questions and discussion, and also provoke sorting work.

'Finished products' are obviously the most familiar to children. Depending on season/availability the following might appear: blackberries, strawberries, raspberries, apples, pears, plums, mushrooms, cabbages, lettuces, carrots, potatoes etc. These could be examined and various records made: *Which have pips inside? Of which do we eat the 'underground bits'? Which one's leaves do we eat? Which are called fruits? Which are called vegetables? Where can we find these things?*

Young children may well answer 'shops' or 'the supermarket' for the last question. This is perfectly valid, and can be used as a passport for 'working back' through how the product gets to the shop, where it is grown etc.

Looking at and discussing these collections provides many opportunities to name the various parts and establish familiarity with words such as leaves, roots, fruits and seeds. Questions to emerge from this activity might include: *How do they get like this? How do they grow? What do they grow from? What makes them grow?*

52   Science Topics for Infants

NC coverage
AT2 Level 1a: *know that there is a wide variety of living things which includes humans*
Level 2b: *be able to sort familiar living things into broad groups according to easily observable features*

b) Let's look at seeds

Seed collection
Make a collection of seeds – this will, of course, vary according to the season. Summer might provide grass seeds, poppy heads, peas, beans, tomatoes, soft fruits. Autumn offers nuts, acorns, conkers, berries (eg hips and haws). Apples, oranges, melons, dates etc can be purchased to add to the collection.

Allow time for the children to appreciate the seeds for their own sake, observing shape, texture and colour. Children enjoy sorting and making patterns or collages with their collections. These observations could lead on to more investigations: *Why are seeds different shapes? What happens to the seeds now? Why do some fruits have lots of seeds* (eg strawberries) *and others only a few* (eg apples)?

Growing seeds
Following on from the children's observations on seeds, it is very valuable for them to have practical experience of how seeds grow. The wider the range of seeds, containers etc, the better, but some seeds (such as orange pips) take a long time to germinate. It is important to ensure lots of variety, with different things going on at different times to maintain interest. It is a good idea to have some very simple books on hand, so the children can compare their testing with pictures.

Have on hand some soil, peat, compost; pots, yoghurt cartons, boxes, saucers; discarded cutlery as 'gardening tools'; beans or other fast-growing seeds.

Get the children to work in groups. Give each group four pots, labelled A – D. Help them to fill the pots with a growing medium and plant a bean in each. They can then experiment to discover what conditions seeds need for growth, by treating the pots as follows:

A   given water at regular intervals and exposed to the light
B   given no water, exposed to the light
C   given water; covered with black paper or put in a dark place
D   given no water and no light

Ask the children to record the treatment given to each pot, and the results. From this, they could be encouraged to draw conclusions about what plants need for growth.

Roots
The above activity showed children what happens 'above the ground'. This experiment looks at what goes on beneath the surface – roots.

Fill a jar with wet cotton wool. Insert several beans between the wool and the glass. Make sure to keep the cotton wool damp. After about a week, roots will be

Living Things – Plants 53

visible – growing downwards from the beans. Turn the jar over. After a few days, the roots will have changed direction and begun to grow downwards again. This is an example of geotropism: the roots are attracted towards the earth by the pull of gravity. This could be explained to the children in very simple terms.

Another 'fun' test is to balance an acorn in the neck of a bottle of water. Make sure the water touches the acorn. The acorn will begin to grow, and its progress can be observed and recorded. Once the roots have really begun to develop, it could be transferred to a pot of soil or peat.

NC coverage
AT2 Level 2a: *know that plants and animals need certain conditions to sustain life*
   Level 2c: *know that green plants need light to stay alive and healthy*

c) Looking at flowers

Some questions might start things off here. *Where do we find flowers? What sort of colours are they? Are they the same all the year? Do they look the same all through the day? Can they live indoors?*

Flower search
Prepare a simple plan of the area immediately outside the school.

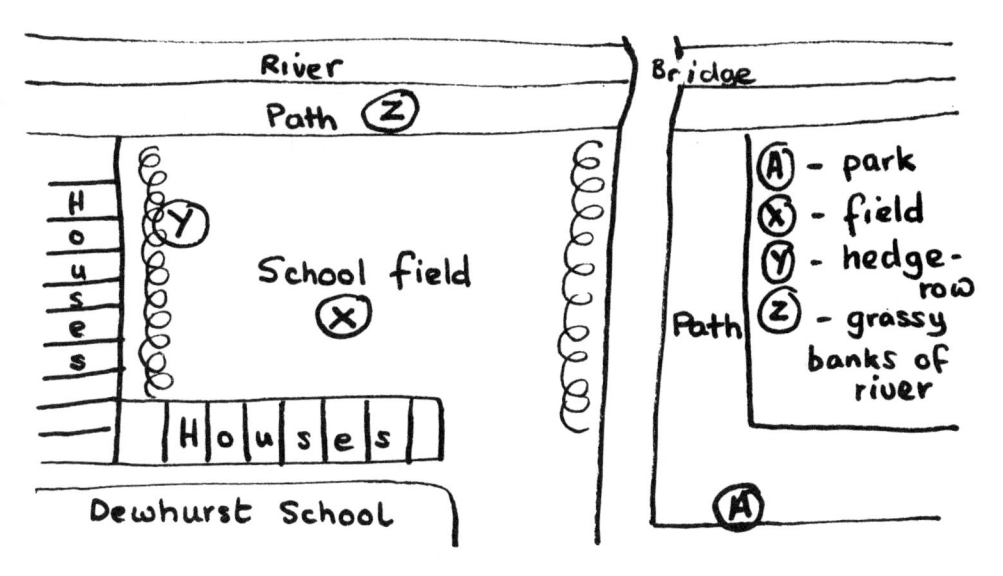

(The school shown on this map is fortunate in that it is possible to take children onto a field, a riverbank, beside a hedgerow and into a park, all without crossing a main road. Most schools have some possibilities, however. Even those in inner cities can often find flowers on wasteland.)

Help the children in a flower search. All flowers found should be carefully recorded and identified (see the *Resources* for some useful flower guides). They can be represented on the map by coloured marks and numbers, showing where different species were found. This would then be linked to a key, matching numbers with flower names. One or two specimens could be brought back to school for further study, but the need for conservation and preservation of wildlife should be emphasised at all times. Another way of recording where plants were found could be as follows:

FLOWERS COLLECTED ON OUTING

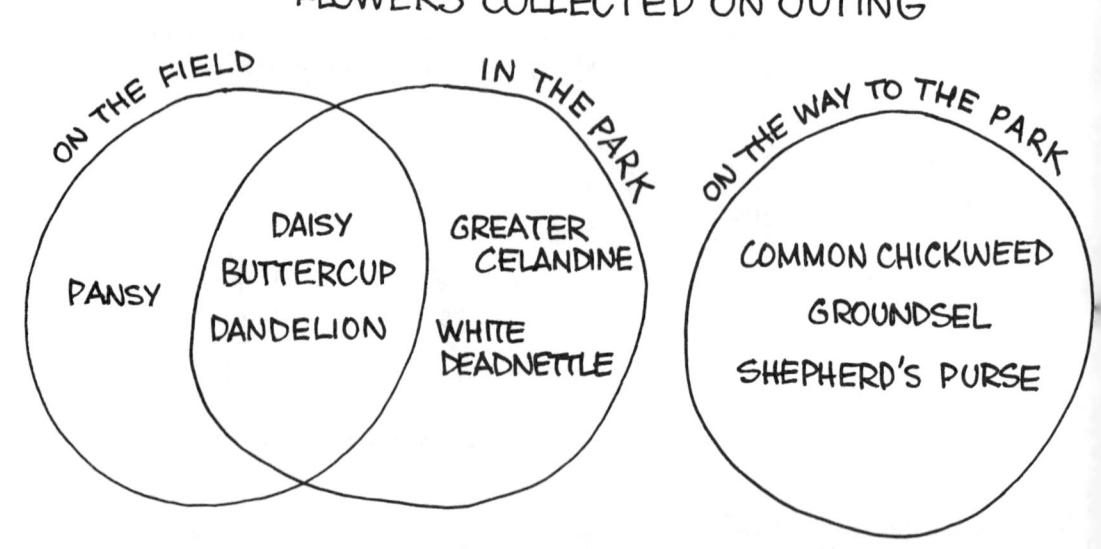

ON THE FIELD | IN THE PARK | ON THE WAY TO THE PARK

- PANSY
- DAISY, BUTTERCUP, DANDELION (field ∩ park)
- GREATER CELANDINE, WHITE DEADNETTLE (park only)
- COMMON CHICKWEED, GROUNDSEL, SHEPHERD'S PURSE (on the way to the park)

If specimens are brought in to school, help the children examine them. Some vocabulary could be introduced at this point: the flower is on a *stalk*; the coloured leaves are called *petals*; the small green leaves under the petals are called *sepals*.

Encourage the children to record their findings by prompting with questions like: *What shape is the flower? What colour is it? Is it smooth or rough? Has it got a smell? What does it look like through a magnifying glass?*

NC coverage

AT2 Level 1b: *know that there is a wide variety of living things which includes humans*
  Level 2b: *be able to sort familiar things into broad groups according to easily observable features*
  Level 2c: *know that different kinds of living things are found in different localities*

d) Rounding up

If the local park keeper likes children (not all do!) they could be invited in to talk about their work. This might also open the way for visits to parks, greenhouses, potting sheds etc.

Make a garden
Some groups might like to make an indoor garden for continuous study. This can be done as follows:

a Line a large, deep tray with pebbles.
b Fill the tray with soil, making a hollow area at one end.
c Put a plastic sheet in the hollowed area and weigh it down with stones. It can then be filled with water to make a miniature 'pond'.
d Add a selection of seeds, plants and bulbs.

Involve the children as much as possible in caring for the garden. Aquatics (plants which float on the water, with roots hanging down) could be planted in the water area. Frogbit is a useful example; it looks like a small water lily, and the leaves die off in late autumn.

NC coverage
AT2 Level 2a: *know that plants and animals need certain conditions to sustain life*
　　 Level 3c: *know that green plants need light to stay alive and healthy*

Cross-curricular links

Seasonal poems are an obvious stimulus for **creative writing** and **English** work. There are 'weather lore' type jingles, or evocative material like *Autumn Fires* by R L Stevenson, *Autumn in Hyde Park* by Alan Ross and *Autumn under the Trees* by Geoffrey Grigson. A re-telling of the Greek myth of Persephone, as an explanation of how the seasons came about, could provide a starting point for drama writing.

　This idea of 'words and nature' could be carried on to enjoyable **music/drama** in the traditional children's singing game *Oats and Beans*.

　Maths is introduced with the measuring involved. **Technology** is needed for construction of the indoor garden. There is a lot of scope for **art** work with seed patterns and pictures. 'Growth' is an excellent theme for **RE**, and the topic could be linked with Easter or Harvest Festival celebrations.

8 Cold

    a) It's cold
    b) The 'shape' of cold
    c) Measuring cold

Anatomy of a topic

Ideally, this topic should coincide with a spell of really cold weather, with ice and snow. The best time for the topic is therefore January/February. The teacher needs to be flexible and prepared to 'seize the opportunity' if the right conditions present themselves. Even without the ice and snow, however, the topic can still have a great deal to offer.

Some outside work is necessary, but this can be restricted to the school grounds. A useful asset is a bird table, or some point where birds can be watched.

Equipment

water	wellingtons	pencils
containers	bird table (or other	scissors
ice cubes	vantage point)	deep freeze
coats	paper	rulers
socks	various materials – wool,	tin (2lb treacle tin
scarves	cotton, cardboard,	is ideal)
gloves	plastic, silver foil,	magic markers
shoes	polystyrene	tape recorder

Resources

- Useful visitors might be a teacher from a field studies centre who could talk about birds and animals in winter; a police or road safety officer who could talk about communication problems caused by fog, ice and snow in winter.
- Viewtech Audio Visual Media stock a video called *Winter*. It describes how animals prepare for winter and survive wintry conditions.
- Pictorial Charts Educational Trust produce some useful posters showing the variations of the seasons.
- 'Cold' has inspired many poems. A good anthology would be useful. 'A patch of old snow' and 'Stopping by the woods on a snowy evening' by Robert Frost are evocative, as is Christina Rossetti's 'January'. 'White Fields' by James Stephens is also good for providing a background to the children's scientific observations and tests.

Pattern of a topic

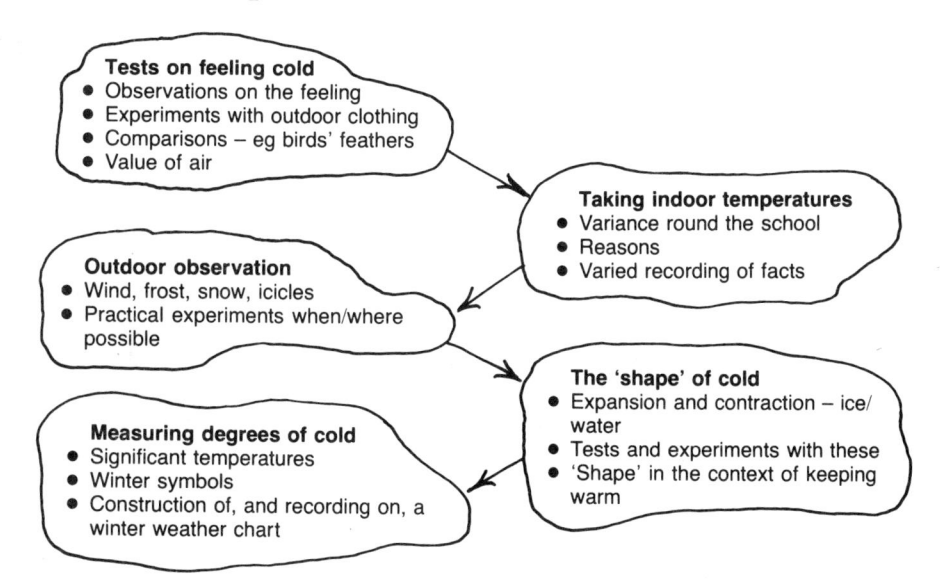

Tests on feeling cold
- Observations on the feeling
- Experiments with outdoor clothing
- Comparisons – eg birds' feathers
- Value of air

Taking indoor temperatures
- Variance round the school
- Reasons
- Varied recording of facts

Outdoor observation
- Wind, frost, snow, icicles
- Practical experiments when/where possible

Measuring degrees of cold
- Significant temperatures
- Winter symbols
- Construction of, and recording on, a winter weather chart

The 'shape' of cold
- Expansion and contraction – ice/water
- Tests and experiments with these
- 'Shape' in the context of keeping warm

a) It's cold

Feeling cold

Start with some group activity. Supply each group with a bowl of water containing ice cubes. The children take turns to immerse their hands in water and keep them there as long as is comfortable, while the rest of the group 'time' them by counting aloud. The times could be recorded in a block graph.

In discussion, focus on what cold feels like: *Why is it difficult to keep our hands in water like this? What did they feel like at first? What did they feel like as time went on? What did they feel like when they were taken out of the water?*

Get the children to observe how they warmed their hands up. *Who put them near the radiator? Did anyone shake their hands about? Did you put them in your pockets? Or wrap them in your jersey or cardigan?* Invite ideas about how we warm up our bodies when they are cold – note these down for practical application later.

From this, encourage the children to talk about other 'cold' situations and times when we feel cold. If it is a wintry day, get the children to put on their coats and go in search of the coldest place in the playground. *Why is that place colder than the others?* (This could lead into a discussion of wind-chill factor.) *Which parts of us felt cold first? Did they have any covering? Does it help to wear a hat? Why?* On returning to the classroom, remind the children of the ideas they had for getting warm. Get them to try these out. *Which are most effective?*

What sorts of clothes keep us warmest?

This follows on directly from the above. Provide the children with various types of material (eg thin cotton, wool, synthetic fibres. . .). Ask them to experiment to find the answer to the question: *Which materials are best for keeping our hands warm?* In further discussion the teacher could introduce the idea that air helps to keep us warm: wearing layers of clothing keeps us warmer than just one garment because air is trapped between the layers; wool is warm because it traps a lot of air in its fibres; a duvet keeps us warm because it holds air in the feathers or fibres inside.

How do birds keep warm?

If you have a bird-table, encourage the children to observe the birds in cold weather. They may notice that: a) birds fluff up their feathers in cold weather – this traps the air to give them extra warmth – rather like a duvet! b) a bird may lift one leg up under its feathers, or tuck its head and beak under one wing. Explain that the bird's beak, legs and feet all have blood vessels but are not covered by warm feathers. These are the areas where they feel the cold most intensely. The children will probably be able to work out the link with their own hands, feet and noses for themselves.

In follow-up work, read the children the following traditional poem:

> *The north wind doth blow*
> *And we shall have snow.*
> *And what will the robin do then,*
> *Poor thing?*
> *Oh, he'll go to the barn*
> *And to keep himself warm,*
> *He'll hide his head under his wing*
> *Poor thing.*

School temperature survey

Groups could take temperature readings in classrooms and in the school hall. The hall will generally be colder. Why? For one group of top juniors the resulting speculation, discussion and testing led to the following 'group report':

The hall was colder than the classroom. When we sat still in the hall we were cold. The hall is bigger and has got more space to heat. A lot of the time there are no people in the hall. We could keep warm in the hall by running about. We can run faster in the hall. Running about makes you warm.

Rounding up

These activities increase children's awareness that clothing, movement and food are all aids to keeping warm; exposure to low temperatures, cold winds, unheated rooms or freezing substances all induce the feeling of cold. These factors can be recorded as follows, with added illustrations and colours to make an attractive display.

Obviously it would be advantageous if this topic could be studied when there is frost or snow about. Ask the children to predict when the frost is likely to be at its thickest on the playground, then check to see if they were correct. This could lead on to reflections on the short days and long nights that occur at the coldest time of the year and the effect of these on the temperature.

Cold 59

> **THINGS WHICH KEPT US WARM**
> Scarves made of wool. Thick coats. Thick gloves. Trousers. Thick socks. Hats.

> **THINGS THAT DID NOT**
> Thin clothes. Gloves which were too tight. Wellingtons without thick socks. Letting our coats be unfastened. Thin shoes.

> **COLDEST PLACES IN THE PLAYGROUND IN A COLD WIND**
> In the middle. At the corner leading to the passage. On top of the climbing frame.

> **LESS COLD PLACES**
> Right beside the classroom wall. By the hedge and the trees. Crouched down behind the logs.

NC coverage

AT3 Level 2b: *know that heating and cooling everyday materials can cause them to melt or solidify or change permanently*

Level 3a: *be able to link the use of common materials to their simple properties*

AT4 Level 2b: *understand the meaning of hot and cold relative to the temperature of their own bodies*

Level 3b: *know that there is a range of fuels used in the home*

b) The 'shape' of cold

Snowflakes

If it snows, get the children to examine the shape of the falling flakes, or catch one and look at it in the instant before it melts. This is not at all easy! Children enjoy making paper 'snowflakes' as follows:

a Cut out a circle of white paper. Fold it in half, then in half again (to make quarters), then once again (eighths).

b Cut a pattern into the edges.

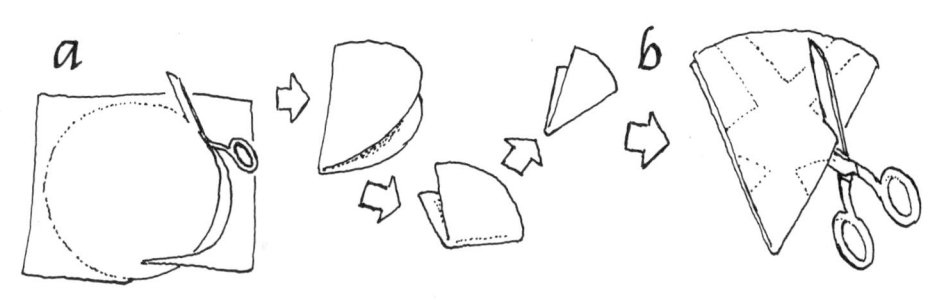

60   Science Topics for Infants

c   Open out the paper. The pattern cut out will appear as a snowflake.

Icicle examination
If the weather is freezing, take the children outside on an icicle hunt. Focus thoughts with questions such as, *Where are we most likely to find icicles? Why are they formed there? How are they formed? When are they most likely to melt? When are they likely to be at their longest?*

Bring some icicles into the classroom for testing. Give each group an icicle on a saucer. Ask groups to place their saucers in different parts of the room and predict – then time – how quickly the icicle melts. As well as recording times, children could note change in the appearance of the icicle – what it looked like at the start, when half-melted, what was left at the end... The icicle's diminishing length in the melting process could be recorded on a chart like this:

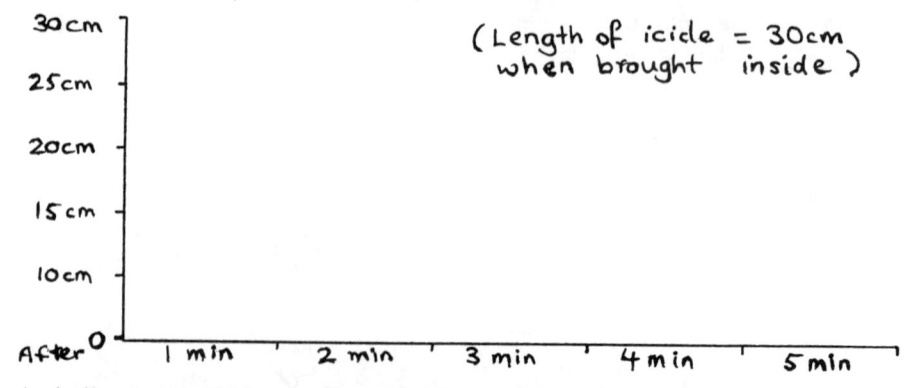

(Length of icicle = 30cm when brought inside)

A similar test could be conducted with a snowball. Its change of shape could be noted as it melts. The children will probably be surprised at how little water is left when the snow has completely gone. This is because snow contains ice crystals with air between them.

Ice-cube tests

Fill a variety of vessels of different shapes and sizes with water. Put them into the deep freeze. Ask the children to predict how long it will take each of the containers to become completely frozen.

The children could use their frozen shapes to do the experiments above, if real icicles or snowballs were not available.

Another line of investigation could be *How can we get the ice out of the containers?* Linked to this would be observation of how the ice changes shape during melting.

If it is a severe winter there may be warnings about burst pipes. Discussion of this problem could lead on to the following experiment, which demonstrates that water expands when it freezes.

The experiment requires a tin (a 2lb treacle tin is a good size), a magic marker, a ruler and access to a deep freeze.

a Fill the tin above half-way with water.
b Make a mark at Point X – the level of the water.
c Measure and record the distance from A to B.

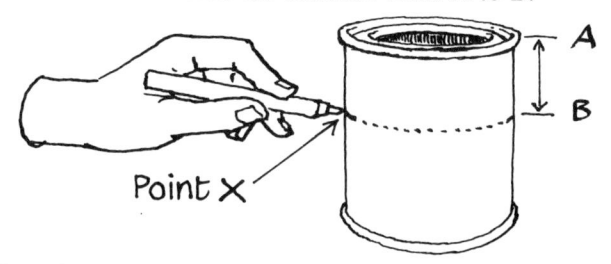

d Put the tin of water into the deep freeze and leave it there until it is completely frozen.
e Take out the tin and mark the new Point X.
f Measure and record the distance from A to B.

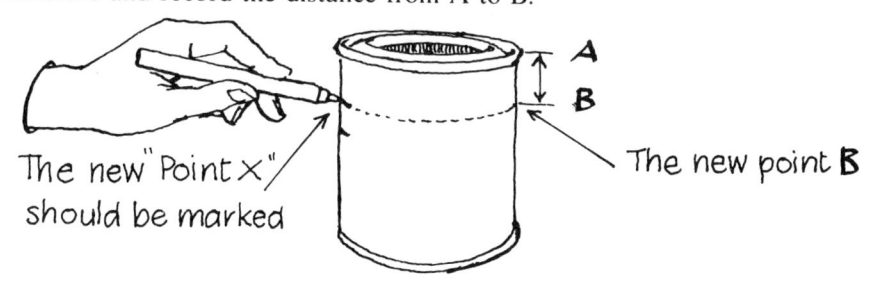

The distance A – B is much shorter when the tin contains ice rather than water. Allow the ice to melt and empty the tin. The children can now see that the mark of the second Point X is higher than the first Point X. This demonstrates that water expands when it freezes.

Does shape help keep us warm?

This activity goes back to examining things which might keep us warm, to find out if 'shape' is significant.

Tests could again be made with a variety of materials including quite unlikely ones. Apart from wool, thick material and thin material, things like cardboard, pieces of plastic and polystyrene could be tested. *How is shape significant here?*

A further development of this could be more testing to see which materials keep an ice cube from melting for the longest period of time. *What shape of container is best? What should the container be made of?*

Children could tape-record their activities as they happen. They could then discuss this recording when it is replayed afterwards.

NC coverage
AT3 Level 2a: *be able to group materials according to observable features*
　　　Level 2b: *know that heating and cooling everyday materials can cause them to melt, solidify or change permanently*
AT4 Level 2b: *understand the meaning of hot and cold relative to the temperature of their own bodies*

c) Measuring cold

Thermometers
Photocopy a simple drawing of a centigrade thermometer. Give copies to groups of children and suggest they use their 'thermometers' to record temperatures which the group have found significant when using real thermometers.

Examples of such measuring and recording might be:

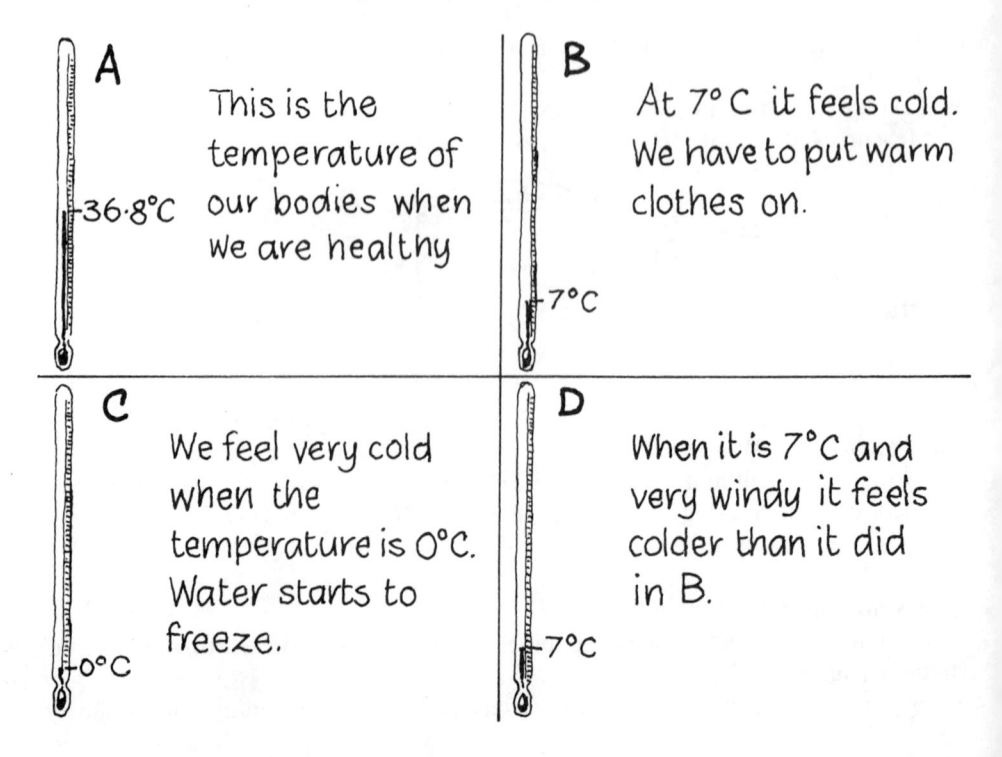

A — 36.8°C This is the temperature of our bodies when we are healthy

B — 7°C At 7°C it feels cold. We have to put warm clothes on.

C — 0°C We feel very cold when the temperature is 0°C. Water starts to freeze.

D — 7°C When it is 7°C and very windy it feels colder than it did in B.

Cold 63

There is of course plenty of scope for extending children's measuring and recording in other areas. These activities make them more familiar with using a thermometer, and give them an idea of what are important temperatures.

Winter weather

This activity with thermometers could be linked to a winter weather chart. This could be kept on a daily basis throughout the period of the topic.

Invite the children to devise the symbols used to show the weather. Here are some ideas:

Snow   Ice   Frost   Sun

Temperature   Thick cloud   Some cloud

Rain   Wind

The symbols could then be attached to a chart like this:

DATE : January 14th	
Time of first weather check: 9.30 am	0°C
Time of second weather check: 3.00 pm	-1°C
Notes on weather	Today got colder as it went on. It started to snow at 2.30pm

At a very basic level the use of a torch as a light source, and a tilted globe, can show that in winter the northern hemisphere is tilted farthest away from the light/heat source.

NC coverage
AT4 Level 1d: *be able to describe the apparent movement of the sun across the sky*
Level 2e: *know that the Earth, Sun and Moon are separate spherical bodies*
Level 3e: *know that the appearance of the moon and the altitude of the Sun change in a regular and predictable manner*

Cross-curricular links

In **English** children can talk and write about severe weather, darkness, bare trees and lack of colour, the need to be 'cosy' and warm. Vocabulary to help them express these features could be introduced, eg: sleet, hail, freezing, hibernate, starving, survival, wild, lonely, bare, blizzard, warmth, central heating etc. Prose and poetry can be prompted by several winter themes: footprints in the snow, the biggest snowman ever, sledging, the day we got stuck in the snow . . . and so on.

Background music for this topic could come from seasonal compositions such as *The Four Seasons* by Vivaldi; *Folk songs of the four seasons* by Vaughan Williams; and *'Saturn'* from *The Planets Suite* by Holst. The latter is very evocative on a wintry day.

RE might focus on taking care of animals and old people in winter; **Geography** could be very well served by looking at 'cold lands' or even developing a topic within a topic and doing some work on Eskimoes and other people who live in cold climates. **History** might look at the development of winter clothes/warmer houses. **Maths** would again be involved in the various measuring aspects of the topic.

9 Heat

a) **You and heat**
b) **Heat and food**
c) **Moving heat**
d) **Deserts**

Anatomy of a topic

The ideal time for this is at either a hot or a cold time of the year. If the former then the hot sun would be a useful reference point; if the latter then heat sources like radiators could be used. Many teachers might consider it advantageous to locate the topic in November and link it with November 5th and further development on the theme of 'fire'.

Equipment

tea cosy	sugar	pieces of metal and wood
tea pot	oxo cubes	various materials (wool,
kettle	other cooking materials	cotton, cotton wool)
clinical thermometer	glasses for hot and cold	bottle with screw-on
classroom thermometer	water	metal top
pencils	spoons	cactus plants
paper	candles	sand
card	matches	pictures/photographs of
heat sources (varied)	gloves	the desert and desert
milk	steel rods (possible use	animals
chocolate	of knitting needles	
butter	here)	
salt	dish for candles	

Resources
- A very useful resource in Harbutt's *Case Study* series is 'Heat', a package containing thermometer, spirit burner, flasks and boiling tubes, insulating materials and various metal rods. Whilst the activity sheets included are aimed at juniors they have minimal text and can be adapted. There are also Teacher's Notes.

Pattern of a topic

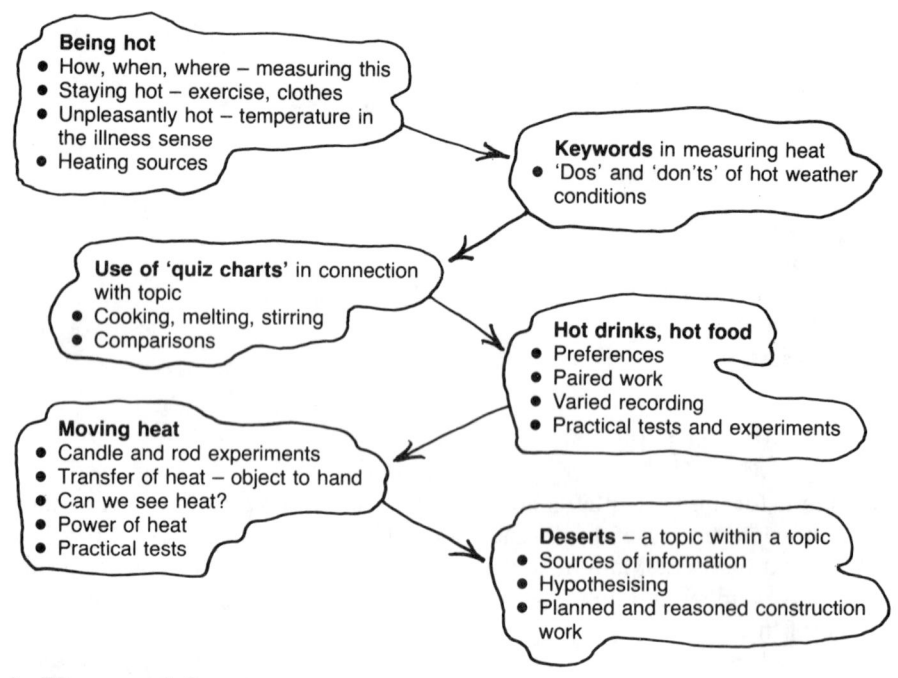

Being hot
- How, when, where – measuring this
- Staying hot – exercise, clothes
- Unpleasantly hot – temperature in the illness sense
- Heating sources

Keywords in measuring heat
- 'Dos' and 'don'ts' of hot weather conditions

Use of 'quiz charts' in connection with topic
- Cooking, melting, stirring
- Comparisons

Hot drinks, hot food
- Preferences
- Paired work
- Varied recording
- Practical tests and experiments

Moving heat
- Candle and rod experiments
- Transfer of heat – object to hand
- Can we see heat?
- Power of heat
- Practical tests

Deserts – a topic within a topic
- Sources of information
- Hypothesising
- Planned and reasoned construction work

a) You and heat

Questions like the following will start off the children's thinking around this topic:
When do you get hot? Where is the hottest place in the classroom? What sorts of things make you hot? How can you make yourself hot? What do you want to do when you are hot? When do you feel hot in a very unpleasant way? How do we measure how hot we are?

Allow plenty of time for the children to suggest ideas and tests for answering these questions, try them out and record their results. If possible, help the children use classroom thermometers to measure temperatures in and around school. Key words in this component are *temperature, thermometer, measure*, plus less 'scientific' terms like boiling, roasting, frying, sweating, scorching, dripping etc.

1 Where is the hottest place in the classroom?
Ask the children to find the hottest place. In summer it might be near uncurtained windows on a hot, sunny day. In winter it might be near the classroom radiators.

2 How can you make yourself hot?
Children may suggest putting on more clothes, running around a lot, or both. This could be extended to look at methods of retaining heat, eg wearing hats and gloves, using a tea-cosy, lagging on water tanks, insulation on pipes and in lofts. This could be extended to look at how we keep houses and classrooms warm. *Do we open or close doors? When? What about windows? What can we do to stop draughts?* Ask the children to describe the sort of heating they have at home. *Which are the*

Heat 67

coldest/warmest rooms? Why? Some children will point out that they have a combination of heating sources eg fire and radiators. *Why might this be? What advantages does it have?*

3 When do you feel hot in a very unpleasant way?
After discussion someone may suggest *When we are ill. Has anyone had their temperature taken? What happened? What sorts of people use thermometers?* At this stage it is sufficient for the children to know that a fit human body works well at a temperature of 36.8°C. When our temperature rises too high, we feel ill. The results of these investigations could be recorded in a variety of ways:

HOW WE KEEP OUR HOUSE WARM:
Coal or coke fire: Marcus, Elaine
Electric fire: Nina, Geoffrey
Gas fire: Alison, Louise, Wayne, Martin
Radiators: Nina, Geoffrey, Alison, Wayne, Martin
Hot air blowers: Elaine, Louise

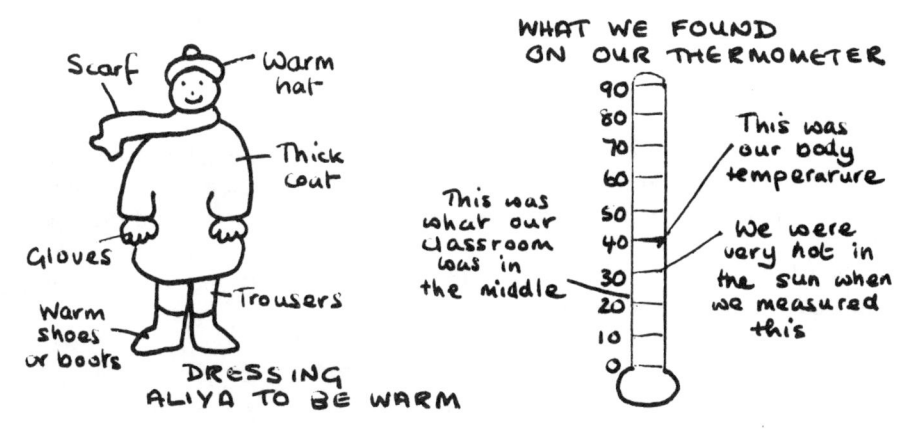

DRESSING ALIYA TO BE WARM
- Scarf
- Warm hat
- Thick coat
- Gloves
- Trousers
- Warm shoes or boots

WHAT WE FOUND ON OUR THERMOMETER
- This was what our classroom was in the middle
- This was our body temperature
- We were very hot in the sun when we measured this

4 How do we keep cool when it's hot?
Invite children to contribute ideas about ways of keeping cool. These could be displayed in a picture chart or collage, illustrated with pictures from magazines or the children's own drawings.

HOW WE KEEP COOL WHEN IT'S HOT
- Fan
- Cool drinks
- Keep in the shade
- Don't do too much in the sun
- swimming

68 *Science Topics for Infants*

Key words to arise would include: *temperature, thermometer, measure* and then a selection of *boiling, roasting, frying, sweating, scorching, dripping* and so on.

NC coverage
AT2 Level 3a: *know the basic life processes common to humans and other animals*
AT4 Level 2b: *understand the meaning of hot and cold relative to the temperature of their own bodies*

b) Heat and food

Eating and drinking
'Favourite hot drinks and hot food' might be the starting point here. Ask children to work in pairs and record (on paper, on tape, by illustration. . .) their partner's preferences. When this has been done, simple bar charts could record class findings.

Heating food and drink
From this, move on to consider how we heat food or drink, and what happens when we do. If you have access to cooking facilities, and plenty of adult help, the children could watch liquids such as water or milk being heated (in a kettle and saucepan respectively). Invite the children to comment on the 'change of state' from cold liquid to hot liquid. Older children could try out a 'quiz chart' like the following when they have watched the practical work.

Look at the picture and then this list of words: boiled, hot touch, temperature

Put the missing word in these sentences. You can find it here.

1. This picture shows us that the water in the kettle is very _____.

2. It shows us that the kettle is being _____.

3. You must never _____ the spout of a boiling kettle.

4. As the kettle boils the _____ of the water rises.

If parental help is available, some simple cooking could take place. Ask children to note changes of state, differences in taste and texture of the ingredients before and after they are subjected to heat. An easy and practical example would be a piece of bread/toast. Another way of using heat sources is to warm a bar of chocolate or a piece of butter and note the results. *What happens when they are removed from the heat source and left to cool for a period of time?*

Hot or cold?

Give each group three cups of hot water and three cups of cold water. Again, make sure that there is plenty of adult supervision. Give the children some salt, some sugar and a crumbled stock cube. Explain that they need to put some salt in a hot cup and a cold cup, then some sugar in the next pair of cups, and so on. Stir the cups. *What happens?* (The substances will dissolve more quickly in the hot water, because the molecules are moving more quickly.) Again the children could record their findings.

What we used

Three cups of hot water   Three cups of cold water

1 spoonful of salt   1 spoonful of salt

1 spoonful of sugar   1 spoonful of sugar

1 oxo cube   1 oxo cube

What we did

salt sugar oxo   salt sugar oxo

We stirred the things in the cups

What happened

The things in the cups of hot water **DISSOLVED FIRST**

NC coverage

AT3 Level 2b: *know that heating and cooling everyday materials can cause them to melt, solidify or change permanently*

c) Moving heat

Does heat move?

a Place a candle on a tray and light it.
b Ask an adult helper to hold a thin steel rod. Drop several blobs of wax from the burning candle on to it.
c Set down the candle in its tray again. The teacher should then hold one end of the steel rod in the flame of the candle. (Be sure to wear a glove or wrap some protective material around the rod.)

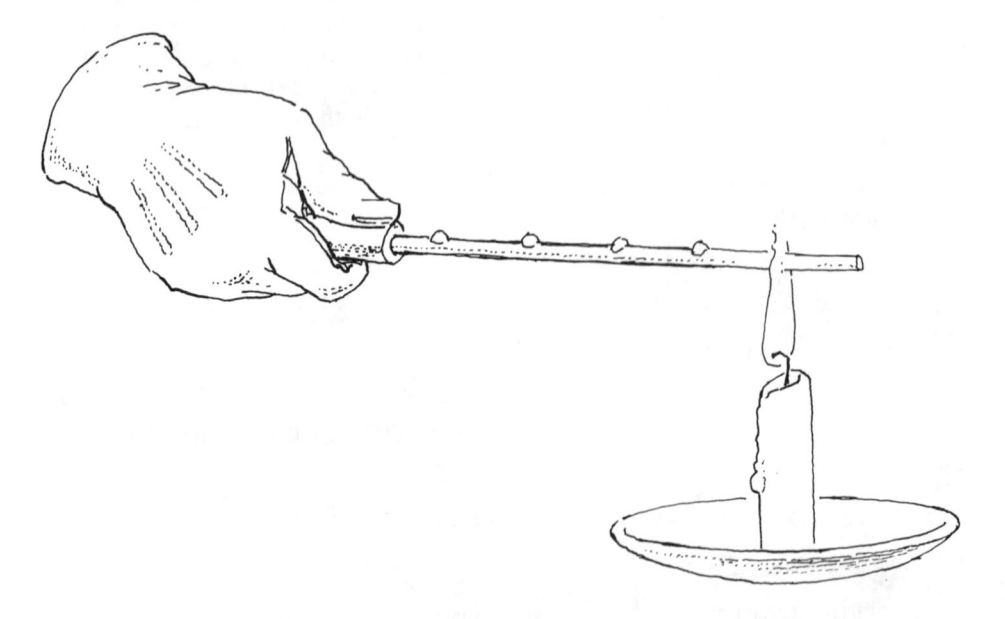

d The children will observe that the blob of wax nearest the candle (blob A) soon melts – followed by blob B, then blob C and so on. This shows that the heat is travelling up the rod. Observant children will be able to offer an answer to the question: 'Why is the teacher wearing a glove?'

Another very simple experiment here would be to light a candle, put it in a bowl and place it on a desk in the centre of the classroom. Again, under adult supervision the children could do some problem solving and record their findings. In doing so they could make the discovery that warm air rises. Their 'problem list' might include the following: *Can we see heat in the air? What does the air feel like next to the candle? What does the air feel like above the candle? How do we know that the heat is travelling through the air? How does this help us to keep warm in our house?*

A final experiment which the children enjoy doing is the 'mystery bottle top'. A bottle with the metal top screwed tightly on is held under the hot water tap for a minute or two. (The hot water should be directed onto the metal top.)

After this the top unscrews more easily. Heat has 'moved' once again. (This is an illustration of metal expanding as it heats up.)

Heat conductors

Now that we know heat moves through things, how could we find out what it moves through best? Find a heat source where there is no danger of burning, such as the top of a radiator. Give the children a piece of wood, a steel ruler, various pieces of material. Invite them to feel the radiator through the material. *Which felt hottest?* Explain to the children, in simple terms, that all materials conduct heat. Those which do it well are good conductors. Those which do not let much heat through are good insulators.

NC coverage

AT3 Level 1a: *be able to describe the simple properties of familiar materials*
    Level 2b: *know that heating and cooling everyday materials can cause them to melt, solidify or change permanently*
    Level 3a: *be able to link the use of common materials to their simple properties*

d) Deserts

This component makes a 'topic within a topic'. It also provides an interesting opportunity to bring together what children have learned so far.

What is a desert?

Almost any kind of weather outside the classroom can start things off here.

    A very hot day – *What must it be like to live where it is as hot as this every day, or hotter?*

    A windy day – *What must it be like to live in a very hot place where strong winds blow?*

    A wet day – *What must it be like to live in a place where it practically never rains?*

    Have some visual stimulus material around the room: photographs of deserts and desert creatures (camel, locust, snake, jerboa, iguana) and people appropriately dressed for the desert; a selection of cacti. Do not include any photographs of houses in the desert, because this is the nub of the problem-solving exercise: *Can you make up your own house for living in a desert?*

    Get the children to work in groups on this. Help them to review some of their learning in the topic so far: too many glass windows in strong sunlight make for too much heat; which type of floor stays cooler; what is the maximum amount of shade to aim for; the value of water and how precious it is in such circumstances; the need to keep out wind and sand. This activity will generate a great deal of group discussion and opinion sharing. The children could record their investigations in writing and pictures, or perhaps make models of their houses.

NC coverage

AT3 Level 3a: *be able to link the use of common materials to their simple properties*
AT4 Level 2b: *understand the meaning of hot and cold relative to the temperature of their own bodies*

Cross-curricular links

There is plenty of appropriate **music**, eg *Ritual Fire Dance* (Falla) and 'The Desert Song' from the *Firebird Suite* (Stravinsky). The BBC record *Out of this world* (BBC REC 225) contains suitable sound effects material.

'Heat' has been evoked in poems and prose. Laurie Lee's *Cider with Rosie* has a lovely descriptive passage which infants will enjoy. Poems like Tessimond's 'A hot day' are evocative. Children enjoy **writing** about this subject. They could go on to link their writing with paintings or drawings and models in **art and craft** work.

Measuring with thermometers and modelling desert houses involves plenty of **maths** and **technology**. There are also links with **geography** in the 'desert' theme: world areas containing deserts could be talked about. **History** might investigate ways invented to keep warm, or cool.

The topic could be linked with 'Fire' – November 5th, a visit to a fire station, stories of St Catherine and Prometheus are just a few of the ideas that could be developed.

10 Buildings

    a) **Collecting and observing**
    b) **Classroom building**
    c) **Practical building work**
    d) **Tools, machines and us**
    e) **Keeping dry**
    f) **Build your own house!**

Anatomy of a topic

This topic requires quite a lot of planning and preparation. One of the main requirements is the organisation and collection of quite a lot of material. In the main this is very easily come by, but an early start should be made to stockpiling! (A list of equipment and material needed follows).

Another preparatory requirement is the planning of 'viewing' visits – looking at the school from the outside, looking at houses and a local street, possible visits to a church and a building site. All of these activities are very rewarding indeed if carefully planned. There is plenty of scope for using the senses, observing and discussing. 'Prepared' teacher tests and experiments are mixed with opportunities for the children to experiment, test, consider, reflect and record. This topic has the advantage of being 'seasonless' – it could be done equally effectively at any time of the year.

Length will depend upon the teacher's discretion, bearing in mind the 'extension' possibilities, and the fact that the scientific work is not done in a vacuum but alongside other interesting cross-curricular aspects. A month would seem a useful time-scale for the topic.

Equipment from within the classroom

paper	Lego	water
pencils	cardboard boxes	wooden board for mixing
card	building bricks and	water receptacles
glue	blocks	ruler
plasticine	string	tape measure
sellotape	tape recorder	

Equipment from outside the classroom

wood	nails	spirit level
tiles	screws	drill

74 Science Topics for Infants

slates	sand	saw
bricks	hammer	spade
roofing felt	chisel	dowelling
rubber	vice	screw hook
wiring	pliers	wire
putty	screwdriver	cotton reel
plaster	spanner	
cement	mallet	

Resources
Expert human resources would be valuable if linked to visits and observations. The school caretaker could be useful when examining the school building; a householder or shopkeeper might be likewise. Visits to a church or building site would obviously be enhanced by prior contact, and meetings, with the vicar and site foreman.

Pattern of a topic

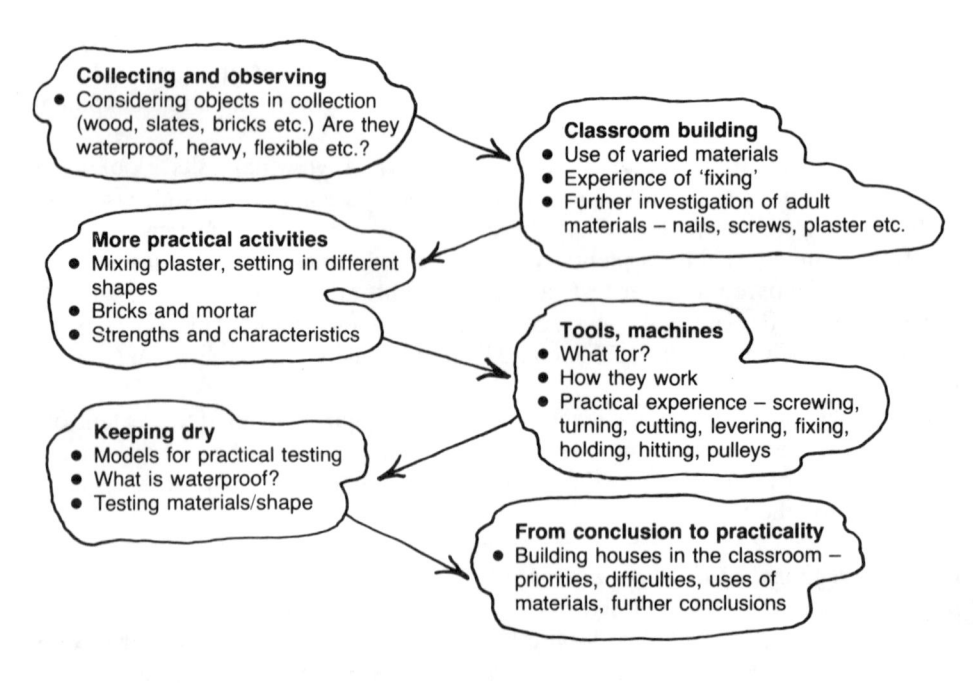

Collecting and observing
- Considering objects in collection (wood, slates, bricks etc.) Are they waterproof, heavy, flexible etc.?

More practical activities
- Mixing plaster, setting in different shapes
- Bricks and mortar
- Strengths and characteristics

Keeping dry
- Models for practical testing
- What is waterproof?
- Testing materials/shape

Classroom building
- Use of varied materials
- Experience of 'fixing'
- Further investigation of adult materials – nails, screws, plaster etc.

Tools, machines
- What for?
- How they work
- Practical experience – screwing, turning, cutting, levering, fixing, holding, hitting, pulleys

From conclusion to practicality
- Building houses in the classroom – priorities, difficulties, uses of materials, further conclusions

A valuable starting point for this topic is guided use of the senses. Take 'seeing' as the first consideration. *What do we see when we look up at houses and schools?* (windows, roofs, chimneys, TV aerials, slates, tiles, gutters, drain pipes). *What can we see when we look either on the level or down?* (doors, windows, locks, porches, walls, ventilation outlets, drain pipes, sinks.) Questions following these observations might include: *What things do we see both up and down? What is the significance of this? What needs to be waterproof? What needs to be transparent?*

What is the most effective kind of roof? What materials are best suited to particular needs?

This discussion invariably brings in other senses: *What noises might we hear from a building in a heavy rainstorm? . . . In a high wind? What noises would we hear in a building which was being constructed? What can we tell when we feel some building materials – in terms of strength, weight, flexibility?*

Once these questions have been discussed, and linked to the children's own observations, their curiosity should have been well and truly aroused and a series of tests, experiments and practical work could be arranged to satisfy it. In short, now is the time to start work on the 'scientific components' of the topic.

Note When observing and discussing in this way it is always useful to introduce focal points which the children will enjoy thinking about.

An example of what is meant here could relate to chimneys. *Does smoke always come out in the same direction? What causes it to change direction?*

Back in the classroom these observations could be displayed. (This sort of visual information would stimulate talk and explanation about wind direction and force.)

a) Collecting and observing

A collection of materials used in buildings could be made. Such a collection might include: wood, tiles, slates, bricks, roofing felt, rubber, wiring, glass, perspex, plastic pipes.

Encourage the children to examine and compare the different materials and talk about their qualities. After they have considered each material, the children could complete a table like the following:

Material	Waterproof	Heavy	Flexible	Transparent	Easily breakable
Wood					
Tiles					
Slates					
Bricks					
Rubber					
Glass					
Perspex					

Invite the children to speculate on where each material is used, using their observations of the material and of houses they have seen. This will start to build up an understanding of the 'where, what, why and how' of the use of such materials in a building context.

NC coverage
AT3 Level 1a: *be able to describe the simple properties of familiar materials*
    Level 2a: *be able to group materials according to observable features*
    Level 3a: *be able to link the use of common materials to their simple properties*

b) Classroom building

This takes the work done above a step further. Begin with a collection of infant classroom equipment: building bricks and blocks, cardboard boxes, pieces of card, Lego, large sheets of paper etc. Along with this collection another could be made – of materials which, at infant level, might be used for 'fixing' – glue, string, sellotape, plasticine.

Invite the children to work in groups. Explain that you want them to build a structure with these materials, and to 'fix' it so that it will be as strong as possible. When groups have finished, they can evaluate the different structures – comments could be written down or tape-recorded. From this, pose the question *How does fixing take place in real buildings?* A close look at some of the school buildings might provide some answers (with teacher guidance): putty, plaster, cement, nails, screws.

NC coverage
AT3 Level 1a: *be able to describe the simple properties of familiar materials*

c) Practical building work

Plaster activities

a Plaster is made from the rock gypsum. It is mixed with water until a creamy mixture ensues, which can be smoothed on to walls, ceilings etc. Give the children small amounts of plaster and invite then to mix it themselves. Stress that only a very small amount of water should be used first, then more added as needed. It's not as easy as it sounds!

   When it has reached the desired consistency the plaster mixture can be spread on pieces of wood. Encourage the children to make impressions and patterns on the wet plaster. These could be examined and decorated.

b Pour wet plaster into a plastic bag, then arrange the bag into a shape. When the plaster has set, discuss what has happened: *What does it feel like? How could this be useful for builders?*

Work with mortar
Mortar is made up of cement, sand and water. Help the children to experiment

Buildings 77

with different quantities of cement, sand and water until they find the most effective mixture. This could be used to cement three bricks together in different ways:

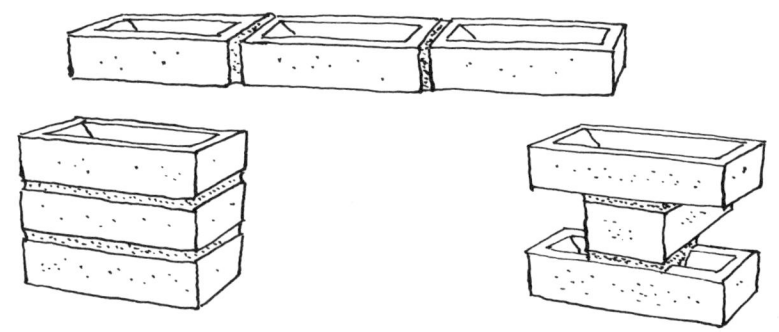

The results would again throw up valuable talking points: *What was the ideal mixture of the three elements to get the strongest mortar? What mixture dried the quickest/slowest? Which bond of bricks is the strongest? Why is this?*

Follow this up with more outdoor observation of bricks used in building.

NC coverage
AT3 Level 3a: *be able to link the use of common materials to their simple properties*
    Level 3b: *know that some materials occur naturally while many are made from raw materials*

d) Tools, machines and us

So far the emphasis has been upon materials but the activities in the last component will have raised the question of tools and equipment.

Make a collection of building tools: hammer, chisel, vice, pliers, screwdriver, spanner, ruler, tape measure, mallet, spirit level, drill, saw, spade, nails, screws.

Encourage the children to discuss the uses of the tools and then sort them into groups:

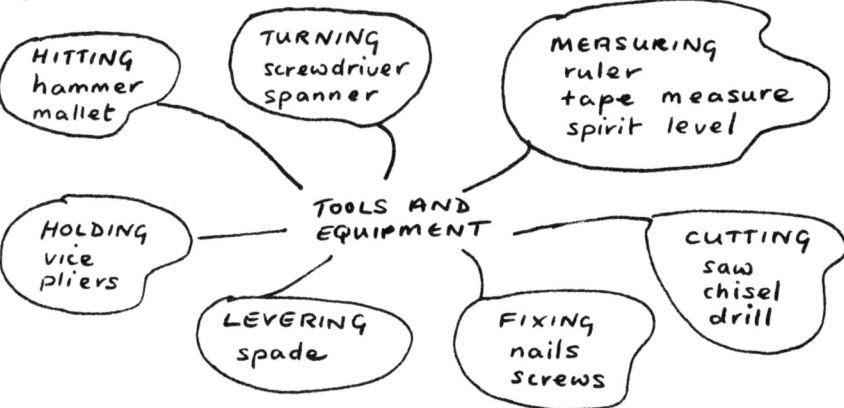

HITTING — hammer, mallet
TURNING — screwdriver, spanner
MEASURING — ruler, tape measure, spirit level
HOLDING — vice, pliers
TOOLS AND EQUIPMENT
LEVERING — spade
FIXING — nails, screws
CUTTING — saw, chisel, drill

(Subgroups are also apparent here and could be developed at teacher's discretion. eg Turning – Screwdriver, Spanner, Drill, Screws.)

78 Science Topics for Infants

If you have plenty of adult help, children could experience using some of the tools, eg hammering a nail, turning a screw, chipping, levering, measuring etc – under close supervision. The teacher could demonstrate using drill, saw etc. These activities will raise many further questions and answers. *How do we put nails and screws in? Which are the most effective in holding things together? Why? Is it easier to push something up a gentle slope or a steep slope? Why? What machines do the work of spades on a building site? What is the significance of this in terms of time, effort, manpower? What picks up heavy weights?*

A marvellous book for infants that fits in beautifully to the work done in this component is *Mr Bear's Chair* by Thomas Graham, published by Hamish Hamilton. The story is set in the house of Mr and Mrs Bear and revolves round his breaking and repairing of a chair. It is delightfully told and features many of the tools and technical details discussed in this component. Children listening to the story at the conclusion of this work will have a nice 'knowing' appreciation of the repairs described and illustrated.

Pulleys

Pulleys make the lifting of heavy loads much easier. This can be illustrated by constructing a very simple pulley as follows:

a Suspend a piece of wood between two desks.
b Insert a screw hook in the bottom of the wood.
c Attach a cotton reel to the hook with some coat hanger wire.
d Get the children to suggest a fairly heavy object from the infant classroom (perhaps a toy bucket full of water?). Attach strong string to the object and pass the other end of string over the cotton reel. Pull down on the string and watch the object rise – with apparently no effort!

Once the equipment is set up, the children could try for themselves, comparing the effort needed to lift the bucket on its own and with the pulleys.

NC coverage
AT3 Level 1a: *be able to describe the simple properties of familiar materials*
     Level 3a: *be able to link the use of common materials to their simple properties*

e) Keeping dry

No work on buildings should overlook the real life adult problem of how we keep the rain out!

1 *What makes the best roof?*
Provide the children with a selection of boxes, various 'roofing' materials (eg kitchen foil, paper towels, cloth, plastic. . .) and strongly-constructed roof frames made of dowelling. Help them to experiment as follows:

a box open at the top. Material 'roof' is stretched flat over the top and fastened at the sides.

b open-topped box with securely-fixed dowelling roof frame. The roofing material is attached at the top and sloped down to the sides.

Encourage the children to predict which roof shape will be most efficient and which materials the least/most waterproof. Then invite them to pour water on their structures to test their predictions. This should be repeated with as many combinations of roofing materials/structures as necessary.

Again this activity could generate much discussion. *Are sloping or flat roofs most effective? Why? Is a real roof tiled from the top or the bottom? Why do the tiles overlap? What is used to bring rainwater from the roof to the ground? What holds the roof on the house?*

Photographs and plans of houses would provide useful back-up. Best of all would be a visit to a real building site.

NC coverage
AT Level 3a: *be able to link the use of common materials to their simple properties*
   Level 3b: *know that some materials occur naturally while many are made from raw materials*

f) Build your own house!

Challenge groups of children to build their own house. Remind them about what they have learned so far. *Think about the roof; how you need to let light in; good foundations; strong walls; a good shape; how you keep it warm; how you go up and down in a house.* (The standard staircase in a house has 13 steps. Apart from discussing such things as energy, parts of the body etc involved in traversing the staircase, some interesting mathematical work could be done on different ways of getting up it – single steps at a time, two at a time, one then two, and so on. Thus some useful work on sequencing could take place.)

Each group might decide on a different way of presenting their ideas. One might be a drawing of a house with written explanations; another might be models; a third might be a tape recording of their ideas.

NC coverage

AT3 Level 3a: *be able to link the use of common materials to their simple properties*
　　 Level 3b: *know that some materials occur naturally while many are made from raw materials*
AT4 Level 2d: *know that light passes through some materials and that when it does not shadows may be formed*

Cross-curricular links

One obvious link is with **maths** and work on simple plans would be instructive and enjoyable. These could be discussed prior to the practical work: *What is a plan? Can we make one using infant apparatus? Can we draw a large, simple plan of the classroom? What would the downstairs plan of a house show? What would a supermarket plan show?* Very simple graphs of the buildings in 'our street' could also be compiled.

For **English** work, children could listen, talk and write stories and poems related to houses, sounds in them and other buildings, adventures in buildings, houses in unusual places etc. A useful book for source material is the Lion paperback *Pictures on a Page* by Pat Wynne Jones.

Buildings and **history** are obviously linked; children could look at photographs of old and new buildings and visit and compare buildings from a range of different periods. Another theme might be *How does a building show its age?* (style, location, materials used, wear and tear). A look on the inside could consider furniture, heating systems, layout.

It might be possible to visit a local church. This would provide opportunities to consider the furniture and architectural features. Talking, drawing and writing could all stem from such a visit, linking with **RE**.

In **geography**, children could look at different types of buildings for different environments. **Art** and **technology** could be involved in making models.

11 Sending Messages and Storing Information

a) Starters
b) Going further
c) Going even further
d) Recording and storing information
e) More experiences – including computers

Anatomy of a topic

Science in the National Curriculum contains statements which are significant for this topic. It emphasises the need for children to 'understand the purposes of recording' and the 'use of simple techniques such as pictograms and drawings' and 'to have an introduction to a wider variety of methods of recording'.

Then there is the comment: 'children's work in all areas should involve, where appropriate, the use of information sources and computers. Where appropriate they should have the opportunity to use tape recorders and television to broaden their experience of science.'

In line with NC philosophy the pattern of work in this topic flows as follows:

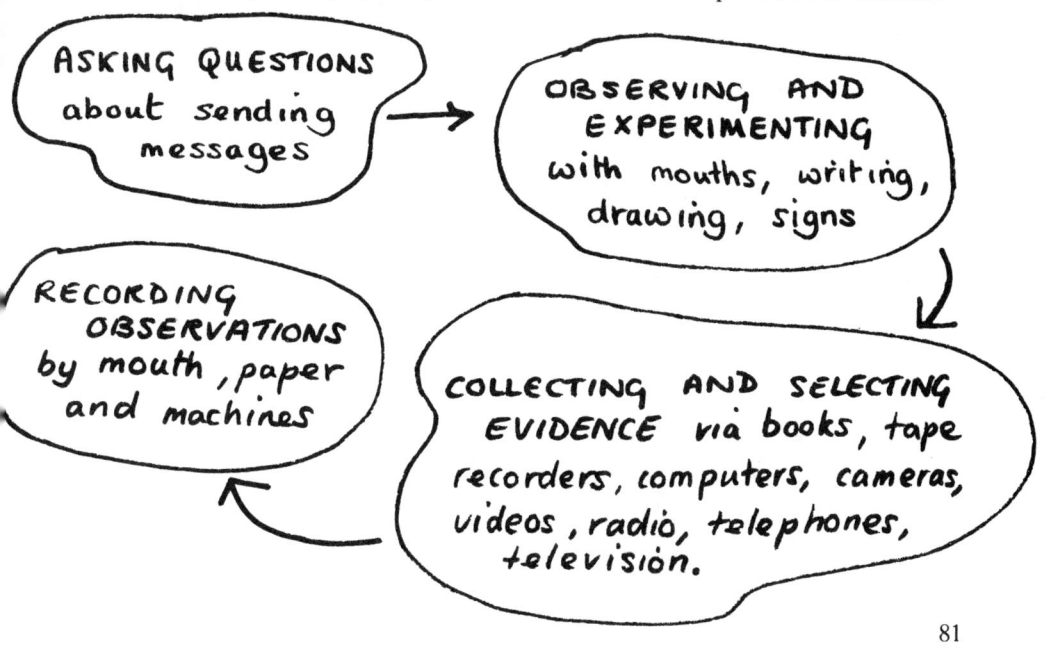

ASKING QUESTIONS about sending messages → OBSERVING AND EXPERIMENTING with mouths, writing, drawing, signs ↓

RECORDING OBSERVATIONS by mouth, paper and machines ← COLLECTING AND SELECTING EVIDENCE via books, tape recorders, computers, cameras, videos, radio, telephones, television.

The time span for 'Sending messages' is flexible but would probably be about four weeks plus. Its location in the school year is equally flexible.

This is a topic where visits and visitors would be very valuable. Visits to a telephone box, a church bell-ringing loft, a photographic studio, a camera shop, a recording studio all have possibilities. Visitors capable of speaking about various communications systems mentioned would be welcome (provided, of course, that they could gear their comments/demonstrations to the level of the children concerned).

Equipment

Few schools will have *all* the items/materials given below. The list aims to indicate the range of possibilities that could be explored.

pencils	telephone (disconnected)	record player
paper	radio	microwave oven
drums	tape recorder	stop watch
bell	camera (polaroid preferable)	digital watch
horn		calculator
simple electric circuits with 'flashing' bulbs	video camera	computer
	video	word processor
telephone (connected)	TV	

Computer software is listed in Component e) *More experiences – including computers.*

a) Starters

Initial work could involve children in discussing and asking questions about sending messages. *How do we pass a message from one person to another? Can we pass this message in different ways? What ways are there?*

The most obvious way of passing a message – by speaking – would be quickly apparent to all. The next step might be to consider how the information in the spoken message could be given in alternative ways:

(Spoken) *Gemma comes to school with her mum and her dog.*
(Written) Gemma comes to school with her mum and her dog
(Drawn)

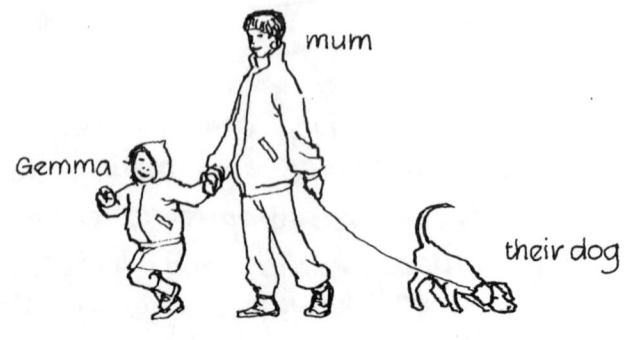

Sending Messages and Storing Information 83

(Acted)   One person 'plays the various parts' to pass on the message. This idea could then be developed a little further:
(Spoken) *Stop!*
(Written) Stop!
(Drawn)

(Acted)

Ask the children if they can think of any other ways of sending messages. (eg telephone, flags, radio. . .)

NC coverage
AT4 Level 1c: *know about the simple properties of sound and light*

b) Going further

Invite the children to consider how a message might be sent over a longer distance (ie where sender and recipient can no longer see each other). In this work the children will move on to 'collecting and selecting' evidence and the following points might feature.

1 By shouting/using cupped hands/making a megaphone.
2 By making a simple code of sounds and then beating them on a drum. Children could decide on the simplest of codes – one beat for 'Yes', two beats for 'No'. A group could then go out of the room and wait for the signal to tell them whether they can re-enter or not.
3 By visual messages – the idea of smoke signals fascinates young children. In discussing these in a 'problem solving' context it will again be apparent that the signals must mean something – hence the need for a known code between both sender and receiver. Talk about when smoke signals would be ineffective – in darkness, fog, heavy rain etc.
4 By flashing lights – the work in this component can be developed in connection with suggestions/instructions in the topic *Electricity and Magnetism*. The children could make simple circuits quite easily and work out how to 'flash' the light. In the context of sending messages *via* flashing lights, introduce the idea of the lighthouse, which flashes a warning to ships. There are nearly 100 lighthouses around Britain. Each has a different code, eg Bishops' Rock lighthouse near the

Scilly Isles sends two flashes every 15 seconds. As well as warning a ship of possible hazards, the different codes give useful information about location.

As with smoke signals, questions could be raised as to when a lighthouse would be ineffective. This could develop into the use of sound signals, eg foghorns.

The children could record their findings in various ways, eg

SENDING MESSAGES
SOUND | **SIGHT**

NC coverage
AT4 Level 1c: *know about simple properties of sound and light*
　　　Level 3a: *know that a complete circuit is needed for electrical devices to work*
　　　Level 3d: *know that light and sound can be reflected*

c) Going even further

Having starting to think along the lines of 'sending messages even further', more collecting and selecting of evidence could take place, eg

1 The telephone – the children might be able to use both a disconnected and connected telephone. They could experiment with how to dial, what to say, how to respond. This could be extended into role play with various 'messages' being given and received. Again the significance of codes should not be missed, with 999 being the most obvious possibility.
2 Discussion and experimentation with a radio – switching on, tuning in, expectation of certain messages at certain times (news, weather, road reports etc). The children might make a simple chart to illustrate how long is spent on each regular item.
3 Comparison of the telephone and the radio. *Can we feed information into both? Can we influence what is to be said on either?*

NC coverage
AT3 Level 3a: *be able to link the use of common materials to their simple properties*
AT4 Level 1a: *know that many household appliances use electricity but that misuse is dangerous*
     Level 1c: *know about the simple properties of sound and light*

d) Recording and storing information (tape recorder, camera, video)

The topic should have progressed now to the stage where the children can be made aware that information can be stored and retrieved by using a variety of devices.

Using a tape recorder
The amount of equipment available is a determining factor here, but work with a cassette tape recorder should be a possibility. Even very young children may be familiar with a variety of devices; some are adept at handling simple machines. Pairs or groups could work on taping messages, then recording and re-playing them.

    Useful recording of this exercise would be for each group to describe exactly what procedures they followed, in words and pictures. From this, the children will realise that they can 'put in' information and 'get it out' at any time.

Camera work
If a polaroid camera is available the possibilities it offers for recording and retrieving information can be explored. A video camera could be explored in the same way.

    If neither of these pieces of equipment is available, a selection of photographs could be provided as the basis for discussion. It is certain that someone in the class will have a video of a wedding, or a holiday or some 'home shot' event.

NC coverage
AT4 Level 1c: *know about the simple properties of sound and light*
     Level 3a: *know that a complete circuit is needed for electrical devices to work*

e) More experiences – including computers

Again, depending upon what equipment the school (or helpful sources) can provide, the children could have 'hands on' experience of machines such as TV sets, record players, microwave ovens, stop watches, digital watches, calculators and computers. The emphasis would once more be on the storage and retrieval of information.

Computers can, of course, be used to support many other science topics. They can be used for recording via a word processor. Gathering and handling information can be done with very simple data-handling programs such as *Branch* which promotes understanding of similarities of groups of objects. (Available from MESU.)

Other software applicable to the infant age group, and relevant to science activities includes: *All about Me* (Northern Micromedia NOR1CC10 – BBC, B, B+, Master 128, Master Compact, Archimedes, RM Nimbus – age range 4+); this would be useful for infant classes doing an 'Ourselves' topic (see page 32). In *Phonin* (ESM ES658 – BBC, B, B+, Master 128, – age range 4+) a push button telephone is connected to the computer for plenty of 'real life' situations.

The Complete Energy Pack (CUP 52133976 – BBC, B+ Master 128 – age range 6 to 9). This is a very detailed pack of resources with substantial science work and cross-curricular activities. It is useful for the topic 'Energy!' in this book (see page 17).

This software is available from: AVP (address on page 179).

NC coverage
AT4 Level 1a: *know that many household appliances use electricity but that misuse is dangerous*
Level 3a: *know that a complete circuit is required for electrical devices to work*

Cross-curricular links

'Sending Messages' has great potential for **drama** work. All sorts of imaginative work could be done here in pairs, groups or individually. Simulated telephone conversations could range over a wide range of situations and emotions, with starters like: *Who IS that speaking? This is Mario and I've got some GREAT news! Would you like to hear something really EXCITING? This is a very important person who wants to speak to YOU...* and so on.

English work, both written and spoken, could also incorporate some giving of simple instructions, eg making a cup of tea, pumping up a bike tyre, dressing a doll, making a simple model etc. Follow-up discussion could focus on the importance of clarity, sequence etc.

'Sending messages through the years' would allow for some **historial** development and could include looking at books, photographs and models. **Geography** could be linked to this by locating where Indians lived, which is the Atlantic Ocean and so on.

In **Art** some exciting work could be produced which ranges from pictures of Indians sending some signals to perhaps a picture sequence showing what happens when a 999 call is made. **Music** and **drama** could be linked via drums, and children's prayers might be a focal point for **RE**.

12 Looking After Our Environment

    a) Litter!
    b) More about litter
    c) Neglect, pollution, waste
    d) Sound pollution
    e) A local project

Anatomy of a topic

Going out and about is important in this topic, so it needs to be planned for a time of year when outdoor work is possible. Extra adult help is important for out-of-school visits and classroom work. Contact with local environmental health authorities can yield considerable dividends in both material and human resources.

Most of the work on the topic could be covered in three or four weeks. A project 'to improve the local environment' might develop from this work, but would clearly take much longer.

NOTE Health and safety considerations are of prime importance here. Extreme caution should be taken in any contact with litter and pollution.

Equipment

large sheet of plastic	sellotape	various 'muffling'
large pieces of card and paper	glue	materials – cotton wool, wool balls,
pencils	scissors	paper, material
scrap material – newspaper, cartons, lolly sticks etc.	Vaseline alarm clock box small garden tools	

Resources

- Two conservation groups which have special affiliation rates for schools are: *Friends of the Earth* and *WATCH*.
- Macmillan Education produce a wallchart entitled *Countryside in Danger*.
- The *Keep Britain Tidy Group* focuses on the need to keep the environment litter-free.
- Two other groups from which useful material can be obtained are *National Society for Clean Air* and *Noise Abatement Society*.

Pattern of a topic

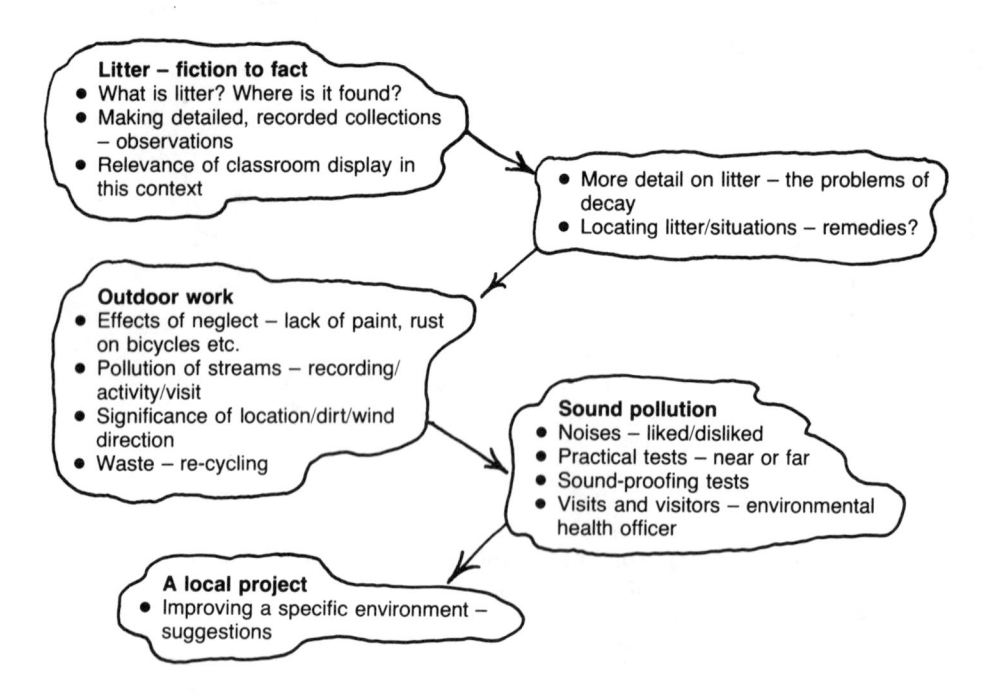

- **Litter – fiction to fact**
  - What is litter? Where is it found?
  - Making detailed, recorded collections – observations
  - Relevance of classroom display in this context

- More detail on litter – the problems of decay
- Locating litter/situations – remedies?

- **Outdoor work**
  - Effects of neglect – lack of paint, rust on bicycles etc.
  - Pollution of streams – recording/activity/visit
  - Significance of location/dirt/wind direction
  - Waste – re-cycling

- **Sound pollution**
  - Noises – liked/disliked
  - Practical tests – near or far
  - Sound-proofing tests
  - Visits and visitors – environmental health officer

- **A local project**
  - Improving a specific environment – suggestions

a) Litter!

To get the children thinking this topic might be introduced by an apocryphal story:

A farmer was walking through one of his fields when he saw a car parked in it. As he got nearer he saw people getting up from the grass. They got into the car and drove away. The farmer was just near enough to read, and remember, the car's number plate.

When he reached where it had been parked he found a pile of litter – plastic bottles and cans, crisp packets, empty cartons, bits of uneaten food. He was very angry because he knew that some of his animals could die if they got some of these things caught in their throats.

The farmer collected the litter into a sack. Next day he asked a policeman friend if he could find out the address of the car owner by knowing the number plate. 'Yes,' said his friend.

Two days later the farmer set out in his car. He had the sack of litter in the boot. When he got to the town he drove to the address he had been given. He walked up a neat front garden and knocked at the door. When a man answered the farmer said, 'You left something in my field the other day, so I've brought it back for you.'

Then he emptied the sack outside the front door, got back in his car and drove away.

'Personalised', and dramatically told, this story 'gets through' to young children and forms a good introduction to practical work.

Litter collection

Spread out a plastic sheet or rubbish sack in one corner of the classroom. Ask the children to form groups and go to different parts of the school and playground on a 'litter hunt'. Stress the importance of safety factors; suggest that only one member of the group handles the rubbish, with their hands inside plastic bags. Another group member could keep a simple record of where and when each item is found.

When the collection is complete, the items can be sorted into groups and numbered, ie 1 = crisp packets, 2 = apple cores, etc. The children's notes on when items were found can be added to this.

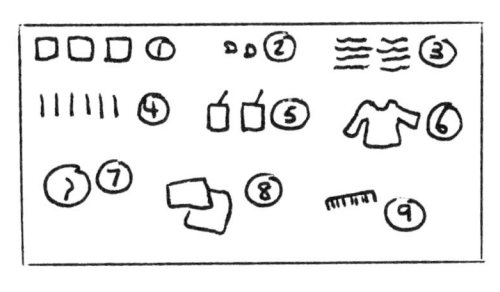

WHAT
1. Crisp packets
2. Apple cores
3. Sweet papers
4. Lolly sticks
5. Drinks cartons
6. A pullover
7. Ball with a split in it
8. Scrap paper
9. An old comb

WHEN
At 9.30 am — 2 sweet papers, 1 drink carton, split ball, some scrap paper, comb
At 11 am — 3 crisp packets, 2 apple cores, more sweet papers, lolly sticks, 1 more drink carton, 1 pullover, more scrap paper

To display where the litter was found, prepare (in advance) a large, simple plan of the school. Help the children locate the items, using the numbers given for different types of litter.

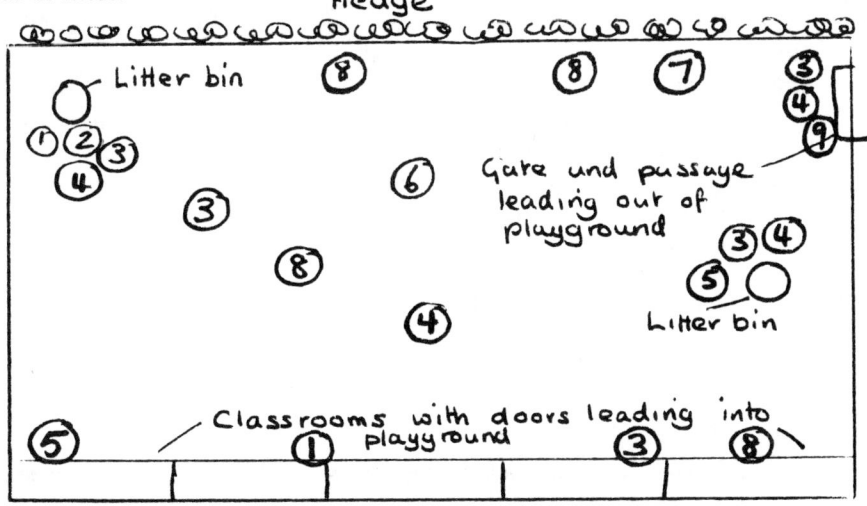

Numbers show where litter items were found, eg ①= crisp packets ②= apple cores, etc.

From this it should be clear where the greatest amounts of litter were found, and this could give rise to a lot of questions: *Where was most litter found? Is there a reason for this? Do the litter bins seem adequate? Could they be improved in any way? Why is litter more likely to be at the edge of the playground? Why was there more litter at 11am than at 9.30am? How could we make sure there was no litter in the playground?*

These questions, in turn, could lead on to problem-solving: *What would be the ideal litter bin? How many should there be in the school playground? Where should they be located? How can we stop people dropping litter?* Children could design 'the ideal litter bin' or create posters encouraging people not to drop litter.

NC coverage
AT2 Level 2d: *know that some waste materials decay naturally but do so over different periods of time*
   Level 3b: *know that human activity may produce changes in the environment that can affect plants and animals*

b) More about litter

The litter collection could be kept and studied over a period of time (at the teacher's discretion). *Which things remain unchanged? Which things change/decay? How long does this take?*

Remind the children of the story which started this topic, and the danger to animals which litter presents, especially when it is hidden in grass. Grazing animals may eat plastic packaging; broken glass could cut their feet. The teacher could extend this to a simple 'chain of events': litter threatens the cow – the cow is injured or dies – the result is no milk. Children readily appreciate the danger to animals here – and also to themselves or younger children.

Encourage the children to look out for rubbish on their way to school BUT ON NO ACCOUNT TO TOUCH OR PICK IT UP. Ask them to look out for different types of 'rubbish': oil stains where cars have been parked, chewing gum on the pavement, chip papers, wrappings etc. As with the school litter survey, this could lead to a lot of questions and problem-solving: *Where was most litter found? (outside shops/pubs/car parks?) What is the reason for this? Are there any litter bins? If so, are they adequate? Who do you think dropped the different sorts of litter? How could we stop people leaving rubbish?*

NC coverage
AT2 Level 2d: *know that some waste materials decay naturally but do so over different periods of time*
   Level 3b: *know that human activity may produce changes in the environment that can affect plants and animals*

c) Neglect, pollution, waste

Out-of-school work is important for this topic. In a walk around the local environment, point out to the children – and get them to observe – the effects of weathering/neglect/pollution, eg erosion of bricks and mortar; flaking paint; rust on railings, bicyles etc.

Stream visit
If there is a stream near school, well-supervised groups could visit it to look for evidence of pollution.

Pollution in streams may be caused by sewage or pesticides washed off the land, or by waste products from industry. Sewage provides food for bacteria in the water. The bacteria then multiply and use up the oxygen in the water that other species need to breathe. Pesticides and industrial waste kill off life in streams. The pollution itself may be invisible, but lack of evidence of stream life may indicate that the water is polluted.

This is obviously too complicated for young children to grasp thoroughly, but they will be able to understand the importance of keeping our streams and rivers clean. They will also be able to observe other signs of pollution, eg rubbish, discoloured water (muddy water is not necessarily always polluted). They could record their observations on a simple tick-sheet, as follows:

```
                    STREAM VISIT
DATE:                       TIME:
WAS THE STREAM :   very clear ◯   muddy ◯   cloudy ◯
DID IT SMELL?      not at all ◯   a lot ◯
Amount of litter in water:  none ◯   a little ◯   a lot ◯
Seen in the bottom:  stones ◯   mud ◯
                     litter ◯   couldn't see ◯
```

Testing the air
Air pollution can be recorded in the following way:

a Take a number of pieces of stiff card. Smear one side with Vaseline or a similar substance.
b Fix the cards at various points around the school, smeared side outwards. Suggested locations are: on the fence nearest a road; facing the prevailing wind; on the roof (enlist the help of the caretaker!); near the main heating source; at ground level.
c Collect the cards after two days. Get the children to compare and record the amounts of dirt on the cards. Discuss: *Which was the dirtiest place? Why do you think this was?*

92 Science Topics for Infants

Waste recyling

Children's observations and experiments for the above will have made them very aware of the problem of waste. Have a supply of 'waste' materials on hand in the classroom for children to use. Old newspapers can be used for printing, cut-out pictures and papier mâché heads; surplus cartons could form the basis for a challenge to children to design a model of practical use – maybe even a receptacle to collect litter!

Your local council or other organisations may have 'bottle banks' and other schemes for collecting and recycling items, which you could discuss with the children.

NC coverage

AT2 Level 3b: *know that human activity may produce changes in the environment that can effect plants and animals*
AT3 Level 3c: *understand some of the effects of weathering on buildings and on rocks*

d) Sound pollution

As young children make generous contributions to noise levels they usually get very interested in this aspect of the topic! As a starter they might be asked to make two lists:

Noises I like   **Noises I hate**

Comparisons will indicate that a noise which gives one person pleasure can be an irritant to someone else. *What sounds does everyone like/dislike?*
From this basis a simple chart of noise levels could be produced. It might look like this:

	db	
Whispering	30	Quiet
Talking normally	50	Fairly quiet
Traffic noise	60	Noticeable noise
Children shouting in classroom	70	Noisy
Loud disco music in room	120	Very unpleasantly noisy
Jet plane taking off	140	Painfully noisy

The teacher could choose whether or not to incorporate the approximate decibel readings. Following some discussion about this list, the children could split into groups and make up their own 'noise lists'. One might look like this:

Looking After Our Environment 93

A sound I heard	Near or far?	Does it go on all the time?	'Nice or nasty?'

With adult help, groups could do 'noise surveys' in the school playground (when full and when empty), in the school dining room, in the middle of the field, at the nearest school point to outside traffic noise. Records of these experiences could again be made.

a Having talked about noises they dislike, the children could be made aware that noise can actually be dangerous. Examples could be pneumatic drills, pop concerts, discotheques. . . (Road menders usually wear protective ear covers, and the children could observe this if there are roadworks nearby.) Research has shown that noise induces feelings of irritability and stress and interferes with blood circulation and digestion of food. Although this is too complex for young children to grasp, they may have experienced adults' annoyance at their own noise-making!

b Although noise *can* be a problem, there are times when loud noises are necessary. *Can the children think of any?* (Examples include fire and burglar alarms, police car/ambulance/fire engine sirens. . .) This could be shown to good effect if the school caretaker were asked to set off the fire alarm at a pre-arranged time.

c How can we reduce noise? This investigation could involve fair testing. Bring in an old-fashioned alarm clock (ie one with a bell rather than a bleep). Set it to go off in the middle of the classroom. Re-set the alarm and put the clock in another place, eg inside the stock cupboard with the door closed, in a cardboard box with no lid, and so on. Get the children to note the loudness and clarity of the alarm each time. As a final activity they could experiment with muffling the clock with a variety of materials, eg paper, cotton wool, cotton material, balls of wool etc. Again, they could note their findings. *Which material was best for muffling the sound?*

NC coverage
AT2 Level 3b: *know that human activity may produce changes in the environment that can affect plants and animals*
AT4 Level 1c: *know about the simple properties of sound and light*

e) A local project

The Science National Curriculum suggests that pupils 'be able to give an account of a project to help improve the local environment'.

It may be useful to give brief descriptions of two such projects done by infant children.

One concerned a border to a school's site. This border ran from the entrance gates to half way along the boundary:

Prior to the attention given to it, this border was unsightly. It contained little of interest, was full of weeds and formed a depository for litter thrown from the 'outside world'. A group of infants weeded and tidied up the area and planted daffodil bulbs. In the spring a magnificent display of daffodils transformed the area. The project has been continued ever since.

The second improvement was to a central courtyard area – a feature of many schools. This was again weeded, tidied up, and with the help of adult friends and teachers a small pond was put in and stocked. It is now a valuable school resource for nature study.

NC coverage
AT2 Level 3b: *know that human activity may produce changes in the environment and can affect plants and animals*

Cross-curricular links

Children respond readily to expressions of concern about the environment. Invite them to design posters to help 'our school' be cleaner, quieter, neater etc. This **art** work could be done in groups, with plenty of opportunity for talk about each group's ideas and finished products.

For **English**, plenty of vocabulary could stem from this topic – pollution, noise, filth, litter, carelessness, waste, vandalism, consideration, quietness, disturbance, traffic.

Technology would be well served by the various constructional activites involved in this topic. **History** might focus on whether it was noisier or less so in times past? (Modern traffic is noisy, but think of the clatter of horses and cart wheels.) What about litter and waste? Children working in mines and factories could be brought into this. **Geography** could be incorporated in a study of various types of pollution – urban, rural, oceanic etc. **Maths** is involved in construction and measurement activities; **RE** work could pursue the theme of caring for others, looking after our school/home/town etc.

Music offers plenty of scope for tests and discussion. What might be considered unpleasant by one person can be quite the opposite to another!

13 Water

a) Wet or dry?
b) Washing, drinking, growing
c) Water: where does it come from? Where does it go?
d) Who lives in water?
e) More fun with water

Anatomy of a topic

In conveying difficult concepts to children it is always helpful to use common happenings and everyday experiences. In a 'water' context such features as condensation, evaporation and solubility are more readily grasped if they are approached through observing weather variations, or practical classroom activities such as washing, cooking etc.

In choosing a time location for this topic therefore the long range weather forecast could be significant! A rainy period would be most helpful. The topic could last from between three and four weeks.

The most significant 'visit' to be made in connection with this topic would be to a pond. This may mean going no farther than the school grounds. It could however mean going farther afield; a local field studies centre would probably offer the best facilities of all. It should be emphasised that pond dipping as an activity should be attended by stringent health and safety precautions.

Equipment

rain coats
rain hats
wellingtons
umbrellas
a selection of materials –
　some waterproof, some not
bowl for water
newspaper
pencils
card
wax crayons
sellotape
handkerchieves
jam jar lids

plastic bottle with the
　bottom cut off
sand
gravel
pebbles
cotton wool
rubber or plastic gloves
bucket
magnifying lenses
notebooks
bottles
large dish for water
spring balance
kettle
low level toilet cistern

various drinking vessels
　including some glasses
jam jars
'thick and thin' materials
　to use in drying
　experiments
various pieces of soap
　and liquid soap –
　washing up liquid
cold and hot water
taps
pipes
water tanks

Resources
- The Slide Centre has a set of slides entitled *Water and its Uses*.
- Philip and Tacey supply a useful piece of equipment for this topic. This is an integral displacement vessel which is divided into two compartments which are separated by a wall with an overflow tap at the top.
- Philip Green Educational Ltd, produce a 56 half-frame filmstrip with teacher's notes entitled *Water* (F03).
- *Pond Watch* is an interesting collection of 25 photocopy masters plus record sheets, posters, OHP acetates, and teacher's notes which would be a useful resource for pond dipping activities. It can be obtained from LDA.
- A useful book for pond dipping is *What's in a Pond?* by P Olney (Puffin).
- For those near enough, an interesting outing might be to the Thames Barrier Visitors' Centre.

Pattern of a topic

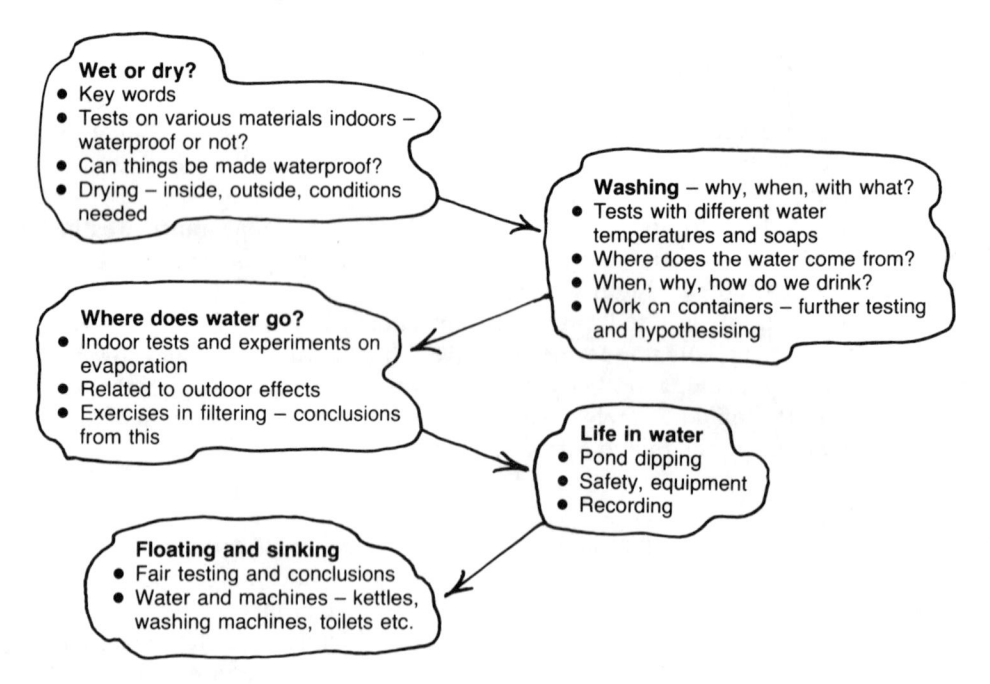

Wet or dry?
- Key words
- Tests on various materials indoors — waterproof or not?
- Can things be made waterproof?
- Drying — inside, outside, conditions needed

Washing — why, when, with what?
- Tests with different water temperatures and soaps
- Where does the water come from?
- When, why, how do we drink?
- Work on containers — further testing and hypothesising

Where does water go?
- Indoor tests and experiments on evaporation
- Related to outdoor effects
- Exercises in filtering — conclusions from this

Life in water
- Pond dipping
- Safety, equipment
- Recording

Floating and sinking
- Fair testing and conclusions
- Water and machines — kettles, washing machines, toilets etc.

It is worth waiting for a rainy day to start this topic. This provides a very 'natural' lead in to the first component.

a) Wet or dry?

Showers generate excitement in the infant classroom. 'Brainstorming' related vocabulary would be one way to start the topic off:

'It's raining . . . pouring . . . cats and dogs . . . bucketing down . . . soaked . . . drenched . . . nearly drowned.

Storm . . . clouds . . . puddles . . . drips . . . splashes . . . dry . . . macs . . . umbrellas . . . wellingtons.

The teacher could then guide the discussion by asking: *How do we keep dry?* The children will probably offer responses like: *We put our coats on . . . We put our umbrellas up . . . We put our hoods up . . . We wear our wellingtons. . .*

Why do some clothes keep water out?

This builds on the opening discussion. Get a child to put on a raincoat and project one arm over the sink or a bowl. Another child carefully pours water over the arm. *Does the water go through?* Invite another child to put on wellingtons and stand in a bowl of water. *Do their feet stay dry?* Children are likely to ask *why* the water doesn't get in. The answer, of course, is that the materials are *waterproof*.

Waterproof and non-waterproof

Spread some newspapers (several sheets thick) on desks. Give the children a selection of materials – cotton, silk, plastic, paper, silver foil, canvas, rubber. Aim to have a mixture of waterproof and non-waterproof materials. Ask them to spread out the pieces of material on the newspaper and give each a number. Invite the children to predict which materials they think will be waterproof, and which not. Then tell them to pour small amounts of water on each piece of material and observe the results.

The children could record their findings as follows:

OUR WATERPROOF TEST

	Did we think it would be waterproof?	Was it waterproof?
PIECE 1	Yes	Yes
PIECE 2	No	Yes
PIECE 3		

RESULTS OF OUR TESTS

Waterproof: rubber, plastic, silver foil

Non-waterproof: cotton, wool, paper

As a follow-up, challenge the children to see if they can change one of the materials from non-waterproof to waterproof. Give them some wax crayons and paper or card. Tell them to crayon all over the paper as thickly as possible, then repeat the test above.

Drying out

The final piece of work in this theme might be to consider what happens when we are caught in the rain without waterproof clothing. *How do we get our clothes dry? Which clothes dry quickest? What things help them to dry quickly?* Provide a variety of materials, some thick and some thin. There should be enough pieces so that the same tests can be tried on each. Get the children to immerse the materials in water, then try out various methods of drying. These could include draping on chairs in the classroom, putting on radiators, hanging on a line outside, subjecting them to blasts of hot air from a hair drier. Once again the children could record their findings.

> Best and worst days for drying outside
> (Dry, sunny, windy)   (Damp, wet, frosty)
>
> OUR DRYING TEST
> We had [A] [B] — two handkerchiefs. We put [A] on the hot radiator. We put [B] on the music trolley. [A] was dry in 5 minutes. [B] was still wet.

NC coverage
AT3 Level 1a: *be able to describe the simple properties of familiar materials*
　　　Level 2a: *be able to group materials according to observable features*

b) Water for washing, drinking, growing

Some opening questions might be: *Why do we get washed? When do we get washed? With what do we wash? What are the different ways in which we can get washed? What are the best ways of getting washed?*

Encourage the children to get their hands dirty with paint, clay etc. Then try various methods of getting them clean and record the results:

> HOW WASHED   RESULTS
> With cold water   Still dirty
> With warm water   Still fairly dirty
> With cold water and soap   Still fairly dirty
> With hot water and soap   Clean
> With hot water and
> 　　　liquid soap   Very clean

Focus the children's attention on the washing process: *What happened to the water after the soap was added to it? What happened to it after the soap had been added and hands washed? How did the soap change when it was in the water? What shape were any bubbles? How could you make more bubbles?*

The question *Why do we get washed?* has obvious links with good health. Ask children to suggest some ideas about when it is important to wash. Examples might be *When we have been handling our pets. After working in the garden. When we are cooking. Before eating food with our hands. After going to the toilet. After working on our bikes. When we have been playing with toys indoors or outdoors.* 'Why' we wash might then be discussed in more detail.

For older infants the teacher might choose to extend this washing theme to consider where the water comes from and take a simple look at taps, pipes, water tanks and means of heating the water.

Drinking

The children will obviously be aware that they want a drink of water when they are thirsty. Discussion on what would happen if there was no water could follow on from this. (This work could be linked to the needs of all things for water explored in the topics: *Living things – Animals* and *Living things – Plants* see pages 42–55.)

Invite the children to get a drink from the tap – but without using a cup. Some may try to get their heads under the tap, others to drink from cupped hands. Neither method is very successful! This could lead on to some interesting discussion and testing.

What do we need to drink from? What sort of qualities does a drinking vessel need to have? What materials would be best to make it from? What shape should it be – and why?

With these questions in mind, help groups to design a drinking vessel, decide what material it should be, and make it. This is not easy! Encourage the children to keep on trying and record their attempts; the aim being to improve and modify the plans until they have the most effective drinking vessel.

PLAN A

We made our drinking water container out of :....

We made it like this :

What we then asked ourselves :

Would it stand ?
Would it leak ?
Would the water soak through it ?
Would the sides collapse when we got hold of them ?

Answers to these questions would be via practical experience, with the aim all the time being to improve and modify the plans until the most effective drinking vessel was reached.

NC coverage
AT2 Level 2a: *know that plants and animals need certain conditions to sustain life*
　　　Level 3a: *know the basis life processes common to humans and other animals*

c) Water – where does it come from, where does it go?

Young children think along simple lines. The question *Where does water come from?* will probably elicit 'a tap' if the question was in relation to drinking, or 'the sky' if it was posed in the context of getting wet.

Disappearing water
Start with an experiment:

a Fill two identical jam jars with exactly the same amount of water:
b Screw a close-fitting lid on to jar X, making sure it is firmly done up.
c Glue a strip of paper to the side of jar Y, with the top aligned with the surface of the water.

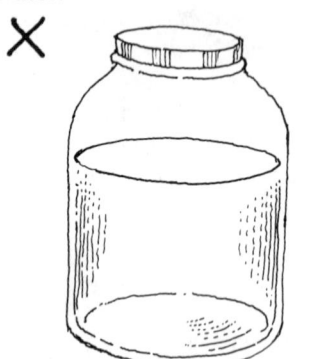

d Put both the jars on to a classroom windowsill and leave them for two days.
e On day three, mark off the water level on Y. Continue to do this on a daily basis.

Quite soon it will be obvious that the water level in jar Y is dropping – the water is 'disappearing'. The children will want to know where the water has gone. Young children can grasp the idea of the water cycle if it is explained very simply.

- water vapour rises from seas, rivers, lakes etc into the sky
- cold air causes the vapour to condense into miniature drops of water which form clouds
- the drops of water join together and become heavy – to form rain
- the rain falls on to the land and into rivers, streams etc. . . and the whole process begins again.

Drinking water

The children may wonder why the water we use comes from a tap. *Why can't we drink rainwater?* This experiment provides an effective answer to the question.

a Put out a receptacle to collect rainwater.
b If possible collect another sample from a stream or pond.
c Fill a third container with tap water.
d Allow the water to stand for a few days, then invite the children to study the jars carefully and compare the three water samples.

Filtering

An obvious follow-on from the previous experiment is to look at how our water is purified.

a Cut the bottom off a plastic bottle and invert it into a drinking glass.
b Fill the bottle with the following layers:

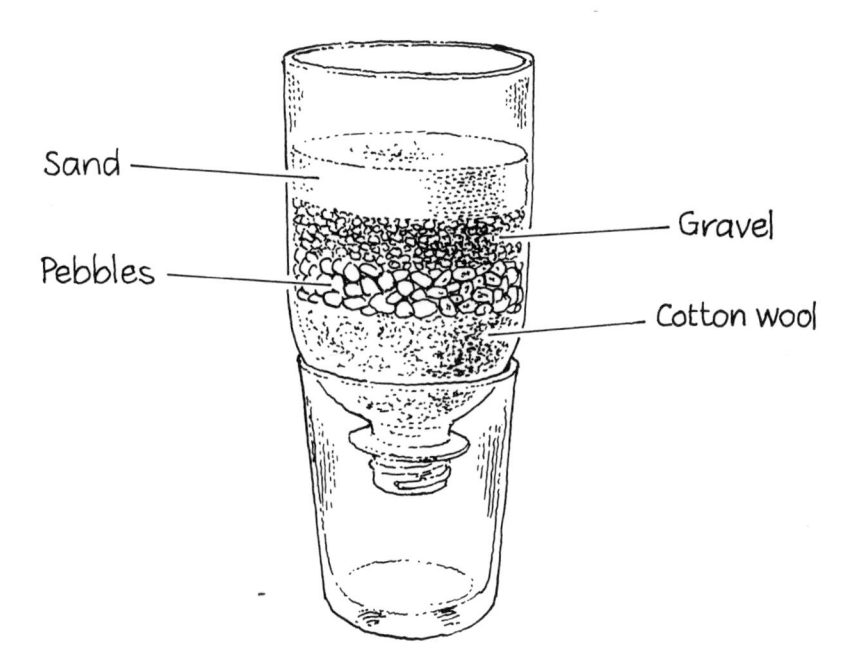

(Diagram showing an inverted plastic bottle filter with labelled layers: Sand, Pebbles, Gravel, Cotton wool, sitting in a drinking glass.)

c Pour dirty water into the 'funnel'.
d Get the children to note what the water is like when it is poured into the funnel, then when it finally drips into the drinking glass. Point out that the water which comes through our taps is filtered in a similar way, and chlorine is added to kill germs.

NC coverage

AT2 Level 2a: *know that plants and animals need certain conditions to sustain life*
　　Level 3a: *know the basic life processes common to humans and other animals*
　　Level 3b: *know that human activity may produce changes in the environment that can effect plants and animals*

d) What lives in water?

This component moves from classroom study to work outdoors. Young children greatly enjoy pond dipping and it can be done in situations ranging from the school grounds to a local field studies centre. Health and safety precautions should be rigorously observed. Children should wear adequate clothing and footwear and appropriate (rubber/plastic) gloves for their work in or near, the pond.

Equipment required includes pond nets (if the real thing is not available a good substitute can be made from a broom handle, strong wire and some nylon tights); plastic containers (margarine boxes); a bucket; magnifying lenses; notebooks and pencils. A good Pond Life book is invaluable (see *Resources*).

On the surface
The first activity might be to watch the surface of the water. The children might see whirligig beetles, water gnats, water skaters and water boatmen. They will probably be surprised to see creatures than can 'walk on water'. Back in school the principle could be demonstrated by floating a dry needle in a bowl of water. (Water molecules hold so tightly together that it appears that there is a skin on the surface.)

Under the surface
The most exciting part of pond dipping is of course the exploration of the water with nets. 'Dippings' are likely to produce creatures such as tadpoles, beetles, sticklebacks, damsel fly nymphs, water boatmen. Scraping the surfaces of plants and stones can yield pond snails and leeches.

The children could examine their finds through the magnifying lenses, record their findings, and then return the creatures to the pond. Recording at this level would be simple and might be done with teacher help as follows:

WHAT WE FOUND IN THE POND

How big	How many legs	What sort of body	Name
2 cm	6 very long black legs	Longer than wide. Part horny wing case	Water Boatman
5-6 cm	None	Fish. Fins. Three spines sticking up.	Stickleback

NC coverage
AT2 Level 2a: *know that plants and animals need certain conditions to sustain life*
    Level 2b: *be able to sort familiar living things into broad groups according to easily observable features*
    Level 2c: *know that different kinds of living things are found in different localities*

e) More fun with water

Floating and sinking

Provide groups with a bowl of water and ask them to collect a variety of objects for testing. They could fill in a simple tick chart to record which items floated and which sank. When they have tested a few objects, children could be asked to predict whether they think something will float or sink.

Floating/sinking is a difficult concept for young children to grasp, but this practical experience provides a useful basic awareness that can be built on later. A helpful follow-up might be to discuss what happens when we get into the bath. When we get in the water rises; we 'push the water out of the way'. When something floats, the water 'pushes back' as it were, strongly enough to support it.

Air and water

Next, try some tests with jars/air in water

a Float a tightly corked jar in water and note what happens.
b Remove the top and put the bottle back in the water. The following is an infant recording of what happened when a group tried this experiment:

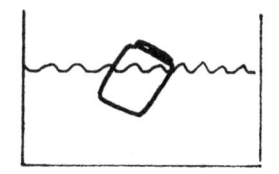

A bottle with a lid floated.

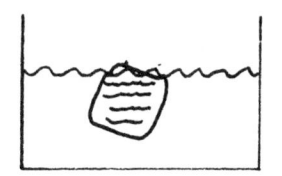

A bottle without a lid filled up with water. It sank. As it sank bubbles came out of it.

Talking points arising from this test could focus on air being all around us even though we don't see it.

Further work could be done by weighing various objects on a spring balance. Then weigh the same objects suspended in a bucket of water. The children will be surprised to find that all the items weigh less when suspended in the water.

Other wide-ranging questions to discuss include: *What machines use water in our houses?* (kettles, washing machines, dishwashers). *How much water do we use when we have a wash?* (practical work using a water measure to fill a sink). *How much water is used when the toilet flushes?* (practical work – filling up a low level cistern while an adult holds down the ball valve to cut off mains supply). *Where does the water go when we pull the plug out of the sink?* (more detective work in and around the classroom).

NC coverage
AT3 Level 2a: *be able to group materials according to observable features*

Cross-curricular links

'Water' is a very popular theme in **RE**. Points to follow up could be the Noah's Ark story (*Genesis* 6, 7 and 8) baptism, being 'clean', Moslem washing before prayer. . .

Children like talking about 'big' things. Storms are a good subject to link water with the children's own experience and some exciting information. There are several recorded instances of freak storms, in which freshwater fish rained on Rhode Island; ants on a town in Romania; caterpillars on Salins in France; herrings in the Isle of Islay. Scientific explanation indicates that enormous updraughts lifted these creatures, bore them away from their place of origin, and later deposited them from the sky in a storm. These accounts offer plenty of stimulus material for creative **writing, artwork** and **drama**.

In **History** the subject of ships is a fruitful topic. Sailors have always been superstitious and sought to protect themselves from storms at sea. African canoes carried the tribe's sacred emblem; Egyptian ships were marked with ☥ the symbol of hope; Greek ships carried the picture of dolphin on them (the dolphin was the sign of safety and salvation). Roman ships had a warrior's figurehead and medieval ships carried an olive branch to plead for a peaceful passage. Many ships throughout history have had an 'eye' painted on them, to 'see' them safely back to shore.

Geographical work could be done with weather observations. 'cooking' might be done by making some iced tea. One quick recipe is: a) Make a weak brew of tea. b) When cool, strain it into a container. c) Put container in fridge. d) Serve with pieces of lemon or sprigs of mint.

Once again, **maths** for measuring, and **technology** for the various models would be well served.

14 Hygiene and Health

a) Staying healthy
b) Food
c) Exercise
d) Rest
e) Teeth

Anatomy of a topic

The National Curriculum advocates that children of this age should be 'introduced to ideas about how they keep healthy' and should 'know about the need for personal hygiene, food and rest'. (*Science for Ages 5 – 16*, DES, August, 1988)

Young children are naturally interested in their bodies. This topic aims to focus that natural curiosity and help develop healthy attitudes and habits in as lively a way as possible. Two ideas for stimulus material are:

a A series of posters with simple messages, which could be placed around the room during work on the topic. The posters might feature a graphic or cartoon-style 'character' eg:

CAPTAIN CLEAN SAYS.... Don't let pets touch your food

b With older infants a number of 'quiz sheets' could be positioned around the room for children to solve as the topic progresses, eg

106 *Science Topics for Infants*

> QUIZ SHEET 1
> To be healthy we all need VITAMINS. Look at this chart.
>
> | VITAMIN A | VITAMIN B | VITAMIN C | VITAMIN D |
> |---|---|---|---|
> | (helps growth and good eyesight) | (good for nerves) | (good for healthy skin and hair) | (good for bones and teeth) |
> | ↓ | ↓ | ↓ | ↓ |
> | butter | milk | oranges | fish oils |
> | milk | eggs | lemons | butter |
> | carrots | meat | grapefruit | bread |
> | eggs | fruit | green vegetables | milk |
> | | fish | | |
> | | fresh vegetables | | |
>
> 1 What drink gives Vitamins A, B and D?
> 2 What is the only vegetable named in these lists?
> 3 What are oranges good for?
> 4 If you had no fish oil, butter, bread or milk which parts of your body would be less healthy?
> 5 Name a vegetable which helps you to grow.
> 6 Which vitamin is needed for healthy hair?
> 7 Are there any 'sweet' things in these lists?
> 8 Which vitamin helps you to grow?

Further examples can be seen in the component on *Teeth* (see page 113). It would be useful to have prepared the sheets before classroom work starts. The number will obviously depend on the age and ability of the children.

It would be helpful if some of the specific vocabulary of the topic was introduced to the children, such as:

> VITAMINS – chemicals in food which we need to stay healthy
> STERILISE – to kill germs by boiling or other means
> SHELF LIFE – the time a packaged food remains fit to eat

The topic should take about four weeks.

Equipment

pencils, paper, card, milk, cheese
various foods/drinks which are 'good' or 'bad' for teeth
a tin of beans or other pungent food which can be easily heated
a heat source (hot plate in classroom or canteen/kitchen stove)
containers of strong-smelling foods
bread (to be allowed to go 'off' or mouldy)
apples and a plastic bag
a real or model skeleton and/or charts showing bones, muscles etc
two teeth
a glass of water
glass of sweet fizzy drink
Licorice Allsorts or similar sweets
toothbrushes

Hygiene and Health

Resources

- Visits from a doctor/nurse/dentist would be invaluable – although these people are normally very busy. A sportsman or woman would also be a useful person to talk about how they keep fit and why it is important.
- If a real (or model) skeleton can be obtained (perhaps borrowed from a local secondary school) it would be very useful for simple identification and comparison of bones.
- The Pictorial Charts Educational Trust produce an excellent series of charts for this topic. *The Human Body* (T40) is a life-size illustration of a 13-year-old, showing skeleton, muscles and nervous system. *Food and Nutrition* (T728) contains one 50 × 76cm chart and six charts of 38 × 50cm. *Food Hygiene* (T27) is a chart showing how food is contaminated by micro-organisms, presented in cartoon style.
- Wayland publishes a series of three books: *What the World Eats – Breakfast, Midday Meal, Evening Meal* by T and J Watson. These books go beyond simple description and include details on: food we need, how much we need, overeating, starvation, eating and illness.
- A collection of toothpastes and packaging would also be useful.

a) Staying healthy

'Gathering and handling information' could be the main activity in this component. Much of the information will emerge from discussion and questioning. A record of the discussions could take the following form:

STAYING HEALTHY

Do!	Don't!
Wash your hands before a meal	Stay in hot sun too long without a top
Wash your hands after using the toilet	Breathe in dust
	Get too near very loud noises
Wash your hands after playing with pets	Put sharp things near your eyes
	Try to read in bad light
Brush your teeth regularly	Drink things that are too hot
	Stick things in your ears
	Let cuts and grazes stay dirty

The significance of material such as this is that it reminds children of basic health precautions which they can take themselves. It also reminds them of some of the different parts of the body which need to be kept healthy.

NC coverage
AT2 Level 1a: *be able to name the main external parts of the human body and a flowering plant*
   Level 2a: *know that plants and animals need certain conditions to sustain life*

b) Food

What we eat

A leading question here might be, *Do we eat the same food all the time?* One group of children might then draw up a menu for their day. It could look like this:

> BREAKFAST: tea, Rice Crispies, an egg, toast and jam
>
> LUNCH (at school): you can choose from: cheese salad, pizza, sausage rolls, potatoes (mashed or boiled), peas, carrots, jelly, rice pudding, cake
>
> TEA: tea, chicken, chips, an apple

This menu could then be discussed by the class as a whole. More questions would stem from it:

Do we all have our meals at the same time? What different sorts of food do members of the class eat? Do we all eat in the same way with the same things? (possibilities include fingers, chopsticks, knives and forks, spoons. . .) *What helps us to like the food we eat?*

Various lists could be drawn up from these questions. One could concern leaving things. In the first instance this could apply to the menu given:

We eat	We don't eat
The inside of the egg	The egg shell
The potatoes	The potato tops which stick out of the ground
peas	
chicken meat	The pea pods
apple	The chicken bones
	The apple core

'Good' smells

Discussion about our appreciation of the food we eat could be extended to focus on the fact that the smell of food is often as important as the taste. The following tests help make this point:

a Heat up some simple, pungent food, eg baked beans. (It may be possible to have a hot plate in the classroom, or to take the children to the school kitchen.)
b Invite the children to describe the effect the smell has on them. The phrase 'makes your mouth water' could be introduced, to highlight the link between taste (the reaction of the salivary glands) and smell.
c Extend this with some classroom 'smelling tests', inviting children to identify various strong-smelling foods (eg cheese, curry, onions) with their eyes shut.

Different foods could be heated and the children invited to describe what happens to them – smell, change of state etc.

... and 'bad' smells

Repeat the test with some unpleasant smells – sour milk, rancid cheese, mouldy bread (all prepared in advance). This is a useful reminder that our sense of smell can warn us if something has 'gone off'. Point out the need to preserve food by keeping it cool, in fridges, and observing the storage conditions.

A follow-up might be to expose a variety of food to the air and record what happens to it. The 'apple test' is one example, eg

THE APPLE TEST – What we did
We cut an apple in two. We put half on a piece of paper on the windowsill. We looked at it every day.

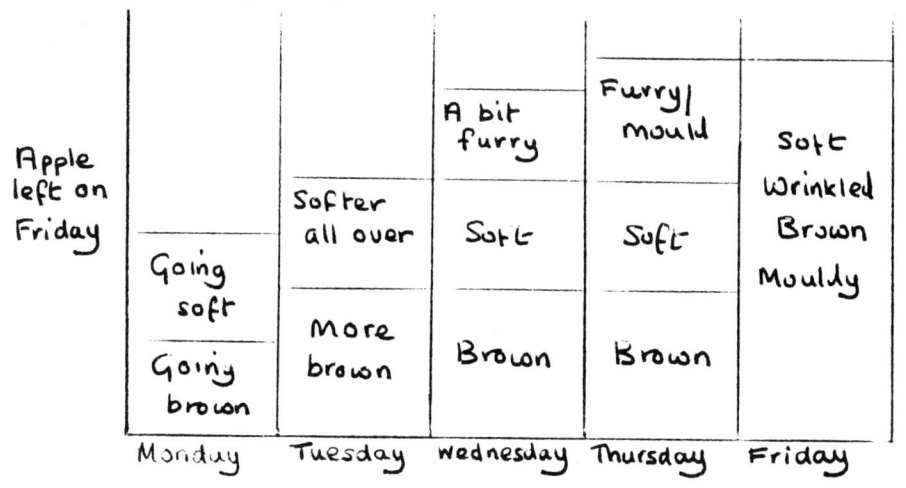

Apple left on Friday			A bit furry	Furry/ mould	Soft Wrinkled Brown Mouldy
		Softer all over	Soft	Soft	
	Going soft				
	Going brown	More brown	Brown	Brown	
Monday	Tuesday	Wednesday	Thursday	Friday	

A variation on this is to immerse different foods in water and note what happens to them.

Food for energy

This time the children could do some tests on themselves. In pairs, they could do a series of exercises – running round the playground, jumping on the spot 20 times, hopping on alternate feet. . . (If members of the class have physical handicaps, try to include some exercises which they can perform.) Before each exercise, partners should take each other's pulse (placing fingers gently on the partner's left wrist, near the base of the thumb) and time the number off. This should then be done after each of the activities, with a rest period before the next exercise.

What happens to the pulse? Children will probably answer that it is faster. From this, point out that when we exercise the body and the heart work harder. Exercise uses up energy, and this energy comes from food. (This simple explanation is appropriate for infants. In fact, energy comes mostly from carbohydrates and fats. Body tissue is made up mainly of proteins. Minerals and vitamins are important for many body processes.) The conclusions could be recorded in the form of a chart, as follows:

> **WHY WE NEED FOOD**
>
> When we play our bodies use ENERGY. FOOD gives us energy. Food helps our bodies to grow, and mends them. These foods are good for us:
>
> meat   fish   poultry   eggs   nuts   cabbages   carrots   parsnips   lettuce   tomatoes   oranges   lemons   grapefruit   apples   pears   bananas   grapes   plums   potatoes   bread   cereals   butter   margarine   cheese   milk

The children could make a large picture collage of the different foods.

NC coverage
AT2 Level 2a: *know that plants and animals need certain conditions to sustain life*
     Level 3a: *know the basic life processes common to humans and other animals*

c) Exercise

In planning work related to this component, the teacher needs to be sensitive towards children who have any physical handicaps.

Begin with a closer look at our bodies and how we use them. Ask for a volunteer to be a 'model'. Get them to stand in front of the class and ask the other children to name the external parts of the body.

Divide the children into pairs and get them to experiment with a wide range of exercises. Children take turns to be 'performer' and 'recorder'. The performer does an exercise, the recorder notes down which parts of the body are most used, as follows:

> Balance – one foot
> Hop – one foot, the other foot
> Stretch – arms
> Skip – legs
> Run – legs
> Jump – legs and knees
> Crouch – legs and knees
> Roll – whole body
> Touch toes – back, fingers
>
> Twist – arms, middle of body
> Handstand – arms and legs
> Climbing – arms and legs
> Press-ups – wrists and arms
> Cartwheel – arms and legs

Ask for comments from the class, *How did you feel after doing the exercise? Which was the easiest? Which was the hardest? Does practice make them easier?*

If appropriate resources are available, show the children a large picture of the human body showing the bones/muscles beneath the skin. This will obviously be useful in drawing attention to what is going on underneath the skin when the exercises are taking place.

The 'health' point that exercise strengthens muscles and makes our bodies work better could then be made.

NC coverage
AT2 Level 1a: *be able to name the main external parts of the human body and a flowering plant*
   Level 2a: *know that plants and animals need certain conditions to sustain life*
   Level 3a: *know the basic life processes common to humans and other animals*

d) Rest

Begin with a 'guessing game' that actually requires a lot of deduction. *What room is this? It is in a house, but not in a school. It's usually upstairs in a house. It usually has a clock in it. You wear special clothes in this room. You lie down in this room. You close your eyes in this room.*

Once the bedroom has been established as the focal point, talk about bedtimes, sleep and so on. Some charts could be prepared, giving this information.

112 *Science Topics for Infants*

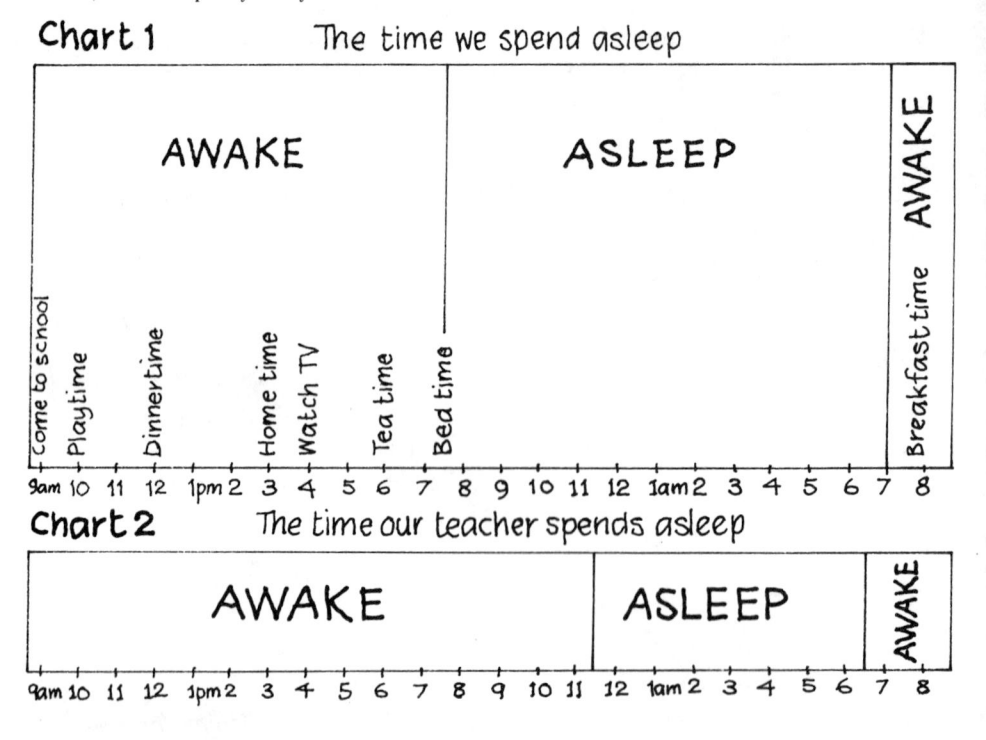

Chart 1 The time we spend asleep

| AWAKE | ASLEEP | AWAKE |

Come to school · Playtime · Dinnertime · Home time · Watch TV · Tea time · Bed time · Breakfast time

9am 10 11 12 1pm 2 3 4 5 6 7 8 9 10 11 12 1am 2 3 4 5 6 7 8

Chart 2 The time our teacher spends asleep

| AWAKE | ASLEEP | AWAKE |

9am 10 11 12 1pm 2 3 4 5 6 7 8 9 10 11 12 1am 2 3 4 5 6 7 8

Obvious conclusions can be drawn from this material. Adults need less sleep than children. Why? This will provide an opportunity to discuss growth, using energy, the need for rest. Invite a small child to stand next to the teacher and invite children to make comparisons. What is the difference in height, weight, in the size of hands, feet and body? This will indicate the growth required from infant school age to adulthood. The next stage in the discussion could be to take this backwards – *Who has a baby brother or sister? How old/big are they? How much do they sleep?*

All this will establish in the children's minds that rest is an essential part of our lives. *What conditions are needed for proper rest?* A class survey of children's own experience could be recorded like this:

Single bed	|||| |||| ||||
Bunk bed	|||| ||
Sleep with brother or sister	|||| |||
Have electric blanket	|||| ||
Have duvet	|||| |||| |||| ||
Central heating in bedroom	|||| |||| |||| |||| ||
Window open	|||| |||| |||| |||
Window closed	|||| |||| ||

Hygiene and Health 113

This could be followed by the question, *What stops us sleeping?* Suggestions might include: being too hot/too cold; feeling sick; toothache; noise; nightmares. From this, a picture of the best conditions for sleep can be built up. We need comfort, the right temperature (neither too not nor too cold); quiet. . .

Another line of enquiry might be, *What happens when we feel tired? What makes us tired?* (lots of exercise, going on a journey, being ill). Point out that people often need more rest when they are ill or recovering. Old people sometimes fall asleep during the day. Children could also talk about their pets and how much they sleep.

NC coverage
AT2 Level 2a: *know that plants and animals need certain conditions to sustain life*
    Level 3a: *know the basic life processes common to humans and other animals*

e) Teeth

Teeth are a good subject for the specific study of a particular part of the body. Top infants may find this especially interesting because some of them will be losing their primary teeth. Inculcation of good dental health habits at this stage is clearly beneficial.

The children might ask for more information about what is happening in the 'change' from primary to permanent teeth. Primary teeth are important for eating, in the development of speech, and for appearance. They usually number 20 and begin to fall out between the ages of 6 and 7, as the roots dissolve. The first permanent teeth are the front ones, and they begin to appear at about 7. The adult mouth usually consists of 32 teeth, made up of incisors, canines, premolars and molars.

Tooth count
Working in pairs, children can do a 'teeth count'. A simple 'tooth' chart can give children an idea of the shape of the mouth and gums and help them to locate the teeth in this context. If this can be duplicated for each child, they could record numbers of teeth.

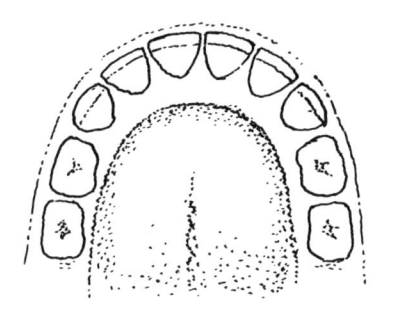

Not only are the numbers noted, but crosses are also put where there are gaps.

Children should now be aware of the external appearance of the teeth. If you have a good diagram of the tooth structure, older children may be interested to learn what is inside the teeth.

Why are teeth important?
Discussion here could be linked to another close look inside mouths and a careful feeling of the surfaces of the teeth. More information could be recorded, with useful vocabulary work as an incidental gain (incisors, canines, premolars, molars).

MORE ABOUT TEETH

Some of our teeth are thin and sharp.
They CUT our food.

Some of our teeth are bigger and pointed.
They TEAR our food

Some of our teeth are flat.
They CRUSH our food.

Our biggest teeth are at the back.
They are flat and broad.
They CRUSH our food even smaller.

Looking after our teeth
Having established the importance of our teeth, the next step might be to consider what threatens them. Two key words could feature here: *decay* and *pain*.

Children could eat a licorice sweet (or some other colourful sweet) and then look in the mirror. They could record how their teeth look. Next they eat a bite or two from an apple, check and record again.

If any children still have their lost teeth then an interesting scrape test could be set up. Requirements are two teeth and two beakers – one containing cold water, the other a very sweet soft drink.

Tie a thread round each tooth and lower it into one of the beakers at the beginning of the topic. During the time span of the topic each tooth could be scraped once a week and a note made of what the scrapings show. At the start of the project place half an apple in a tightly-sealed plastic bag. This too could be regularly examined over the same period.

Hygiene and Health 115

From these tests and observations the children will note that 'something' forms on the teeth. The teacher can explain that this is PLAQUE. Sugary foods help bacteria in the plaque to make an acid which attacks teeth and causes DECAY. The apple in the plastic bag gives an idea of what decay looks like. The teacher could then show, on a picture of the tooth, how the path of DECAY leads to PAIN.

So far children have learned that we need our teeth. We do not want to suffer pain and lose them. So how can we keep them healthy?

Refer back to the licorice/apple comparison. Point out that some foods are good for our teeth, others aren't. Ask for suggestions and draw up two lists 'good for teeth' and 'bad for teeth'.

The children could illustrate this list with colourful drawings; they could go on to practise the correct way to brush the teeth, and perhaps draw a picture of it.

This is a good opportunity to comment on the value of regular visits to the dentist.

Quiz sheets
Examples of quiz sheets related to this topic are as follows:

QUIZ Tick the things that are good for your teeth. Put a ring round the things which are bad for your teeth.

QUIZ Put the correct word in from this list:—
GUMS · TOOTHBRUSH · TOOTH · DENTIST · APPLE · CUT
1. I brush my teeth with a _____.
2. The _____ keeps my teeth healthy.
3. An _____ a day is good for teeth.
4. This is a _____.
5. These sharp teeth _____ our food.
6. Our teeth are in our _____.

116 *Science Topics for Infants*

NC coverage
AT2 Level 1a: *be able to name the main external parts of the human body and a flowering plant*
  Level 3a: *know the basic life processes common to humans and other animals*

Cross-curricular links

There is plenty of scope for remembered observation in **writing** and **talking** about a visit to the dentist. Good **drama** possibilities exist here too with the children acting out the parts of dentist, patient, mum, dad etc. Imaginative writing might be encouraged by ideas like: *The Terrible Tale of a Tooth* where 'a tooth' tells his or her story of life in the mouth of one who cares nothing for dental hygiene.

Maths features in the various counting and recording activities with regard to children's teeth. Graphs might be drawn to show when the children visited the dentist, how many teeth are missing from various mouths, anybody who has got permanent teeth etc. Records of food eaten by the class over the past two days also yield more statistics to be talked about in the 'good' and 'bad' categories.

At a more advanced level the **history** of dentistry makes fascinating reading and there are several facts which are both informative and fun to use with young children. Travelling dentists of past generations moved round England and set up their booths in market places. They then pulled out aching teeth to the sound of a beating drum which was used to drown the yells of the patient! Cave men had good teeth because they ate little sugar. Romans who ate a lot of honey suffered accordingly.

Technology could be brought in through collecting various toothpastes and toothpaste wrappers. *What makes them attractive? How does one claim to be better than another?* The children could then make up a name and wrapper for a 'new toothpaste' of their own.

There are a whole range of **artwork** possibilities. One obvious one is making posters to promote good health.

15 Now and Then

a) **We are different**
b) **Young and old and in-between**
c) **Other living creatures**
d) **Long, long ago**

Anatomy of a topic

The infant teacher will be aware that life "now and then" offers the scope to consider features as varied as personal differences to dinosaurs! This topic seeks to present the 'variance' idea along with some conception of 'time'. It is helpful to make the work more concentrated than with some other topics; the time taken could be a maximum of three weeks.

Equipment

pencils	laths for frames
paper	selection of photographs
card	(showing a wide
glue	variety of people,
paint	animals and children)

Resources

- 'Human resources' are especially valuable here. Some parents or grandparents who get on well with young children could be invited in to tell of significant events in their lives.

- A collection of objects related to the children's own 'time lines' would also be useful – teeth, a tricycle, invitations to a birthday party etc.

- Philip Green Educational produce a film strip on dinosaurs; Galt Educational have a dinosaur frieze (between 2 and 3 metres long); Philip and Tacey supply plastic templates of prehistoric creatures. These are supported by information/work cards.

- A visit to the Natural History Museum is well worthwhile. The Dinosaur Museum, Icen Way, Dorchester, Dorset DT1 1EW, has fossils, skeletons, and life size models. There are party rates and a service for schools.

Pattern of a topic

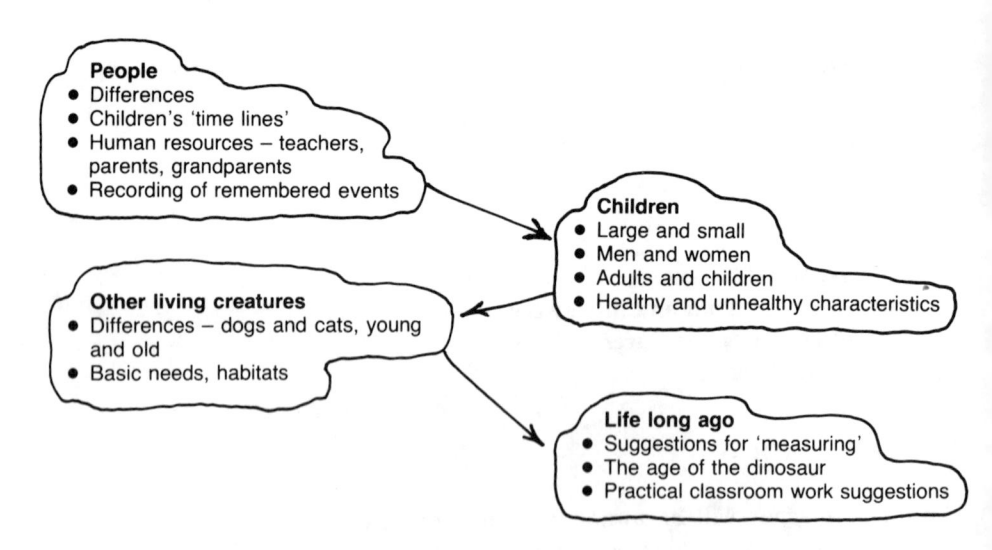

People
- Differences
- Children's 'time lines'
- Human resources – teachers, parents, grandparents
- Recording of remembered events

Children
- Large and small
- Men and women
- Adults and children
- Healthy and unhealthy characteristics

Other living creatures
- Differences – dogs and cats, young and old
- Basic needs, habitats

Life long ago
- Suggestions for 'measuring'
- The age of the dinosaur
- Practical classroom work suggestions

a) We are different

If children have already done work on physical differences a brief reminder of this could begin this component.

Individual differences

Invite volunteers to stand in front of the rest of the class and be 'examined'. The aim is to remind them of 'difference' in terms of height, weight, hair, eyes, size of hands, feet and so on.

After this introductory work the next step could be to highlight other sorts of differences by a series of individual charts. One idea is a 'this week' chart, eg (assuming it is a Wednesday):

MARTIN	SATURDAY	SUNDAY	MONDAY	TUESDAY

Ask the children to suggest what could be filled in. Entries might include food eaten, favourite TV programmes watched, visits or other special activities done at the weekend, anything special done at school, activities done with special friends and so on. This will reinforce the idea of people being different.

Timelines

Draw up a birthday 'time line' to put round the wall. This may span 12 months if the class is chronologically arranged, or longer if the school operates some other grouping system.

The timeline could look something like this:

```
   SEPTEMBER          OCTOBER              NOVEMBER
   |     |          |    |    |              |
  1st   3rd        4th  14th  16th          16th
 Martin Louise    Marcus Lucy Kassie        Nusrat
```

All the children are listed alongside their birthdays. From this, not only will another 'difference' be noted, but a sense of time in the context of being 'older/younger' will be introduced. With this in mind the children, with the help of teachers at school and parents at home, could draw up their own individual time lines. An example might be as follows:

Each marked off span (x) represents a year (to fill in as appropriate). The measures between years should be the same for each child.

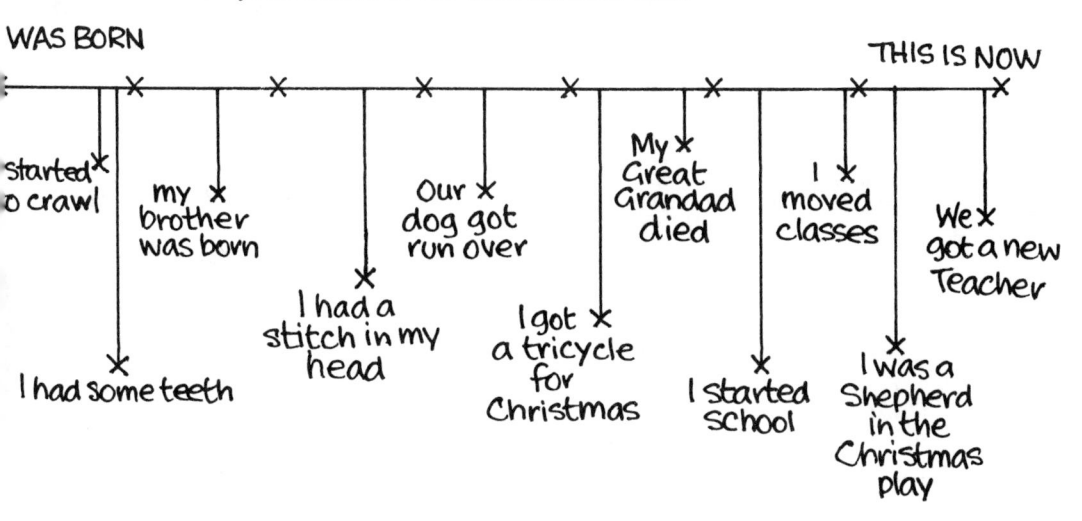

WAS BORN ————————————————————— **THIS IS NOW**

- Started to crawl
- my brother was born
- I had a stitch in my head
- Our dog got run over
- I got a tricycle for Christmas
- My Great Grandad died
- I moved classes
- We got a new Teacher
- I had some teeth
- I started school
- I was a Shepherd in the Christmas play

This activity, and the results, should promote a lot of discussion and raise some interesting points. *When does everybody's timeline start? Could the teacher's time line be put on a piece of paper the same length as the pupils'? Why not? How would a Mum's timeline be different to her child's? On the example shown, the dog and great grandad's timelines ended on certain dates – why?*

From all of this the children should begin to grasp the concept of time – in the sense of birth to death. This point could be developed by a few other timelines – a teacher, a parent, a famous personality known to the children and about whom some statistics are available.

NC coverage
AT2 Level 1b: *know that there is a wide variety of living things which includes humans*

b) Young and old and in between

Make a class collection of as many photographs of people as possible. These could be from newspapers and magazines as well as home sources.

Invite the children to arrange the 'home' photographs in groups. These might be babies, grown-ups, under 10s, male and female. This will again emphasise differences, but in a way sensitive to the owners of the photographs.

The collection from newspapers and magazines could be used more freely. Draw up another time line, of say 0 to 75. Ask the children to place examples from the selection at the age they find most appropriate. Other groupings might be – people doing active things; people who look old, pairings of people who look as different as possible. In each case, ask the children to explain their decisions, eg *What makes you think that person is old?* etc.

Again a good deal of discussion could be generated from this work, with the following talking points emerging: *The differences between small and large children. Differences in size of men and women. Differences between adults and children. Differences between healthy and unhealthy people. How do people look as they get older? When are people most active?*

NC coverage
AT2 Level 1a: *be able to name the main external parts of the human body and a flowering plant*
Level 2b: *be able to sort familiar living things into broad groups according to easily observable features*

c) Other living creatures

To provide a visual stimulus for a discussion, display some pictures of pets, including, if possible, small puppies or kittens.

Encourage the children to talk about their pets, and about other animals as well. Again questions might be useful: *Do all dogs look alike? How is a young dog different from an old dog? How are kittens different from cats? Name some ways in which cats and dogs are different to us. Name some ways in which cats and dogs need the same things as us* (food, rest, exercise, home etc.).

Make a collection of photographs of animals and invite the children to sort them. A 'contrasting pairs' group could be made up. Baby animals could be linked with photographs of baby people and 'old with old' in the same way. More pictures and books could be used to show animals in their specific habitats.

NC coverage
AT2 Level 1b: *know that there is a wide variety of living things which includes humans*
Level 2b: *be able to sort familiar living things into broad groups according to easily observable features*

d) Long, long ago

The work in this topic so far has encouraged children to think about differences between themselves, differences between people, the effects of growth and ageing, differences and similarities in comparison with other living creatures.

The 'time' concept which has been a parallel feature of the topic could now be developed further. In the context of their own time lines, those of adults will seem very long to children. The teacher could point out, however, that some living things were on the earth so long ago that no living human being ever saw them. A chart like the following might form the basis for discussion aimed at helping the children understand what 'long ago' means...

1 cm   could have been the measure to show 1 year in each child's life
         so:-
10 cm   = 10 years
1 M   = 100 years
10 M   = 1,000 years
100 M   = 10,000 years   } Measurements which can be
1 Km   = 100,000 years   } looked at on a ruler,
10 Km   = 1,000,000 years   } or paced out
100 Km   = 10,000,000 years
1000 Km = 100,000,000 years
1500 Km = 150,000,000 years AGO...

Now we are back to the time of the DINOSAURS!

Obviously the concept of 150,000,000 years ago is beyond the comprehension of young children, but this 'build up' will make an impact because children are fascinated by anything 'big', whether in number or size.

Young children are also very interested in dinosaurs and will soon start asking questions: *What was the world like at the time of the dinosaurs? What were the dinosaurs like? Where are they now? What happened to them?*

A valuable resource here would be a classroom collection of books, pictures, charts etc about dinosaurs. There are many suitable titles available. The following is just a small selection: *Exploring the Age of the Dinosaur* by D Lambert (Piccolo); *Dinosaurs* (Ladybird); *Dinosaurs* (Macdonald Starters); *Dinosaur's Book of Dinosaurs* and *How Life Began* by Althea (Dinosaur Publications). For further material, see the Resources section. Encourage the children to look at the books and materials throughout the topic, and to discuss and share the information they discover.

It may be helpful to have some basic background information:

- At the time of the dinosaurs the world was covered with huge lakes and muddy marshes. The climate was warm.
- The word dinosaur means 'terrible lizard'.
- Not all dinosaurs were huge. Some were very small and ate lizards. Others ate twigs and leaves. Some ate meat – they preyed on the leaf and insect-eating species.

- Some of the largest dinosaurs were:
  Diplodocus – 27m in length, it was heavy and slow-moving.
  Tyrannosaurus – 12m in length, this was the biggest meat-eating animal that ever lived. Its head was as big as three men standing on top of each other! Its teeth were 16cm long.
  Stegosaurus – 9m long. It had protective spikes on its back.
  Triceratops – 9m long, with spear-like horns.
- Much of our knowledge of dinosaurs comes from reconstructions based on fossils and bones. When the dinosaur died, the bones were covered by mud. This mud slowly turned into rock – the bones turned into fossils, and a few of these fossils have been discovered by archaeologists.
- Nobody knows why the dinosaurs ceased to exist. Theories include: changes in the environment (the winters became too cold, the landscape become drier); meat eaters gradually ate all the plant eaters; other creatures ate the dinosaur eggs.

Children could support their research with some practical activities:

1 They could measure and pace out the size of different dinosaurs in the playground. This could lead to making scale models – with one child as the 'scale' for comparison. If time and resources allow, the models could be built on lath frames, and perhaps displayed in the school hall. Alternatively, smaller models could be made in plasticine, and set in a reconstruction of what the environment might have been like at the time of the dinosaurs.
2 The children could collect rocks and fossils, or visit a museum where these are displayed.
3 The dinosaurs became extinct because they could no longer survive. This links with the theme of taking care of ourselves and taking care of our environment.

NC coverage
AT2 Level 2a: *know that plants and animals need certain conditions to sustain life*
   Level 2d: *know that some waste materials decay naturally but do so over different periods of time*

Cross-curricular links

In **English** there is plenty of 'dinosaur fiction' available for this age group. Some good titles are: *Desmond the Dinosaur* by Althea (Dinosaur); *Meg's Eggs* by H Nicoll and J Pienkowski (Picture Puffin); *Danny and the Dinosaur* by Syd Hoff (Young Puffin). Children also enjoy **creative writing** about this subject.

Movement, mime, and drama could be done to percussion sounds made by the children themselves, or to appropriate noises from *Out of this World* (BBC sound effects record REC 225 BBC). Other useful background music for this theme could come from *Carnival of the Animals* by Saint-Saëns and Mussorgsky's *Night on the Bare Mountain*.

Maths is involved in work on size, scale, estimation, measuring and time. **RE** might prove the theme that despite our differences we all have the same feelings and needs, and emphasise tolerance. Birth and death could also be dealt with here, perhaps with regard to animals and pets.

16 Moving

a) **Ourselves and movement**
b) **Toys and us**
c) **Rolls and wheels**
d) **Air and movement**
e) **Moving creatures**
f) **Classroom collections**

Anatomy of a topic

This is a topic which can be developed at any time of the year and there is a great deal of learning 'fun' in it for young children. A variety of displays are an important facet of the topic and these need to be planned and prepared well in advance. It should be noted that they are likely to be displays which are constantly being added to. There is further work with toys in Topic 3 *Energy*.

Equipment

card	soap	a teacher's car
chair	simple finger puppets	a blow football
pencils	(from 'Letterland'?)	arrangement
paper	cocktail sticks	drawing pins
dowelling	scissors	small object to draw circles
thread/string	magic markers	round (a film container?)
matchbox	elastic bands	hair drier
plasticine	as wide a variety as	bricks/wood – for
toilet roll	possible of moving toys	minibeast coverage (see
ruler	and objects	component d)
coins	straws	photographs of moving
wooden surface	'loads' of books for moving	things and creatures
wooden blocks	various objects which	(see component d)
water	will roll (see component c)	

Resources

- Technology Teaching Systems supply a wide range of primary school science/technology equipment. As well as a useful selection of material for gears and wheels, they produce a *Move it Pack* which concentrates on power from fluid and air.
- BP Educational Service produce a resource pack – *Making Work Easier*. This

124 *Science Topics for Infants*

investigates things like screws and pulleys via booklets, work cards and work sheets. The booklet from this pack can be bought separately for £2.25 and the whole thing, booklet included, currently costs £16.00.
- On a theme of transport, there are several good sites for visits depending upon the school's location, eg: The London Transport Museum; The Ffestiniog Railway Museum; The Lakeland Motor Museum; The National Maritime Museum. Movement, in the sense of machines, could form the focus for a visit to the Science Museum.

Pattern of a topic

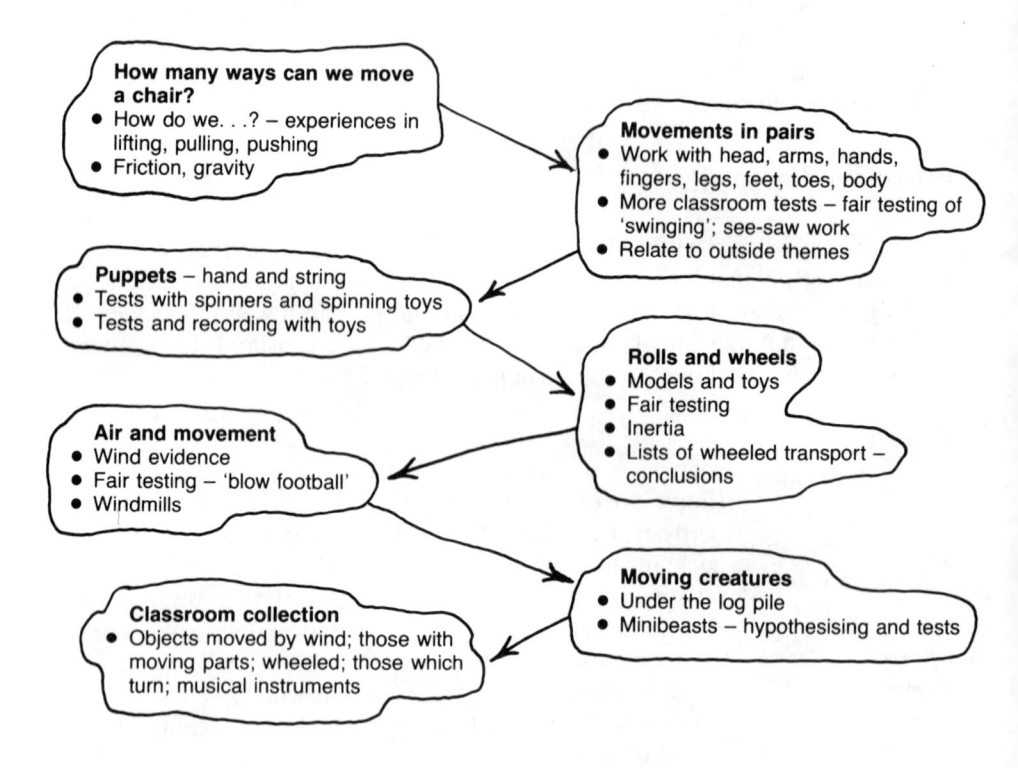

How many ways can we move a chair?
- How do we...? – experiences in lifting, pulling, pushing
- Friction, gravity

Movements in pairs
- Work with head, arms, hands, fingers, legs, feet, toes, body
- More classroom tests – fair testing of 'swinging'; see-saw work
- Relate to outside themes

Puppets – hand and string
- Tests with spinners and spinning toys
- Tests and recording with toys

Rolls and wheels
- Models and toys
- Fair testing
- Inertia
- Lists of wheeled transport – conclusions

Air and movement
- Wind evidence
- Fair testing – 'blow football'
- Windmills

Moving creatures
- Under the log pile
- Minibeasts – hypothesising and tests

Classroom collection
- Objects moved by wind; those with moving parts; wheeled; those which turn; musical instruments

a) Ourselves and movement

How do we move things?
One way to start work on this topic would be to put a classroom chair in the middle of a cleared space and seat the children round it. Place four coloured cards on the floor:

RED

BLUE

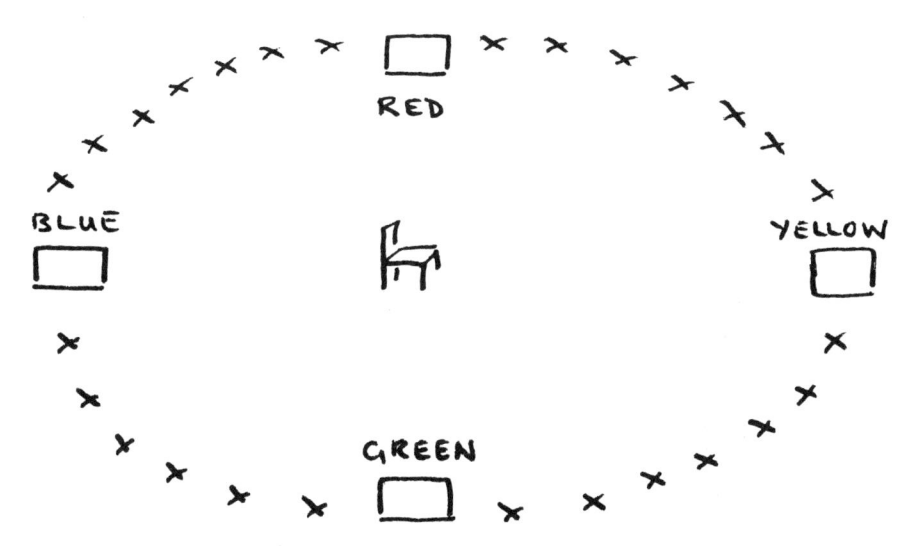

YELLOW

GREEN

Invite several of the children to move the chair. The teacher could suggest that each new 'mover' tries to move it in a way not previously used. This is a record of what was done in one such exercise:

1. The chair was lifted up.
2. It was pulled on its back legs.
3. It was pulled on its front legs.
4. It was laid down with its back on the floor.
5. It was carried to the red card.
6. It was dragged on one leg to the green card.
7. It was pushed to the yellow card.
8. It was laid flat on the floor and pulled to the blue card.
9. Martin laid the chair down and gave it a big push and let go of it.
10. Louise and Lucy lifted the chair up and then let it fall.

Lifting, pulling, pushing, friction and gravity all featured in this simple exercise. This could give rise to a lot of questioning and testing: *Is it easier to drag the chair along a carpeted or uncarpeted floor? Is is easier to lift the chair onto a desk or lift it down from a desk? If we make a slope is it easier to drag the chair up or down the slope? If we lie the chair flat is it easier to pull it or push it?*

126 *Science Topics for Infants*

NC coverage

AT4 Level 3c: *understand that forces can affect the position, movement and shape of an object*

This lifting, pulling, pushing activity could be extended to include all sorts of objects in the room which can be moved by the children in one of these ways. The following chart illustrates this:

HOW DO WE ....?	LIFT	PUSH	PULL
Hang our coats up?	✓		
Close the classroom door?		✓	
Open the classroom door?			✓
Open the windows?		✓	
Close the windows?			✓
Take the lid off the brick box?	✓		
Flush the toilet?			✓
Lock the toilet door?		✓	
Unlock the toilet door?			✓
Open the drawers?			✓
Close the drawers?		✓	
Move our tables?	✓	✓	✓

How do we move ourselves?

Divide children into pairs and ask them to *see how many ways you can move. You can move bits of you, all of you, both of you together.*

Movements might include: walk, run, jump, crawl, kneel, lie, hop.

Movements of individual parts might be:

Head – up, down, side-to-side
Arms – bend, stretch, lift, flap, forwards, backwards, sideways
Hands – shake, bend, up, down, sideways
Fingers – stretch, bend, cross, move all together or one at a time or in twos or threes
Legs – bend, stretch, kick
Feet – bend, up, down, sideways, press, lift
Toes – wriggle, bend
Body – stretch, bend, lean, sag, curl

Children could draw a record of some of these activites, eg for paired activity:

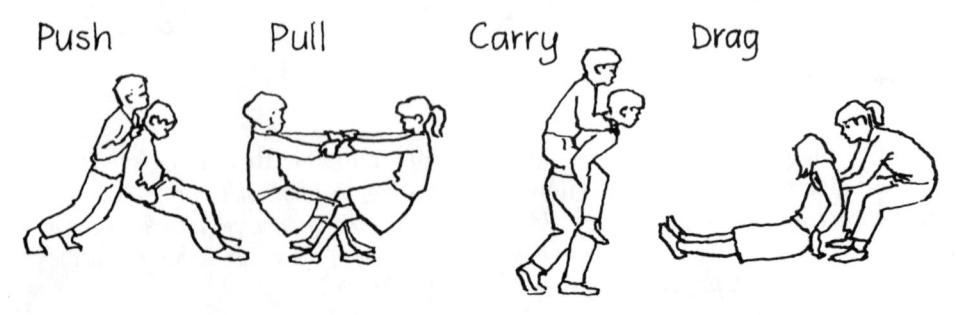

Push   Pull   Carry   Drag

Everyday movements

Discuss with the children what lifting, pulling and pushing they do throughout the day – at home as well as at school.

A wide range of suggestions might be forthcoming here – *pulling up the bedclothes, lifting the cat, going upstairs and downstairs, getting clothes from a wardrobe, pulling the curtains back.* Playing with toys involves movement, and this will be developed later.

Playing on a swing

Again, plenty of questions could arise from this: *How do we keep the swing going? Is it harder to pull or push to start it? What keeps it going? Does it swing to the same point every time?*

These questions could be tested on a real swing if there is one nearby. A simple model could also be made for classroom tests, as follows:

a Put a piece of dowelling between two desks and clamp or hold it firmly.
b Suspend a matchbox from the dowelling with string. Place a small doll or piece of plasticine in the box.
c Start the swing in motion and get the children to observe and note what happens.

(Whenever the load goes up, gravity pulls it down again. The string stops it falling to the floor.)

See-saw!

How do we get a see-saw going? What keeps it moving? What happens if one person is heavier that the other? Again, testing on the real thing would be ideal, but if this is not possible a classroom model could be used to illustrate the principle.

a Put half a toilet roll on a flat surface. Centre a ruler on it and place a coin on each end until it is balanced.
b Add another coin to one end and note what happens.
c Try pushing the two coins nearer the centre until the see-saw balances again.

More tests could be done with more coins.

Moving on different surfaces

Get the children to move about on a well-polished surface (eg the hall floor), first in socks, then wearing shoes. Ask them to describe how it feels and compare the different sorts of movement.

Experiment with moving an object over different surfaces. *How far and how easily can a wooden block slide on a dry surface? On a wet surface? On a wet and soapy surface?* The children could record their results and this 'slipping and gripping' work might lead on to discussion about tyres and safety on wet or icy roads.

128 *Science Topics for Infants*

NC coverage
AT4 Level 1b: *understand that things can be moved by pushing or pulling them*
    Level 2c: *understand that pushes and pulls can make things start moving, speed up, slow down or stop*
    Level 3c: *understand that forces can affect the position, movement and shape of an object*

b) Toys and us

As many infant schools now use the delightful and effective 'Letterland' reading materials, the finger puppets linked with this are an excellent starting point. Some very basic string puppets could be made next and the children could experiment with lifting and lowering arms and legs.

Another simple toy which could be examined is the game spinner, made as follows:

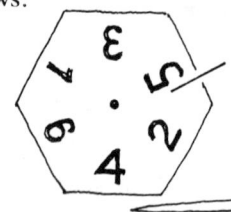

Six sided piece of card with appropriate numbering.

Cocktail stick put through centre of card.

Give all the children a chance to try the spinner. Then the following questions might be asked: *How do we work the spinner? Which fingers do we use? What action must they take? Can we spin both ways? Does it make a difference what surface we are spinning on? How can we keep it going as long as possible? Is a sharp or blunt end best? Can we alter the card to make it better?*

More discussion could then take place on the wide range of toys the children possess and how they are used. Some simple recording of these might be done. One infant class and teacher produced the following:

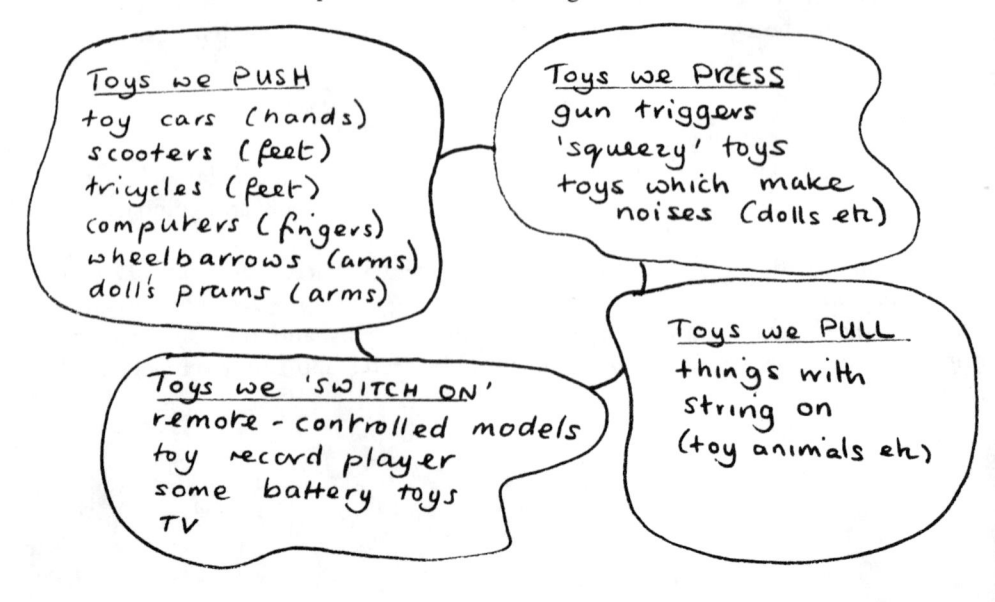

Toys we PUSH
toy cars (hands)
scooters (feet)
tricycles (feet)
computers (fingers)
wheelbarrows (arms)
doll's prams (arms)

Toys we PRESS
gun triggers
'squeezy' toys
toys which make noises (dolls etc)

Toys we 'SWITCH ON'
remote-controlled models
toy record player
some battery toys
TV

Toys we PULL
things with string on
(toy animals etc)

NC coverage
AT4 Level 2c: *understand that pushes and pulls can make things start moving, speed up, slow down or stop*

c) Rolls and wheels

The starting point for this work could be 'looking at a teacher's car'. One facet for particular study might be the wheels (not forgetting the spare wheel).

What are wheels for? How are they attached to the car? What makes them go round? Why are there four of them? Why do the wheels have tyres on? How do the tyres make the ride in the car safer and more comfortable? What others things have wheels and tyres?

Back in the classroom the children could experiment with a toy lorry.

a 'Load' the lorry with a book or bricks.
b Attach an elastic band to the front.
c Pull the lorry along and note what happens.
d Variations might be to try the lorry with no load, or upside-down.

After several tests the children may be able to draw the following conclusions: *The harder the pull the more the elastic stretches. It is harder to start the lorry moving than to keep it moving. If the lorry is turned over and pulled with its wheels in the air, it is very much harder.*

From this the children will be aware that the heavier something is the more force it takes to get it moving; still objects won't move until some force is exerted on them. (The key word here is *inertia* which comes from the Latin, for 'lazy'.) Links can also be made with 'forces' in models and human beings.

Things with wheels
The children could move on to do some more observing, testing and recording. One possibility is to make a list of things with wheels:

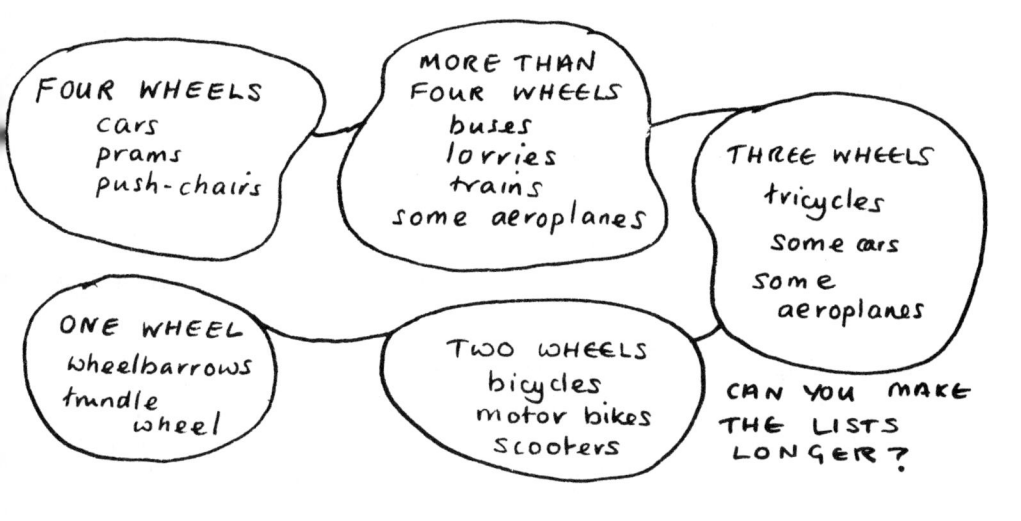

FOUR WHEELS
cars
prams
push-chairs

MORE THAN FOUR WHEELS
buses
lorries
trains
some aeroplanes

THREE WHEELS
tricycles
some cars
some aeroplanes

ONE WHEEL
wheelbarrows
trundle wheel

TWO WHEELS
bicycles
motor bikes
scooters

CAN YOU MAKE THE LISTS LONGER?

There are lots more discussion possibilities here about the relative sizes of wheels to objects; types of tyres; safety; solid and inflated tyres.

Things which roll

More tests could then be done by the children to find other rolling objects (eg roll of sellotape, cotton reel, toilet roll, rolling pin, round bread board, 10p piece, empty treacle tin, PE hoop and so on).

A 'track' of children's paces could be constructed:

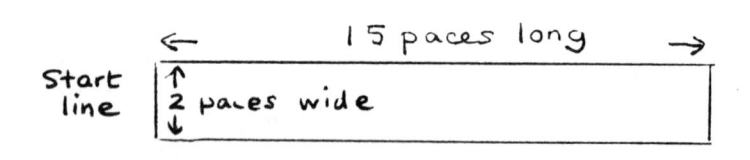

```
                  ←  15 paces long  →
Start line  ↑
            2 paces wide
            ↓
```

Help the children roll the various items along the track and note how far they travel. The results could then be examined in another way: *Which was the easiest object to move down the track? Which was the easiest to keep straight? Was the heaviness of the object important? Was the size of the round part important? Could we apply the same force to each object?*

NC coverage

AT4 Level 1b: *understand that things can be moved by pushing and pulling them*
    Level 2c: *understand that pushes and pulls can make things start moving, speed up, slow down or stop*

d) Air and movement

Begin by asking *what do we notice on a windy day?* If it happens to *be* a windy day, the children may find some answers simply by going outside or looking out of the window. If not, they may remember observations such as: leaves swirling in the air; clothes flapping or pressing against us; clouds racing across the sky; gusts of rain. The sounds the wind makes should not be forgotten.

Blow football

This could lead on to some fair testing in the classroom. Requirements are: a table or desk top; a selection of straws; a table tennis ball; four pieces of dowelling; four blobs of plasticine.

Make two plasticine and dowelling 'goals' – one at each end of the table.

Position the children round the table to play 'blow football'. As well as being great fun, the game can provoke some useful observations: the most successful players will be those who keep the straw close to the ball, and those who blow the strongest. The position of the ball is also important, moving with the wind or being

Moving 131

repelled. 'Refinements' to the game could be made by putting coverings of various material over the table and noting the difference this makes.

Several children could be asked to give accounts of the game (perhaps these could be taped). 'How the goals were scored' might be one feature discussed; another might be how easy – or otherwise – it was to keep the ball on the table. The different material coverings would be a significant factor here.

A simple windmill

The next piece of testing the children could do would involve each of them making a very simple windmill. This could be done as follows:

a Take a square of paper. (If using A4 the square can be 21cm on all sides.)

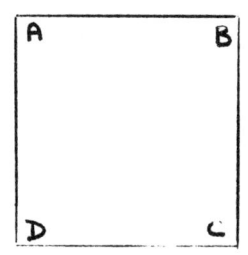

b Take hold of A and C, bring together and fold.
c Take hold of B and D, bring together and fold.
d Open out the paper and draw a circle in the centre (a film container – radius 2cm – is a possible object to use here).

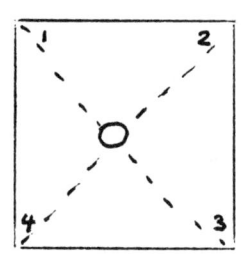

e Cut along the folds of the paper until the edge of the circle is reached.
f Fold 1, 2, 3, and 4 in that order into the middle of the circle and glue each one down. Thus:

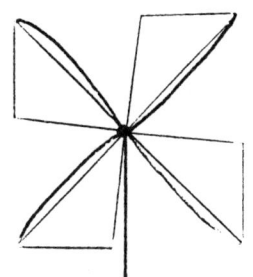

g Put a drawing pin through the centre of the windmill and attach it to a piece of wood (dowelling about the length of a ruler).

Help children to make more examples, using different kinds of paper and card. Tests can then take place to note which paper turned best when the windmills were exposed to wind. Indoor and outdoor tests could take place to determine performance, and 'extreme conditions' might be used – i.e. with a hair drier. Perhaps this time the children could record their observations and test results on tape.

NC coverage
AT3 Level 1a: *be able to describe the simple properties of familiar materials*
AT4 Level 2c: *understand that pushes and pulls can make things start moving, speed up, slow down or stop*
   Level 3c: *understand that forces can affect the position, movement and shape of an object*

e) Moving creatures

One of the highlights of a visit to any field studies centre is exploration of the 'log pile'. Here old pieces of wood can be lifted carefully to reveal the teeming world of minibeasts underneath. Movement is so agitated and frenzied that it sometimes seems as if the whole previously hidden surface is alive. With the help of the teacher, children can recognise different species: centipedes, worms, woodlice, spiders, millipedes, ants.

Schools without access to a field centre can create their own 'log pile' of pieces of wood and bricks. These should be left in a grassy area of the school grounds for two or three weeks before inspection. They could then be examined 'in situ' or by bringing them into the classroom and putting them on a piece of paper before turning them over. The children's observations and discussion might be guided by some questions: *Does the movement of these creatures make any noise? Would it take the minibeasts long to cross the classroom? Why might this be? In what different ways do they move? Which are the quickest/slowest movers? What sort of different shapes are they?*

The next task might be to make lists – this could be done orally with the teacher writing down the suggestions. These again could be based on questions: *What other very small creatures can you think of? What are the biggest, heaviest creatures you can think of? What are the fastest moving. . .? What are the slowest moving. . .? How many fish can you name? How many birds can you name?*

NC coverage
AT2 Level 1b: *know that there is a wide variety of living things, which includes humans*
   Level 2c: *be able to sort familiar living things into broad groups according to easily observable features*

f) Classroom collections

A tremendous variety of things linked with movement can be collected and displayed in the classroom. (Where actual objects cannot be displayed it is usually possible to find photographs.) Here are some ideas for collections and displays:

Things the wind moves
leaves, litter, hats, windmills, kites, gliders, paper aeroplanes, flags, smoke, clouds

Things which move on wheels
cars, buses, lorries, trains, bicycles, tricycles, scooters, prams, wheelbarrows, all sorts of toys

Big machines with moving parts
washing machines, dishwashers, spin driers, cement mixers, vacuum cleaners, fan heaters

Small things with moving parts
scissors, cake mixers, electric pencil sharpeners, whistles

Things we can move by turning
screws, nuts, bolts, keys in locks, wind-up toys, screw bottle tops, lids on jars

Musical instruments where we can see movement
recorder, drum, triangle, viola, piano, trombone.

Other children and adults can be invited to contribute – the resulting display may contain very unusual and interesting items.

NC coverage
AT3 Level 2a: *be able to group materials according to observable features*
AT4 Level 3c: *understand that forces can affect the position, movement and shape of an object*

Cross-curricular links

'Moving' in the re-locating sense, is traumatic for both children and adults. 'Moving day' offers lots of scope for **mime** and **drama**; and **creative** as well as **descriptive writing**.

There are also possibilities for **RE** here. Moving to a new area often makes children apprehensive because they are afraid they will be lonely. Suggestions as to how we should behave in welcoming new people could further the RE theme.

Moving clearly offers exciting possibilities for **music** and **drama**. The children could devise their own music to move to, using simple percussion instruments. Suitable recorded music could be *Nellie the Elephant*; Glenn Miller's *Tuxedo Junction*; *Post Horn Gallup*; *The Man on the Flying Trapeze*; and *Run Rabbit Run*.

How weather, climate and local environmental conditions influence movement could be pursued in **geography** (Arctic snow/dense tropical jungle, etc.) The **history** of transport from human to horse to powered machines could be developed, with varying speeds/distances/times bringing in a **mathematical** element. **Art** might feature a 3D collage of 'things which roll' and children's own depictions of their favourite toys.

17 More about Materials

a) **Making collections and comparisons**
b) **What about metal and glass?**
c) **Changing materials**
d) **Using materials**

Anatomy of a topic

A very important aspect of this topic is for teacher and children to build up collections of materials to work with. Many of the materials discussed will already be in classrooms; some can be found easily at home; others can be collected in the local environment without too much difficulty. (A practical point – it is worth warning the cleaners that there will be a lot of objects in the classroom.) This topic is suitable for any part of the school year, and should last about four weeks.

Equipment

Boxes (for A4 paper/ shoe boxes)
coloured paper
everyday pocket/handbag contents – envelope, drawing pin, whistle, keys, handkerchief, pen, purse, money
PE hoops
stones
pebbles
pieces of rock and brick
a selection of classroom materials – staples, drawing pin, paper clips, scissors, sellotape, gummed squares, rulers, straws, rubbers, elastic bands, files, plimsolls
a metal knife
metal ruler
various metal objects – aluminium, copper, lead, steel, brass, chrome, iron, zinc, tin, spoon, candlestick, wires, door handles, hinges, pencil sharpeners, filing cabinet, trowel, sweet tins
glass windows
glass bottle
pencil
pen
magic marker
chalk
pastel crayons
wax crayons
spectacles
mirrors
polyfilla
gravy powder
coffee
wool
cotton
nylon
silk
satin
PVC
leather
glue
wooden blocks
potatoes
candle
screwdriver
steel file
nail
screw
water container
magnet
sponge cake mix
ground rice
water (hot and cold)
jelly cube
Oxo cube

Alka-selzer tablet
candle
a collection of wooden
  things – toys,
  matchsticks, bark,
  branches, old clothes
  pegs, boxes, broom

handle, rounders bat,
twigs, walking stick,
blocks, chair, drawer,
shelf, hammer
a selection of plastic
  items – Lego, tooth
  brush, watering can,

lunch box, dust pan,
hard balls, combs,
bottles, plastic cutlery,
cups, carrier bags,
raincoats, wrapping,
wellingtons

Resources

- CLEAPSS School Science Service is a useful source of advice and equipment for primary science. In connection with this topic their Guide L173, *Construction Kits* suggests useful kits for all ages.
- Technology Teaching Systems Ltd produce MDF packs for primary school use. 'MDF' is a by-product of timber manufacture which can be cut and glued. It is useful for construction type activities related to this topic.
- Pictorial Charts Educational Trust has an excellent chart – *Structures and Materials* which measures 76 × 100 cm.

Pattern of a topic

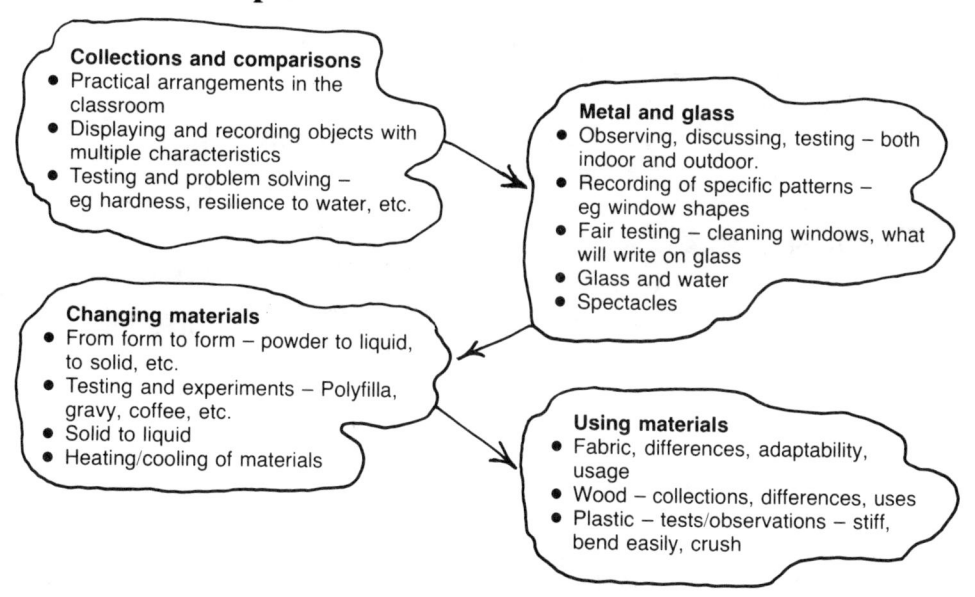

Collections and comparisons
- Practical arrangements in the classroom
- Displaying and recording objects with multiple characteristics
- Testing and problem solving – eg hardness, resilience to water, etc.

Metal and glass
- Observing, discussing, testing – both indoor and outdoor.
- Recording of specific patterns – eg window shapes
- Fair testing – cleaning windows, what will write on glass
- Glass and water
- Spectacles

Changing materials
- From form to form – powder to liquid, to solid, etc.
- Testing and experiments – Polyfilla, gravy, coffee, etc.
- Solid to liquid
- Heating/cooling of materials

Using materials
- Fabric, differences, adaptability, usage
- Wood – collections, differences, uses
- Plastic – tests/observations – stiff, bend easily, crush

a) Making collections and comparisons

Young children enjoy collecting, sorting and studying the results. Perhaps the best way to develop this is to start indoors and finish outdoors.

Shiny or dull?
Collect a number of cardboard boxes (A4 copy paper boxes/shoeboxes, etc) and

paint each one a different colour. Search pockets, handbag, desk drawer, etc, and come up with some of the following articles – pen, purse, coins, keys, handkerchief, whistle, envelope, drawing pin, etc.

Children and teacher study these items and decide on a label for each of them – rough, smooth, shiny, hard, dull, bendy, stiff, soft, etc. As each item receives a label put it into one of the coloured boxes, and give that box the appropriate label.

Split the children into groups. Ask them to look around the classroom area and make further collections of items which can be categorised by being put into appropriate boxes.

A problem will certainly arise. *What about objects which could fall into more than one category?* Invite suggestions from the children. One way of doing it might be to take some PE hoops and cover them in paper the same colour as the boxes. Place the hoops on the floor so that they partially overlap. Items that fall into more than one category can be placed in the centre of this simple diagram:

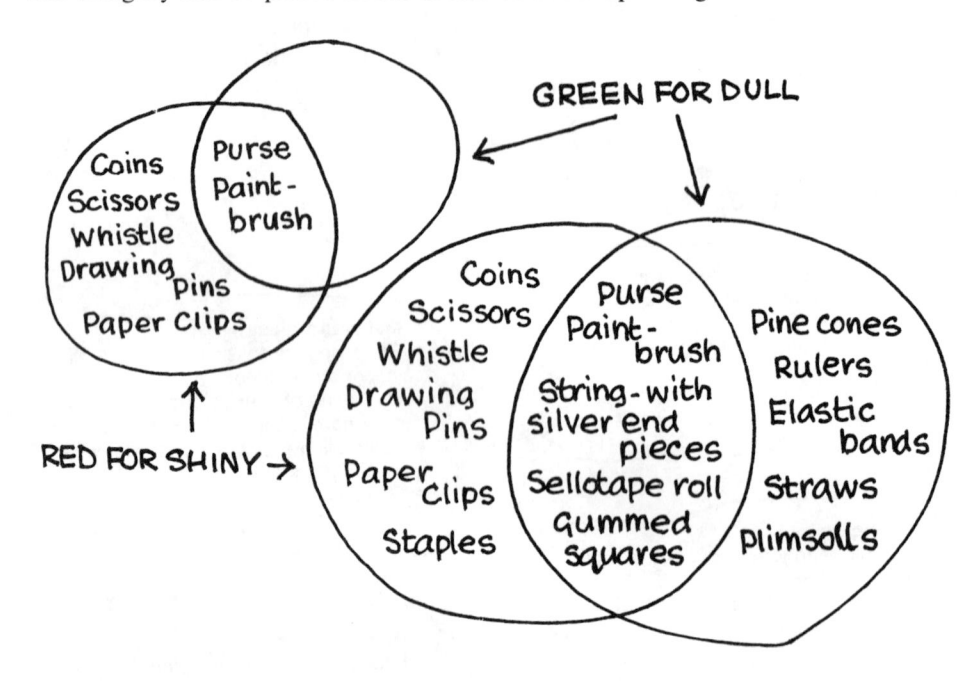

This arrangement makes it obvious that some things are shiny, some are dull and some are both. This is one way of showing that information.

Throughout this activity the children can feel, look, evaluate, compare and contrast the materials they have collected.

Rocks and stones

Now move on to some outdoor collecting. Stones, pebbles, pieces of rock and brick could be collected from as wide an area as possible – school grounds, local field/waste ground/park, seaside (from holidays), building sites, quarries, etc. Clearly time, location and opportunity will determine where the collection comes from.

The first selections and comparisons could be made in a way similar to those with the indoor materials. Stones/rocks could be boxed according to dull, shiny, rough,

More about Materials 137

smooth, hard, etc, criteria. Overlapping hoops could then extend the presentation as before.

From this point testing and problem solving could advance. *How could we test the hardness of these rocks?* Suggestions might include dropping them or hitting them against each other. Emphasise that for a fair test it's important to do the same thing to each rock in turn.

A simple 'scratch test' would be a good starter. Invite the children to think about what to scratch with – another stone, a coin, a knife from the school kitchen, a ruler, a screwdriver or steel file, the end of a pair of scissors, a finger nail. These things could be discussed and evaluated. Once the children have decided on a 'scratcher' the tests and results could be recorded.

A further test could be to see what happens to the pieces of rock when they are put in water. Another check list could be drawn up:

ROCK AND WATER TEST
Did it stay solid?
Did it crumble?
Did the water soak into it?
Did it stay the same weight when wet or dry?
Did it change shape in the water?
(Ticks could be inserted after the testing)

ROCK NUMBER 1
Did it stay in one piece?
Did the water run off it?

Spread out a number of 'test collections' in the classroom. These can be both indoor and outdoor collections; in each one place an 'odd man out'. Working in groups, the children must find the 'odd men' and say why they don't fit. A simple example might be: coin, nail, screw, pebble, handkerchief, brick, wood.

NC coverage
AT3 Level 1a: *be able to describe the simple properties of familiar materials*
 Level 2a: *be able to group materials according to observable features*
 Level 3c: *understand some of the effects of weathering on buildings and on rocks*

b) What about metal and glass?

Many of the materials which are important to our everyday lives could be studied. Two are chosen here but teachers could extend this list or select entirely different materials.

Metal and glass offer contrasting possibilities for observing, discussing and testing.

Metal detectors!

Metals (aluminium, copper, lead, steel, brass, chrome, iron, zinc, tinplate) could be introduced to the children by asking them to do some detective work. Show them some metal objects – a spoon, a brass candlestick, the electric wires exposed from their plastic covering in a length of wire. Then ask them to search the classroom for other objects made of metal. They will make some mistakes, but eventually a list should be built up – door handle, hinges, small pencil sharpeners, keys, legs on the teacher's chair, filing cabinet, trowel for indoor gardening, etc.

Once the children have a better idea of what metals look like, invite them to feel them and again make comparisons between the feel of metal objects and other things like wood, cloth, plastic, etc. They might then move on to sound tests and compare how metal objects like filing cabinets, sweet tins, etc, sound when they are hit with spoons. Comparisons with other objects could again be made.

Once this indoor work has been completed the children could explore the school buildings and grounds and find more metal objects. They could also recall metal objects at home. Photographs of 'really big' metal things from newspapers and magazines could be added to the list.

As a result of these activities the children will gain an idea of the qualities of metals and how useful they are in our everyday lives. A final activity might be to do some testing to show metals are different. Divide the children into groups. Give each group a magnet and a variety of metals, and ask them to test and record which will respond to the magnet and which will not.

Glass around us

Moving from metals to glass, the danger of touching broken glass is perhaps the first thing that needs to be stressed. The first activity here could be to record the glass windows in the classroom, eg:

WINDOWS IN THE CLASSROOM

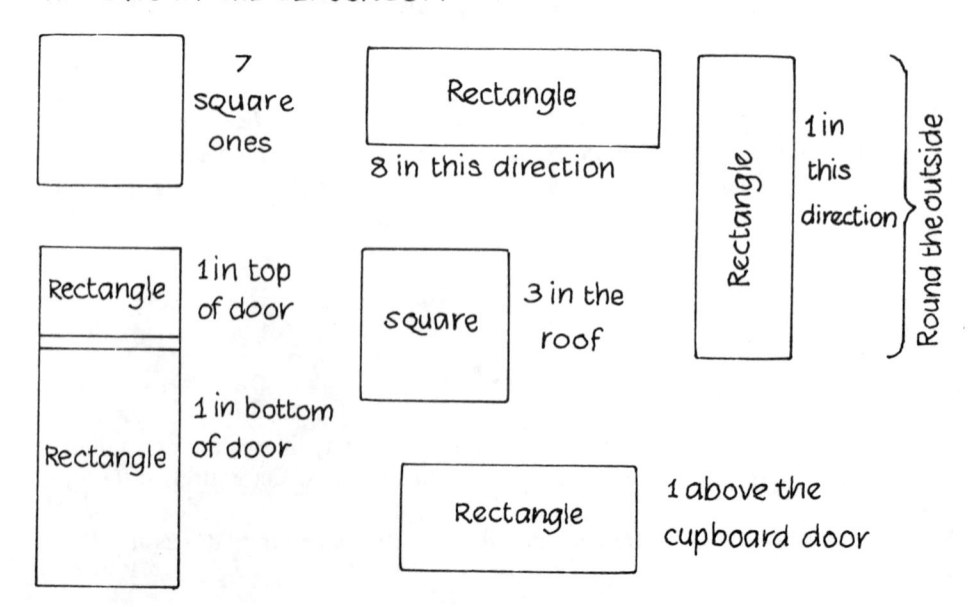

More about Materials 139

Focus children's attention by asking: *Is all the glass the same kind?* There may be some reinforced glass in the classroom ceiling or doors (ie glass with wire running through it) or frosted glass in a window. Once this information has been recorded a number of questions could be posed: *Why do we use glass? Why is the glass not all the same? What is the difference between ordinary and reinforced glass? Why is the glass in the roof reinforced? Is any window dirtier than the others? Is any window cleaner than the others? Could there be reasons for this? Are the roof windows dirtier than the side windows?*

After discussing these questions the children could do some 'fair tests'. One could be discovering how best to clean a window. Processes and materials could be tested here, and records of activities kept. (The teacher should be aware of safety considerations.)

The next lot of tests might be to find out how best to see a reflection in one of the windows – what conditions, material, situations are necessary. A taped commentary might be kept as a record here.

A final test could be to see what things are best for writing on glass, eg pencil, pen, magic marker, wax crayon, etc. Children could record their predictions and test results on a simple tick chart.

Questions to focus children's attention on other aspects and qualities of glass might be: *What other glass objects can we find? What happens when we look through a bottle full of water lying on a book? What happens when we look through somebody else's spectacles?*

Glass in the context of mirrors offers plenty of scope. For more suggestions see Topic 2 *Light, Colour and Shade*.

NC coverage
AT3 Level 2a: *be able to group materials according to observable features*
    Level 3a: *be able to link the use of common materials to their simple properties*
    Level 3b: *know that some materials occur naturally while many are made from raw materials*

c) Changing materials

The aim of this component is to let children have some experience of starting with a material in one sort of 'form', and by doing something to it, changing it to another sort of form.

Bring in a selection of powders, eg Polyfilla, gravy powder, coffee, sponge cake mix, ground rice, etc. Invite the children to investigate the substances and fill in their results in a simple chart:

POWDER	COLOUR	FEEL	SMELL
Polyfilla	grey/white	soft	none
Gravy powder	brown	softer	none

140 *Science Topics for Infants*

Ask the children to test the materials by adding first cold water, then hot water to a sample of each. (Work out the amount of water to add from the instructions for use.)

①
MATERIAL	MIXED WELL WITH COLD WATER	SMELL	RESULT
Polyfilla	Yes	None	went creamy then very hard
Gravy powder	No – had bits in it	None	watery mixture with bits in
Coffee	No – would not mix very well	A little	some powder still on top of water

②
MATERIAL	MIXED WELL WITH HOT WATER	SMELL	RESULT
Polyfilla	same as with cold water		
Gravy powder	mixed much better	Strong smell	ordinary gravy
Coffee	Yes	Strong smell	frothy top

During these tests the children will have experienced feeling, mixing, stirring, smelling and in some cases (with teacher guidance) tasting.

For the next activity, start with some more solid materials – a jelly cube, an Oxo cube, an Alka-selzer tablet . . . Again, using cold and then hot water, the children could test the materials and record their findings.

A final activity in this component could be to light a candle and observe the results. Ask the children to note the starting shape of the material, what happens when it is burning, the products and the final result. (Close teacher supervision is needed here.)

NC coverage
AT3 Level 2b: *know that heating and cooling everyday materials can cause them to melt, solidify or change permanently*

d) Using materials

Work in this component could involve making another collection of materials, which could then be used for experiments.

Fabric
Make a collection of as many pieces of fabric as possible – wool, cotton, nylon, silk, satin, PVC, leather. Invite the children to feel and smell the fabrics and discuss

More about Materials 141

their findings. Next introduce a sorting exercise, asking the children to suggest how the materials could be grouped – by colour, design, feel, strength. If the latter is the yardstick, pulling and stretching tests could take place.

The next test might be to discover *Which materials make the best dolls' clothes?* Some fabrics can be shaped more easily than others around a toy, attached by pins and glue. Other factors can also be considered: *Can the chosen material be seen through? Will it tear easily? Does it fray?*

Finally the fabrics could be made into a collage by sticking pieces onto a large piece of card to form a picture or an abstract design. Questions posed in this exercise might be: *Does the same type of glue work well for all of them? Do they match well in colour and texture? Which materials stand out as being most 'different'?*

Teachers who wish to develop this still further could consider experiments with printing (using wooden blocks, potatoes, etc) and more extensive sewing – joining materials to make life-size garments.

Wood

Observation and collection of wood could result in several activities:

a Make a collection of wood and wooden items: twigs, matchsticks, bark, branches, old clothes pegs, boxes, broom handle, rounders bat, toys, walking stick, blocks, chair, drawer, shelf, etc. Invite children to study the items – the feel, smell, weight, etc.

b Form groups and ask each group to go around the school and find four things made of wood. When the class is re-united it is interesting to see the range of items they have located.

c *Where and what do wooden things come from?* Ideally, some out-of-school work would involve looking at trees. Children could record what and where trees are in the local vicinity. If this is not possible, some books about trees, and photographs, would be a useful resource.

The collected bits and pieces of wood and offcuts could give children opportunities to try hammering in nails, sticking pieces together, putting in screws and so forth. (This will need a lot of adult supervision!)

Plastic

Once again sorting might be one of the first options:

PLASTIC THINGS WHICH ARE STIFF

Toys Lego
Toothbrush
Watering can
Lunch boxes
Dust pan
Hard balls

PLASTIC THINGS WHICH BEND EASILY

Combs
Empty drinks bottles
Plastic knives
Forks and spoons
Cups, Rulers

PLASTIC THINGS WHICH WE CAN SQUEEZE AND CRUSH

Carrier bags
Raincoats
Wrapping
Wellingtons

Another series of groupings could be according to 'rooms in the house where the object would be most likely to be used' or 'people most likely to use the object'. Simpler groupings could be made of colour, shape, size.

Some tests might then be done in groups or pairs to establish why plastic is such a valuable material in everyday use. Tests, and discoveries, here might include – doesn't break when dropped, will bend rather than snap, will withstand scratching, is waterproof, is light in weight.

NC coverage
AT3 Level 1a: *be able to describe the simple properties of familiar materials*
   Level 2a: *be able to group materials according to observable features*

Cross-curricular links

A reading from *The Iron Man* by Ted Hughes would be appropriate here. It could lead on to **creative writing** and **drama**, eg the puppet who came to life, the tin man (from *The Wizard of Oz*). Other stories and **music** could be linked, eg Andersen's *The Tin Soldier* and *The Sorcerer's Apprentice*.

Art, Craft and Technology have virtually unlimited opportunities here, particularly if a good collection of varied materials has been made. 'Construction' could range from the very small to the life size, and various materials could be painted or printed on. These activities could involve use of a wide range of implements – needles, brushes, hammers, staplers, etc.

This topic involves a lot of **maths** work; sorting, measuring and possibly weighing. There is also plenty of scope for **history** in considering how different materials have been used for things over the years, eg ships – wood to steel, toys – tin to plastic. **Geography** and **environmental issues** could be linked with trees; possibly destruction of the rainforests.

An interesting possibility for **RE** could be to focus on the Tower of Babel story – how difficult it is to use materials well in building, even without the problem of everybody speaking a different language.

18 Home and School

a) Looking
b) Touching and feeling
c) Smelling and tasting
d) Listening
e) Jobs and equipment
f) The journey from home to school
g) Improving our environment
h) More about homes

Anatomy of a topic

This topic is far-reaching in terms of work covered, and in terms of National Curriculum application. It probably needs a minimum of four weeks. Although it is not linked to a particular time of year, the topic does involve a lot of work in the playground, so it would be best to avoid severe weather. Several visitors who could offer useful contributions are suggested in the *Resources* section below.

Equipment

pencils
paper
card
classroom building
  equipment
stones
seeds
fruits
leaves
petals
tins
plastic bottles
classroom furniture and
  equipment

Resources

- Royal Society for the Prevention of Accidents produces a large amount of useful material. A catalogue of resources is available.
- Reckitt Household and Toiletry Products provide free material – including a kitchen information poster and a poster about germs in the kitchen.
- Domestos Hygiene Advisory Service offer free information about hygiene at home.
- Pictorial Charts Educational Trust produce a very useful poster: *The Built Environment* (Chart G109 76cm × 100cm).

Human resources who could be called upon for this topic might include: the Headteacher – who may well have plans of the school; an architect – who could comment on buildings such as schools and houses; the caretaker – who could tell

144 *Science Topics for Infants*

the children about his or her duties; and various people concerned with the home to school journey – a parent, a crossing patrol person, a police officer . . .

Pattern of a topic

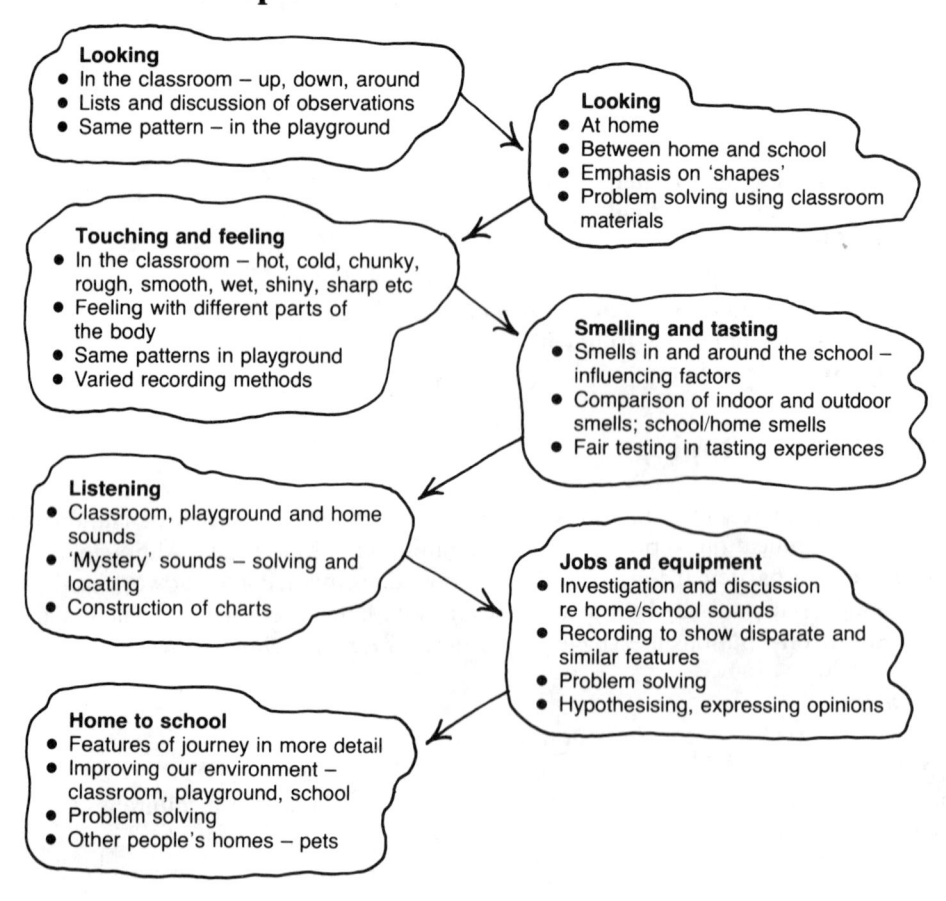

Looking
- In the classroom – up, down, around
- Lists and discussion of observations
- Same pattern – in the playground

Looking
- At home
- Between home and school
- Emphasis on 'shapes'
- Problem solving using classroom materials

Touching and feeling
- In the classroom – hot, cold, chunky, rough, smooth, wet, shiny, sharp etc
- Feeling with different parts of the body
- Same patterns in playground
- Varied recording methods

Smelling and tasting
- Smells in and around the school – influencing factors
- Comparison of indoor and outdoor smells; school/home smells
- Fair testing in tasting experiences

Listening
- Classroom, playground and home sounds
- 'Mystery' sounds – solving and locating
- Construction of charts

Jobs and equipment
- Investigation and discussion re home/school sounds
- Recording to show disparate and similar features
- Problem solving
- Hypothesising, expressing opinions

Home to school
- Features of journey in more detail
- Improving our environment – classroom, playground, school
- Problem solving
- Other people's homes – pets

a) Looking

This component could have as its core the theme of 'looking' in both school and home. *What do we see when we look around us?*

In our classroom

Looking up
roof, curtain rails, light shades, light bulbs, joins in the roof, wires, pipes, clock, skylight, hooks, rack for balls, blackboard

Looking down
floor, tiles, carpet, baskets of PE shoes, switches and sockets, doormat, shelves, chair legs, rubber ferules

Home and School 145

Looking around
radiators, tables, chairs, coat racks, 'Letterland' letters on the walls, pictures, windows, door, set of drawers, Ginn Maths 'Big Books', doll's house, pencil boxes

These lists could be compiled by the teacher from the children's observations. The whole activity could be turned into an 'I-Spy' game . . .

In the playground

Looking up
sky, clouds, trees, telegraph poles, telegraph wires, roof tops, chimney pots, TV aerials

Looking down
playground, stones, painted lines, holes, sinks, concrete, soil, paving stones, path, netball post bases

Looking around
windows, glass doors, walls, hedge, brick wall, netball posts, wire fence

After these records have been made, invite children to describe what they remember seeing when they look 'up, down and around' in their bedrooms, and outside their front doors. Observations could be listed and sorted.

Looking at shapes

Extend the 'looking' theme by inviting the children to look out for shapes at school and at home. They could then relate the shapes they see around them to some of the shapes of classroom building toys; eg

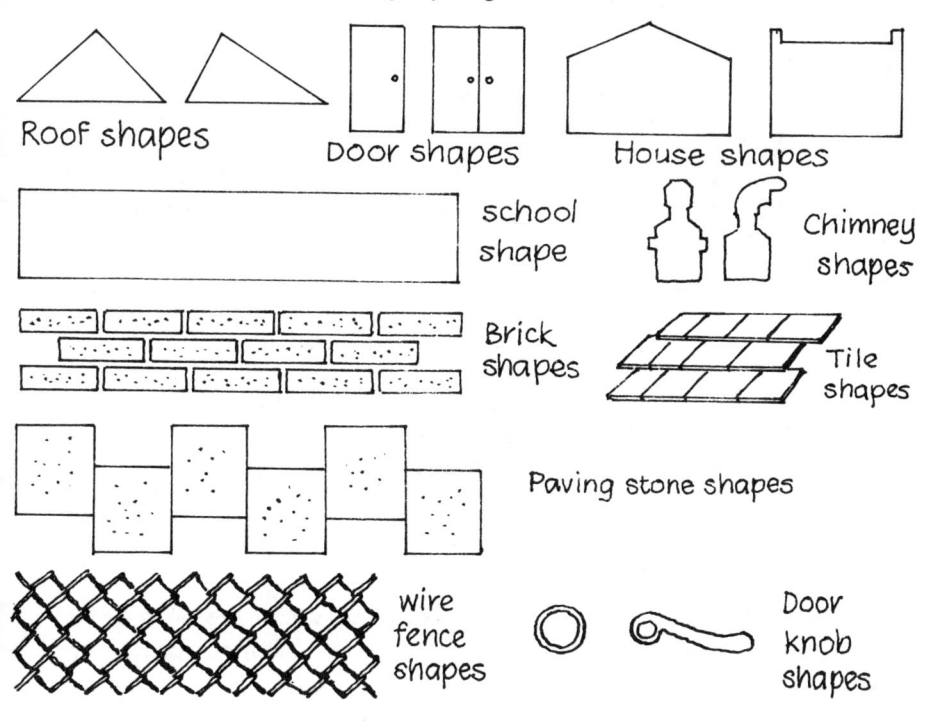

Roof shapes   Door shapes   House shapes

school shape   Chimney shapes

Brick shapes   Tile shapes

Paving stone shapes

wire fence shapes   Door knob shapes

146 *Science Topics for Infants*

A more specific study of shapes might include careful observation of windows, recording numbers and locations:

Most of the windows in our school are this shape.
But some are this shape:

These are the shapes of windows some people had in their homes

Some of us saw a window this shape on our way from home to school. It was in a church.

Talking about the sorts of houses the children live in could result in more recording:

We live in flats. Lee, Helen, Louise, Lisa.

We live in houses that are all joined together — Raymond, Martin, Steven, Nina, Ellen, Rajiv, Kevin

We live in a house joined on one side Melissa, Natalie, Lucy, Nusrat, Scott, Greg

We live in a house that stands by itself Kevin, Adam, Nicolas, Carlie

We live in a house that stands by itself and has no upstairs Jodie, Theodora, Janine, Gemma

Further work on shapes might focus on collecting things we can see when we look down outside. The 'shapes' included here might be varied stones, seeds, fruits, leaves, petals, tins, plastic bottles etc.

Having looked at homes, school and shapes at such length the children could then move on to some problem-solving work. They could use *Lego* and other classroom building materials to make some 'buildings' in the classroom. Questions asked in connection with this work could include: *How many different-shaped buildings can we make? Are all the roofs the same shape? Which are easiest to build? Which are the most difficult – and why? How does a tall building differ from a lower one? How tall can we build? How can we make a building stronger?*

NC coverage
AT3 Level 1a: *be able to describe the simple properties of familiar materials*
    Level 2a: *be able to group materials according to observable features*
    Level 3a: *be able to link the use of common materials to their simple properties*
    Level 3b: *know that some materials occur naturally while many are made from raw materials*

b) Touching and feeling

What can we feel?
Start by making a 'touching and feeling' chart related to the classroom. Ask the children to suggest a number of categories and then, in groups, test various surfaces and objects around the classroom and fill in the chart according to their experiences, eg

HOT – Radiator – Cloth on radiator
COLD – Floor – Window – Door – Window frame – Clock – Milk packets
CHUNKY – Pine cones – Stones
ROUGH – Door mat – Hessian – Desk top – Paper towels
SMOOTH – Jam jars – Tins – Plasticine
WET – Sink – Bottom of taps – Milk
STICKY – Glue – Part of the floor – Door handle
SHARP – Scissors – Pencil points – Staples
PAINFUL – End of pins

How do we feel?
The next piece of testing could be to compare the experience of touching things with different parts of the body. Work done to complete the 'touching and feeling' chart will have been done with the fingers. Encourage children to try feeling with elbows, with the bottom of feet, the backs of hands and, in groups, the back of the neck. The children's observations on these experiences could be recorded on tape. Once all the groups have done this, comparisons could be made.

148 Science Topics for Infants

Suggest the children try the same thing at home and report the findings back to the class.

Much will depend on the season and the weather here. Experiments could include: 'feeling' wind direction with a wet finger; feeling rain briefly with and without a hat; 'feeling' the temperature at different locations in the playground.

In groups or pairs, children could take turns to shut their eyes and feel a mystery object or surface, trying to guess what it is. There is a great deal of scope here for experiments with both large and small objects. Children could record guesses, reality and number of right answers.

NC coverage
AT3 Level 1a: *be able to describe the simple properties of familiar materials*
Level 2a: *be able to group materials according to observable features*
Level 3a: *be able to link the use of common materials to their simple properties*

c) Smelling and tasting

Children react very quickly – and violently – to an unpleasant smell. Useful work can be done to 'refine' this response and develop a more discriminating use of the sense of smell.

Everyday smells
(NOTE: Children should never be allowed to sniff glue, solvents or any other chemicals.)
The classroom offers many opportunities for encountering different smells: coats on a wet day; a polished floor; flowers; soap; old books . . .

This experience could be developed outside the school, eg *What smells come from the school kitchen before lunchtime? Where are they strongest? How far away do we have to go before the smell is lost? Does wind direction make a difference? What 'outside' smells are there?* eg cut grass; tarmac; car fumes . . . smells of the neighbourhood which impinge upon the school whether it be in an urban or rural environment. *Can we tell which direction the smells come from?*

This work in school could be supplemented by discussion of the many varied smells which the children encounter in and around home. Some interesting recording of such smells related to one group's experiences during the autumn term, both indoors and outdoors:

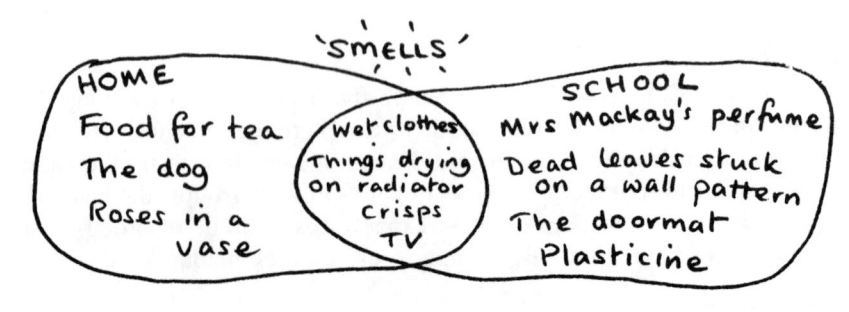

'SMELLS'

HOME
Food for tea
The dog
Roses in a vase

Wet clothes
Things drying on radiator
Crisps
TV

SCHOOL
Mrs Mackay's perfume
Dead leaves stuck on a wall pattern
The doormat
Plasticine

> THIS WEEK: STRONGEST OUTDOOR SMELLS
>
> Near home
> rockets and fireworks
> traffic smells
> piles of dead leaves in garden
> smells of Halloween lanterns
>
> At school
> the canteen
> the paint which was put on the fence by the garages

Tasting is an area where health and safety considerations should always be strictly enforced. There should be no tasting of anything picked outside. Within the school tasting would obviously be valuable in cooking activities and considerations of texture, sweetness, sourness, stickiness, smoothness could all be applied.

NC coverage
AT2 Level 2d: *know that some waste materials decay naturally but do so over different periods of time*
AT3 Level 2a: *be able to group materials according to observable features*

d) Listening

Ask groups of children to note six sounds they can hear in the classroom; then six in the playground. Help them to use a tape recorder to describe what they hear – some of the sounds themselves may also be heard. Young children often find a good descriptive word more easily if they are saying it rather than writing it down.

> GROUP 1's CLASSROOM SOUNDS
>
> The door opening – a rattling, squeaky sound
> Lots of people talking all at once – a jumbly sort of sound
> The tape recorder being switched on – click
> Louise sneezing – a funny, sploshy sound
> Someone using the class pencil sharpener – a grinding sound
> Opening the milk packets – a tearing, plopping sound

150 *Science Topics for Infants*

> GROUP 2's CLASSROOM SOUNDS
> Feet on the playground – made it sound very hard
> Cars going slowly up the lane – a jerky, rough sound
> The bell ringing indoors – it sounded a long way off and muffled
> The wind blowing – a noise you could make with your mouth
> Shouting – you wanted it to stop sometimes
> A big ball bouncing – if you shut your eyes you kept waiting for it to go again

Refinements to these listening exercises could be listing high and low sounds inside and outside; sounds which are constant or intermittent; sounds which give 'clues' when we have our eyes shut; 'mystery' sounds. The children could also do tests to find the sort of sounds different materials make; how far away they have to be before they stop hearing a sound; how easy or difficult it is to pick out one particular sound when there are lots of others going on at the same time. Charts of common sounds at home/in school could also be drawn up.

NC coverage
AT4 Level 1c: *know about the simple properties of sound and light*
    Level 3d: *know that light and sound can be reflected*

e) Jobs and equipment

Work on this component could start with some investigating and discussing. The end product of this might be a record of equipment used in school and at home, noting some things which are common to each, eg:

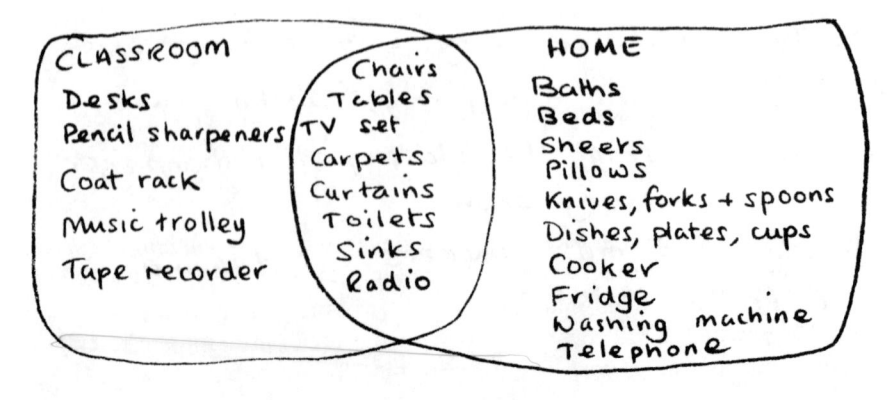

CLASSROOM	(shared)	HOME
Desks	Chairs	Baths
Pencil sharpeners	Tables	Beds
Coat rack	TV set	Sheets
Music trolley	Carpets	Pillows
Tape recorder	Curtains	Knives, forks + spoons
	Toilets	Dishes, plates, cups
	Sinks	Cooker
	Radio	Fridge
		Washing machine
		Telephone

Once this list has been drawn up useful work could stem from it. The children could produce some 'material' titles – Cloth, Metal, Wood, Plastic, Pot etc and then sort the various pieces of equipment into the right families.

They could then categorise the equipment into things which need power (radio, TV etc); things which depend on water (sink, toilets); and those which have to be dealt with manually (pushing music trolley, making beds etc).

From this could stem some problem-solving and 'fair testing' – *How do we reduce noise when we push the music trolley? At what distance is the tape recorder best for recording sounds? What kind of water/additive is best for washing dirty cups? What is the best arrangement of classroom chairs to watch TV?* (consider distance, number, situation of TV regarding windows, curtains etc).

Another possibility might be to consider a number of pieces of equipment in terms of which are most necessary. Scoring here might be done on a 1 to 10 basis. eg:

Bed	10
Radio	5
Cooker	10
Telephone	6
Video	4 etc.

NC coverage
AT3 Level 2a: *be able to group materials according to observable features*
      Level 3a: *be able to link the use of common materials to their simple properties*

f) The journey from home to school

Spread several large sheets of paper on the floor and sellotape them together. Invite the children to help prepare a simple 'Home to School' route map for the class. Locate the school at the centre and draw the map to a scale that will encompass all the children's journeys. The idea of scale and the convention of having North at the 'top' of the paper could be introduced.

Once the map is in place the children could describe and trace their particular routes to school. They could be marked with coloured lines, arrows etc on the map. A more sophisticated development would be to add 3D models/boxes etc at points the children consider significant.

Focus attention on safety aspects of the journey to school. *What things help us get to school safely? Where are they?* Help the children locate things like traffic lights, crossings, routes which avoid main roads, road crossing patrol points etc.

Other things which could be noted include the location of public telephones, street lights, fire hydrants, post boxes, waste bins, bottle banks etc.

152   Science Topics for Infants

NC coverage
AT2 Level 2a: *know that plants and animals need certain conditions to sustain life*
AT3 Level 3a: *be able to link the use of common materials to their simple properties*

g) Improving our environment

This is an ideal area for group work. As far as possible allow each group to choose its brief, do its 'fair testing' and work out its own conclusions. At the end of these activities each group could report back to the rest of the class and further discussion and exploration might develop.

Suggested group themes and developments might be:

Group 1 Classroom

How can we make our classroom more attractive?
- **Should we have more rules?** Making sure coats are hung up tidily; outdoor shoes put in racks; tables kept neat; litter put in waste basket; waste paper basket emptied when full; milk corner kept clean and tidy; sinks kept clean. WE can do all of these things.
- Additions. *Can we display more flowers/plants/objects brought in by us? Can we make posters to remind ourselves to keep the classroom attractive? What sort of pictures do we want on the walls?*
- Things WE can't do but which seem important: *What colour would suit the classroom best? Why? Could the floor area be made more attractive – carpets, some comfortable chairs? Are the bookshelves neat and well cared for?*

Group 2 Classroom

Is our classroom safe and healthy?
- Air. *Is the room warm/cool enough? Are there sufficient blinds and curtains? Do the windows open properly? Which are the best ones to open to let in fresh air?*
- Light. *Can we move the tables and chairs so that everybody can see properly? Where should the light come from? Can we avoid strong sunlight reflecting from our desks? Can we make the most of the classroom space?*
- Moving around. *Is it easy and safe to move around the room? Are there things which could be rearranged/moved to a better place/taken outside? Can everybody see properly when they are moving round?*
- Noise. *Can the classroom be made quieter? How? Are there noises we should get rid of altogether? What? How? What are the noises it is vital that we should hear?*

Group 3 Playground

How could we improve the playground?
- Additions. *Paint markings and boundaries; get more apparatus and seats? Are there places and opportunities for quiet, 'gentle' games as well as noisy, rough ones?*

h) More about homes

Many of the children will have pets, and there may also be a class pet. Invite the children to talk about the animals' homes (eg hutch, kennel, tank, cage. . . .). *Do they all have the same sorts of homes? What things do different animals need?*

Birds' nests

If possible, let the children look at or examine some real examples of birds' nests. If the real thing is not available, they could look at photographs and illustrations of nests. *What are they made of? How are they made?*

Make a collection of nest-building materials: dried grass, twigs, mud, stones, moss, straw, lichen etc. Encourage the children to experiment with these materials to make birds' nests. As they build, ask the children to discuss what qualities they think the nest should have (eg strength, stability, comfort . . .). They could devise ways of testing their nests for each of these qualities. *Where would the nests be safest?* The children could record the results of their observations and experiments in a number of ways.

Unusual homes

Ask the children for some examples of 'unusual' human homes (eg lighthouse, houseboat, tent, windmill . . .) and talk about what it might be like to live there. *What would it be like inside a lighthouse, where everything is round? Would you like to live in a tent? Why/why not?* and so on. The discussion could be extended to homes in other countries and how they are adapted to suit the environment (eg an Eskimo igloo, flat-roofed houses in hot countries . . .). The children could make models of some of these 'unusual' homes.

NC coverage

AT2 Level 2a: *know that plants and animals need certain conditions to sustain life*
    Level 2b: *be able to sort familiar living things into broad groups according to easily observable features*
    Level 2c: *know that different kinds of living things are found in different localities*

Cross-curricular links

Thinking about 'homes' offers considerable scope for **RE** and discussion of people who have no homes, eg refugees. A useful quotation is *'Yes, we have a home, but no house to put round it'*. The following is adapted from a prayer for a Canadian school:

154   *Science Topics for Infants*

> *This is our school*
> *Let peace dwell here.*
> *Let us be content,*
> *Let there be love here*
> *For each other,*
> *For life,*
> *For God.*

Maths is included in measurement, estimations, maps and plans. Maps and plans also include **geography** and work on direction. The **history** of schools or houses offers many opportunities for further work. **Technology** is involved in models and plans.

A topic in **art and craft** which would include many other subject areas might be a 'homes' frieze. This could be constructed with the 'inhabitants' on the background, and the appropriate house or home attached over each one, in such a way that it forms a 'flap'. Then children can be challenged to guess 'who lives where?' before lifting the flap to find out.

19 Festive Occasions

DIWALI
a) Bridges
b) Masks
c) Party time
d) Incidentals

EASTER
a) Decoration
b) Hats
c) Eggs
d) Out and about

MAY 1ST
a) Wood
b) Cushions
c) Shoes
d) Out and about

Anatomy of a topic

This topic takes three separate festive occasions – one for each term of the school year – and approaches them through science based activities. The three occasions are Diwali, Easter and May 1st.

Equipment
rulers
desks
straws
paper
books (same size)
clay
'scratching tools'
water
candles
cardboard rolls
torches
mirror

scissors
elastic bands
thread
string
turnips
knives
eggs
tissue/tracing/sugar/
    A4 paper
glue
staples
paper clips

onion skin
wax
water paints
matchsticks
bit of sponge
potato
cotton swabs
sticks
piece of wood
needles
sandpaper

156 *Science Topics for Infants*

various soaps	sellotape	various pieces of material
a spray deodorant	card	(cotton, satin etc.)
tights (clean/dirty)	cotton wool	shoes
air-tight containers	sand	binoculars
pencils	boxes	milk bottles
magic markers	dye	magnifying glass

Resources

Various books and records are noted in relevant components.

DIWALI

'Diwali' is the Hindi for 'row of lights'. This great autumnal Hindu festival offers tremendous scope for children's imaginations – 'the faculty for forming images in the mind, the artist's creative power' and some excellent 'starters' for scientific work.

a) Bridges

One of the most dramatic features of the Rama and Sita story is when Rama gets animals of all kinds to build a bridge to Lanka. When this is done Rama, Hanuman and his monkey army cross it to rescue Sita, who is being held captive there by Ravana.

Take two desks and separate them by a gap. Ask the children how this gap can be bridged.

a Can it be done with rulers? What if one ruler is too short? How can a ruler bridge be strengthened? What needs to be done to the ends if weight is applied to the middle?

b Can a bridge be made of straws? How many are needed? What other materials are needed? What has to be done with the straws?

c Can string be used for a bridge? How much is needed? What else is needed to construct a string bridge?

d Can we make a bridge with paper? How can we strengthen paper? (by folding, or 'corrugation')

From these ideas the children can investigate something a little more complex. Bridges built by counter-balancing (cantilevering) can be devised using very basic materials.

Get nine hard-backed books of exactly the same size. Start by setting up four of the books as follows:

Festive Occasions 157

1 and 2 are separated by a distance (X ⟵⟶ Y) which is twice the length of each book. The gap could be designated 'the river'.

Challenge children to use the five remaining books and, by balancing and adjusting them on piles 1 and 2, make a bridge which crosses the river. The bridge must balance and 1 and 2 can't be moved.

Although teacher guidance is needed to start with, the children quickly learn what is required.

The 'solution' looks like this:

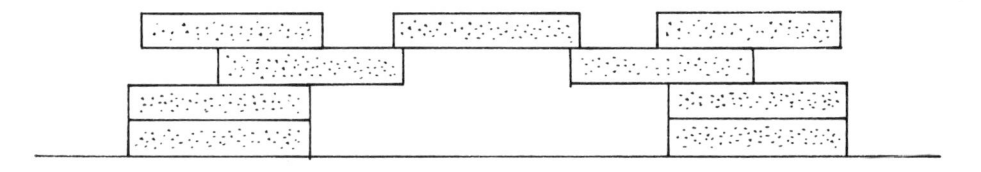

If the children have done work on expansion and heat (see Topic 9 Heat) this can be linked to bridges. During hot weather the metal parts of a bridge expand. *Why then do bridges not crumple and break?* (Small gaps are left in bridges when they are built to allow for this.)

NC coverage
AT3 Level 2b: *know that heating and cooling everyday materials can cause them to melt or solidify or change permanently*
Level 3c: *be able to link the use of common materials to their simple properties*

b) Masks

Another of the features of Diwali is disguise – Surpanaka, the ugly giantess who changes into a beautiful young woman; Ravana, the ten-headed demon king who becomes a deer and then an old holy man.

Disguise
The children can make some disguises of their own in the form of masks. A basic pattern helps here:

a Fold a square of whatever material is used in two.
b Draw in the mask outline:

c Cut out the mask shape, making holes for the eyes and for where string or elastic needs to be threaded through:

Much testing and adaptation stems from this basic format: *How can the mask be made to fit an individual? Is it held best by string or elastic? What is the best material to use? What would be best if the mask was to be painted? How and when is the painting best done?*

With this type of mask the wearer looks through holes. Some follow up work can be done on looking through 'other holes': curled up finger and thumb, top of a milk bottle, both ends of a pair of binoculars, a magnifying glass, a camera viewfinder, a small funnel, a toilet roll. The children can make other suggestions and record observations.

Turnip lantern
Cut the lid off a turnip and scrape out the inside to leave a strong shell. Eyes, nose, mouth and carrying holes can then be made:

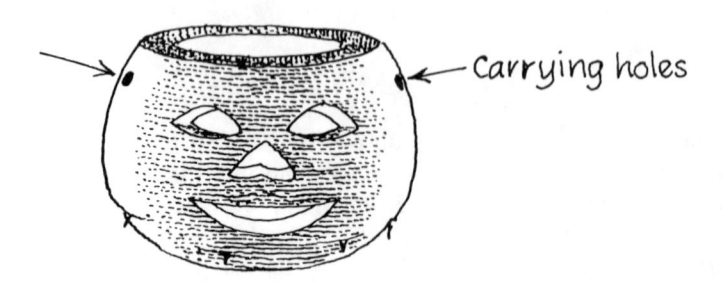

Insert a candle in the turnip; make a wire handle and cut two holes in the lid to allow smoke to escape. (A lot of adult supervision is needed in these activities!)

Scientific links to follow up include: *What is the best material to use for carrying the mask and why? Could we see the light if we had not cut eyes, nose and mouth holes? What could we see with the lid on and the candle out? Could we use anything else to create light inside the mask? What would happen to the lit candle if we carefully covered all the holes cut in the turnip?*

NC coverage
AT3 Level 3a: *be able to link the use of common materials to their simple properties*
AT4 Level 2d: *know that light passes through some materials and that when it does not shadows may be formed*

c) Party time

Diwali is a time of family visits, fairs, fresh starts, hope for the future. Its party atmosphere is reflected particularly in light.

Lamps
The traditional Diwali light is a clay lamp. With adult help, children can make lamps of their own.

a   Start with two ovals of clay, one slightly larger than the other.
b   Scratch the centre of each shape and stick the two together with slurry (a mixture of clay and water) so that the smaller oval fits into the larger one.
c   Turn up the edges at the tip of the inner piece and all round the outer to make a boat shape:

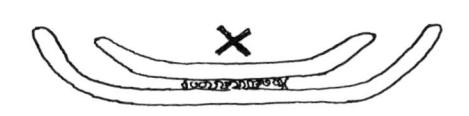

d   Insert a candle at point X.

Lots of questions can be linked to this activity: *How do we scratch the clay? What works best in doing the scratching? How do we make slurry? What proportion of clay/water gets the best results? When must the turning up of the edges take place? How do we 'fix' the candle?*

Tape recording of these questions and answers can be done as the work takes place.

A simple 'light show'
Teacher and children, can create their own 'visual spectacular'.

Requirements are several cardboard rolls, a large mirror, two or three torches. Prop up the mirror and get children to hold cardboard rolls at angles to it as follows:

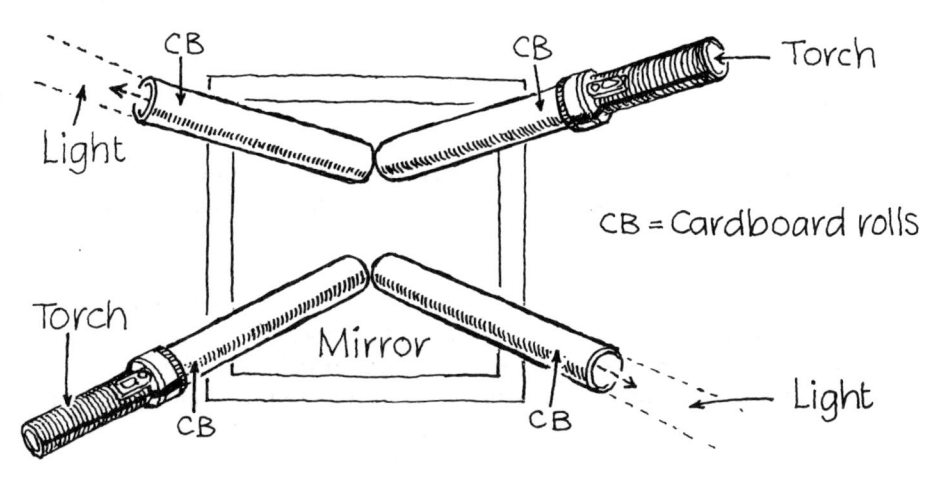

If the tubes are angled correctly, the light bounces off the mirror at the end of the tube which is receiving it, and is reflected back up the other tube.

This can provoke lots of thought and ideas about how to use light in an imaginative way for displays.

NC coverage
AT3 Level 3a: *be able to link the use of common materials to their simple properties*
AT4 Level 3d: *know that light and sound can be reflected*

d) Incidentals

Many stories are associated with Diwali. There is the theme of strength portrayed in Rama's ability to lift the giant golden bow which takes 150 men to pull on a carriage. Another theme is Krishna's victory over Naraka, the demon of Filth who never washed or cleaned. Then there is the story of Vishnu appearing as a giant big enough to step across the world in two strides.

These are all exciting themes for young children – and they also provide many science 'starters'.

Strength
A variety of questions can provoke scientific work here: *How can we test each other's strength? What do we need to make us strong? What muscles can we feel in our bodies? What can we tell about their movements? How can we combine our strengths? How can we improve our strength?*

Cleanliness
To commemorate the demon of Filth's defeat by Krishna, Hindus make an annual celebration of taking scented baths and wearing new clothes.

Some useful scientific work can stem from this. A selection of soaps can be experimented with – *Which gets the best lather? Has the pleasantest smell? Is most/least effective? How long does a piece of soap last if used X number of times a day? Does the water temperature make a difference?*

This work can be recorded in various ways and stimulate more questions: *Why do we need to wash? Why are we offensive to others if we don't? When do we most need to wash?*

This aspect of personal hygiene can be taken further by a simple experiment. Requirements are a deodorant, some clothing, two air-tight containers, and teacher preparatory work!

Place a pair of clean tights (or socks, T shirt etc) and a pair of dirty ones on a table. Spray each with a deodorant and get the children to smell them. Put both in separate air-tight containers for several days and then re-expose them: *How does the clean garment now smell? What about the dirty garment?*

The significance of 'masking' unpleasant smells as opposed to eliminating them by washing is then readily apparent to the children.

Size

Much work on this has been done in other topics (eg *Ourselves, Health and Hygiene*). The ideas of 'giant' strides, breaths, jumps etc and what is required to achieve them, how we feel after them, changes in our bodies etc can all be explored here.

NC coverage
AT2 Level 2a: *know that plants and animals need certain conditions to sustain life*
AT3 Level 3a: *be able to link the use of common materials to their simple properties*

Cross-curricular activities

Diwali offers many opportunities in **art** and **craft**. Hindu families often decorate floors at this time with patterns of coloured rice flour paste, various coloured and powdered chalks. The patterns are intended to attract the blessing of Lakshmi. Children could try their own decorative patterns and make some 'Happy Diwali' greetings cards.

The story of Rama and Sita has many episodes which might be acted out by the children. **Mime** accompanied by readings is very effective here.

RE could consider the similarities and differences of the great festivals of Diwali, Christmas and Hanukah.

Two inexpensive and invaluable books for use with this topic are *Diwali* from the Ginn 'Celebrations' series; and *Diwali* from the Macmillan 'Festival' series. Both books are full of facts and provoke many cross-curricular ideas.

EASTER

Several aspects of Easter lend themselves to scientific work.

a) Decoration

Episodes from the Easter story have been depicted by artists in a variety of media over the centuries. Showing the children some examples can lead on to some interesting experimentation and creative work.

Stained glass
The best way to introduce the idea of stained glass would be to take the children to a local church, cathedral or public building where there are some colourful examples. (NOTE: The technique of blending colour with glass was perfected in

162 *Science Topics for Infants*

the 11th century. Before that, window gaps in churches were sometimes covered with decorated vellum.)

Back in the classroom, the children can make their own stained-glass window, as follows:

a Make a 'template' window of thick card, with a number of apertures, eg

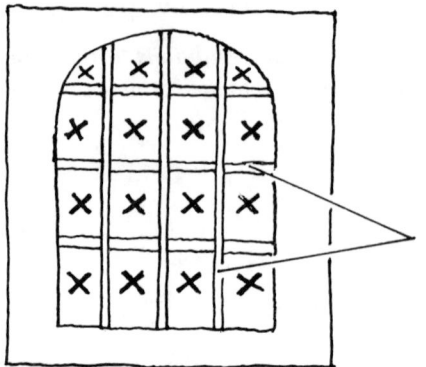

Sections marked **X** for use with different papers.

The thick card frames should be quite substantial.

b Give the children a variety of paper: tissue paper, tracing paper, A4 sheets, silver foil, sugar paper, cellophane . . . Ask them to try the paper to see which gives the best results (ie which is the most transparent).

When all the panels are filled in, the frame could be mounted on a real classroom window to give a 'stained glass' effect. Questions which might arise could include: *What sort of paper is best? Why is this? Would the window look as good if it were mounted on a wall? Why not? What do we need to make a stained glass window look good? Is artificial light as good as daylight?*

Making bigger

A reproduction of Leonardo da Vinci's famous masterpiece, *The Last Supper*, could lead on to work on scale. Leonardo's fresco was painted on the refectory wall of a monastery in Italy. The work took four years to complete, and has lasted for 400 years, with the help of careful restoration.

Begin with a problem-solving exercise: *Look at this picture. How can we make it big enough to put on the wall, but copy it exactly?*

One idea is to 'build the picture up' in sections, by copying each quarter carefully on to a separate piece of A4 paper. The children may need help to do this. When completed, the four pieces could be stuck together, and the enlarged picture mounted on the classroom wall.

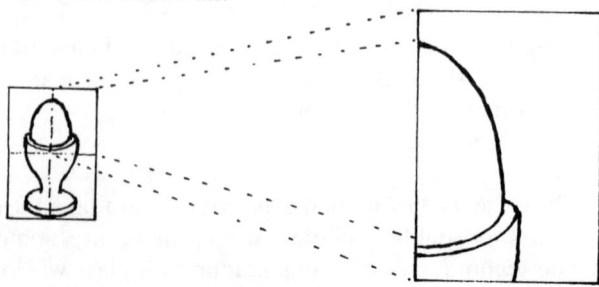

Festive Occasions 163

NC coverage

AT3 Level 3b: *know that some materials occur naturally while many are made from raw materials*

AT4 Level 2d: *know that light passes through some materials and that when it does not shadows may be formed*

b) Hats

'Easter bonnets' could provoke some useful work on hats. To start with, ask every child to bring a hat of some sort to school. These could be examined and a record made of their various features:

Brought by

HAT CHART	MEN'S	LADY'S	EITHER	LIGHT	HEAVY	HARD	SOFT	WARM	COOL	COLOUR
Martin	✓				✓	✓		✓		RED
Kassie			✓	✓			✓	✓		BLUE
Aliya		✓		✓				✓	✓	YELLOW
Lucy	✓				✓	✓			✓	GREEN

Once this work is complete, the children could discuss which of the hats in the collection would be best for a 'special occasion' like an Easter Parade. More sorting could then take place and two groups – one of 'special' hats and one of 'ordinary' hats could be made. The next question might be: *What makes a hat special? Could any of the ordinary hats be made special? How?* Provide the children with a variety of paper, card etc and fastenings (glue, staples, paper clips, sellotape). Invite them to try out different ways of making a 'special' hat.

NC coverage

AT3 Level 2a: *know that plants and animals need certain conditions to sustain life*

c) Eggs

The first thing most young children associate with Easter is probably eggs – of the chocolate variety. Give groups a real egg (warn them to hold it carefully!) and encourage them to examine it. *What does it feel like when you hold it? Is it rough or smooth? What does it sound like when you tap your finger against it? What can you hear or feel when you shake it?*

Break the egg onto a plate or saucer. *How is the outside different from the inside? What colours can we see when the egg is opened like this? What is the difference in the feel of the egg when it is broken?* Point out how easily eggs can be broken – *how are they protected?* Provide some examples of egg boxes. Points considered might be: *Are they all the same size? If not, why not? What shape are they? How is the shape important? How do they fasten? Are they easy to tear or break? Will they stand a lot of weight? What happens if they are dropped on the floor?* The children could try out some practical tests to find the answers to these questions, using hard-boiled eggs as test material. Records of the findings could be made. The next practical work could be for the children to devise some egg 'protectors' of their own.

Give each group an egg (hard-boiled) and a box. Provide a variety of packaging/packing materials, eg cotton wool, crumpled paper, sand, polystyrene, sellotape. Invite the groups to experiment by placing the egg inside and stuffing/sealing the box with different materials to find out which makes the most protective packaging for the egg. Each parcel should be tested:

a by dropping it from shoulder height
b by subjecting it to pressure (eg from a pile of books or heavy object)

Point out that for a fair test the groups need to drop the egg from the same height each time, and use the same amount of pressure. At the end, groups could record and discuss their results.

Remind the children how the inside of the egg was made more secure – by boiling it until it was 'hard'. Crack the shell of one of the eggs to demonstrate how different the contents are now. Having observed this 'change of state', invite the children to suggest other ways in which eggs are used and cooked: poached, soft boiled, scrambled, fried, used in cakes and biscuits . . .

Decorating eggs for Easter

Children enjoy decorating hard-boiled eggs. This can be done in a number of ways, and the following selection can lead to some interesting 'scientific' observations.

1 Draw pictures/patterns/faces on the eggs with magic markers or felt-tipped pens.
2 Smear the egg with glue and stick tiny pieces of fabric all over it.
3 Paint the egg with water colour wash. Before this is quite dry, add another coat, applying this with sponge, cotton wool, potato etc to give a mottled effect – like a wild bird's egg.

The following methods should be done or prepared by the teacher, with the children observing:

4 Dye the egg red. Draw a pattern on the egg in pencil and scrape away the dye from chosen parts of the pattern. (The colour red is traditional in Eastern European egg decorating. It symbolises blood and love.)
5 Wrap the egg in onion skins and boil for 10 minutes. Allow it to cool, then remove the skins to reveal a golden orange egg.
6 Drop hot wax onto the egg. When the wax is hard, place the egg in a cold-water dye. Allow the egg to dry, then peel away the wax to reveal the pattern underneath where the wax has resisted the dye.

NC coverage
AT3 Level 1a: *be able to describe the simple properties of familiar materials*
   Level 2b: *know that heating and cooling everyday materials can cause them to melt or solidify or change permanently*
AT4 Level 3c: *understand that forces can affect the position, movement and shape of an object*

d) Out and about

Eggs symbolize new beginnings and there are plenty of these about in the natural world when it is Easter and Spring. If at all possible an outing in the locality should be part of the project.

NC coverage
AT4 Level 1b: *know that there is a wide variety of living things, which includes humans*
   Level 2a: *know that plants and animals need certain conditions to sustain life*

Cross-curricular activities

John Wesley's famous poem is one good starting point for work in **RE**:

> Do all the good you can,
> By all the means you can,
> In all the ways you can,
> In all the places you can,
> At all the times you can,
> To all the people that you can,
> As long as ever you can.

Teacher and children could work on some simple ideas for **drama**, with themes like 'New beginnings', 'The good turn', 'We all need friends' etc.

Geography could include a look at the Holy Land, and **maths** will feature in activities which involve measuring. Background music could be drawn from *Jesus Christ Superstar* by Tim Rice and Andrew Lloyd Webber, and there are some good Easter hymns in the second volume of the BBC's excellent *Come and Praise* anthology.

May 1st

a) Wood

The old tradition of 'dancing round the maypole' was originally a pagan fertility rite, associated with tree worship. Although this information is clearly not appropriate for infants, linked traditions provide a useful starting point for work on wood.

The maypole was usually made of elm, ash, pine or birch. There may be opportunities for some basic 'tree spotting' in a nearby park or woodland. If the hawthorn is in blossom, point out that it was once thought to bring good luck, and used for decorating doorways and windows.

During this out-of-school work, make a collecting of sturdy sticks (being very careful not to damage any living trees or plants). Back in the classroom, the children could experiment with these basic 'walking sticks' in a number of ways. (If it is not possible for the children to do so, perhaps the teacher could collect some suitable sticks and bring them into school.)

Questions to answer include: *Why are walking sticks needed? Who by? What height or length should the stick be? How thick should it be? What does it need at each end? What is the best way to smooth the stick? What tools or equipment could be used? What happens if the stick is too bendy? How can we test the strength of the sticks?*

Encourage the children to devise their own tests to find the answers to these questions. It may be useful to bring in a couple of 'real' walking sticks for comparison.

Moving on from walking sticks, another feature for discussion and experiment would be to test various pieces of wood collected for their relative hardness and decide which were best for very simple 'carving'.

NC coverage
AT3 Level 1a: *be able to describe the simple properties of familiar materials*
    Level 2a: *be able to group materials according to observable features*

b) Cushions

In days gone by, some villages raised funds to pay for their May Day celebrations by making a display of 'cushions' which invited contributions. These 'cushions' were made out of clay, with flowers stuck in them to form patterns or pictures.

Help the children make some miniature cushions of new clay and experiment with pressing various objects (twigs, lego, pencils, paint sticks etc.) into the clay to make patterns. This could then lead on to the making of proper cushions.

Provide varied scraps of fabric; foam or flock for stuffing; scissors, needles, thread, sandpaper. As the cushions would be made up of patches of material sewn together, the first 'test' could be one of strength. A chart could be drawn up to indicate the results:

MATERIAL STRENGTH TEST

	Easily torn by hand	Easily 'clicked' by end of scissors	Result when rubbed with sandpaper	Result when trampled on
Cotton				
Satin				
Silk				
Wool				
Plastic				

The children could be asked to suggest other ways in which the material could be tested for its strength and durability. Material for cushions needs to be stretched over the 'stuffing'. Invite the children to devise stretch tests for the various materials. Two charts could be used here:

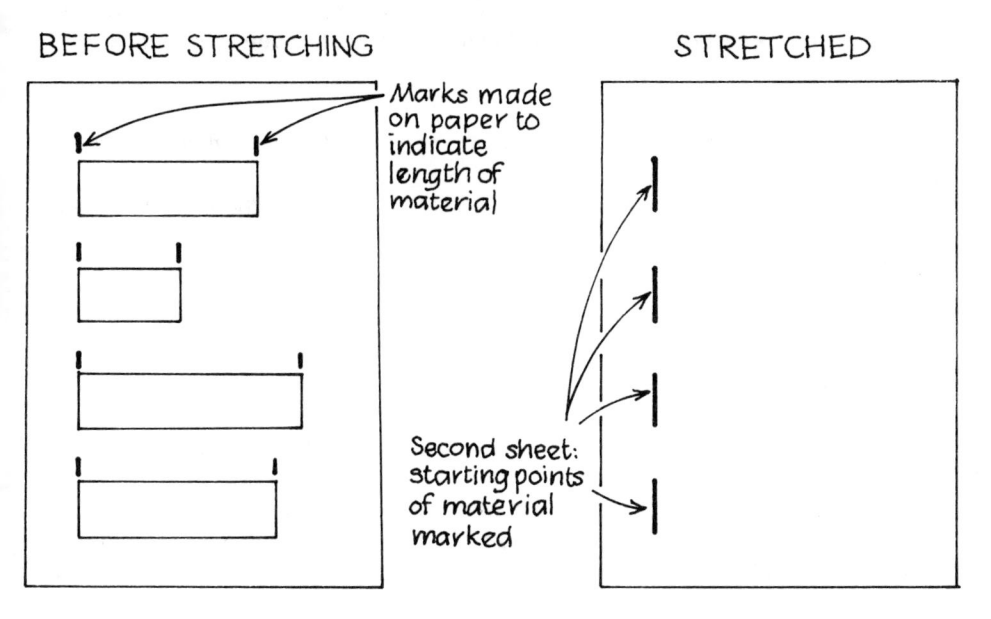

BEFORE STRETCHING   STRETCHED

Marks made on paper to indicate length of material

Second sheet: starting points of material marked

On the second piece of paper or card the 'starting point' of the material could be marked. Then while one child holds firmly at this end, another could pull the material to see the amount of stretch. A third child could mark this off on the paper. When these two tests have been carried out, the best suited pieces of material could be sewn together to make one or two cushions.

NC coverage

AT3 Level 2a: *be able to group materials according to observable features*
    Level 3a: *be able to link the use of common materials to their simple properties*
AT4 Level 3c: *understand that forces can affect the position, movement and shape of an object*

c) Shoes

What do we need, to dance well round the maypole? Among the many possible answers here the teacher should ultimately aim for 'comfortable shoes'.

This could give rise to some interesting class work. *Are all our shoes the same length and width? Are all our feet the same size? What happens if a shoe is too big? What happens if a shoe is too small?*

The children could split into groups; large pieces of card could be spread on the floor and each group could trace round, first, one foot of each member, secondly one shoe of each member. Both should be right feet. When this has been done the feet and shoe outlines could be cut out with owner's names being written on the back. 'Shoes' and 'feet' shapes could then be exchanged with another group who, without looking at the names, have to match the two together. The children could also try on shoes which are too big/too small and describe their experiences.

NC coverage

AT4 Level 1a: *be able to name the main external parts of the human body and a flowering plant*
    Level 1b: *know that there is a wide variety of living things which includes humans*

d) Out and about

Take the children on a tour of the local environment and ask them to assess the 'quality' of the streets, landscape etc.

This assessment could be done according to a predetermined set of criteria. The educationalist Eric Midwinter devised a 'streetometer' for assessing the quality of streets in Liverpool. He chose ten features, each of which was given a 'score' from 0 – 10. The features were: fresh air, noise, safety, landscape, condition of buildings, wirescape, floorscape, parking, advertisements, litter.

This example could be simplified or adapted to suit local circumstances and knowledge. Encourage the children to suggest aspects of the environment they would like to assess.

Back in the classroom, the children could discuss their assessment and perhaps offer suggestions as to how the local environment might be improved.

NC coverage

AT2 Level 2c: *know that different kinds of living things are found in different localities*

Level 2d: *know that some waste materials decay naturally but do so over different periods of time*

Level 3b: *know that human activity may produce changes in the environment that can affect plants and animals*

Cross-curricular links

This topic offers many possibilities for **art and craft** work – a 'collage' of a village celebrating May Day in times past is one possibility. Simple **drama** and **role-plays** could be enacted around traditional themes (Robin Hood featured in many May Day plays).

For **music** the English Folk Dance and Song Society (Cecil Sharpe House, 2 Regent's Park Road, London NW1) offers useful information on folk songs. Appropriate classical music includes Stravinsky's *Rite of Spring*, *From Bohemia's Woods and Fields* (Smetana), music for *A Midsummer Night's Dream* (Mendelssohn) and *Waltz of the flowers* by Tchaikovsky. **Technology** and **maths** come into the work on wood. The **history** of May Day can be explored.

20 Calling Earth

a) Season chart
b) Weekly chart
c) Light chart
d) 'Where has the water gone?'
e) The moving shadow
f) How far?
g) Soil
h) Air, air everywhere

Anatomy of a topic

This topic differs from the others in this book in that it seeks to provide eight components which can be referred to at any period of the year and linked to work in one of the more specific topics.

Equipment
card
rulers
pencils
coloured pencils
chalk
sellotape

tape recorder
rounders post and base
   (or something similar)
soil
sieves
various pieces of rock

jam jars
boiled egg
milk bottle
taper

a) Season chart

Make a durable seasonal chart out of stiff card, as follows:

SEPT	OCT	NOV	DEC	JAN	FEB	MAR	APR	MAY	JUN	JUL	AUG
AUTUMN			WINTER			SPRING			SUMMER		

This can be mounted in the classroom as the basis for a year's work on seasonal change. Teacher and children could fill up the columns in a variety of ways. One possibility is a colour code:

ORANGE: warm enough for no coats
RED: hot enough for shirts and dresses
BLUE: need raincoats
BLACK: need warm coats

This would build up a simple and colourful record of the year's weather. Other seasonal patterns could be recorded according to local circumstances. The 'country year' is one starting point:

January, February, March – hedging, lambing, ploughing
April, May, June – sowing, cultivating, haymaking
July, August, September – market garden crop harvesting, cereal harvesting, haymaking again
October, November, December – fruit harvesting, ditching, tool and machine maintenance

NC coverage
AT4 Level 1d: *be able to describe the apparent movement of the Sun across the sky*
Level 2e: *know that the Earth, Sun and Moon are seperate spherical bodies*
Level 3e: *know that the appearance of the Moon and the altitude of the Sun change in a regular and predictable manner*

b) Weekly weather chart

Groups of children could take turns to record the weather for a week at a time, and their observations could be recorded on a chart, as follows:

RAIN	25ml					
SKY	☁☁					
WIND	W →N→ E S					
VISIBILITY	FAIRLY CLEAR					
TEMP	11°C					
	MON	TUES	WED	THURS	FRI	

Readings at 9:30am each day

Again, these records could be kept for a year.

NC coverage
AT4 Level 1d: *be able to describe the apparent movement of the Sun across the sky*
Level 2b: *understand the meaning of hot and cold relative to the temperature of their own bodies*

c) Light chart

In order to appreciate the differences in light throughout the year a monthly set of readings could be taken and recorded. Measurements could be taken at 9am and 3pm every Monday of each month at school. Colours could be used to record different light intensity: BLUE – very bright; GREEN – bright; BROWN – dull; GREY – dusk; BLACK – dark.

NC coverage
AT4 Level 1d: *be able to describe the apparent movement of the Sun across the sky*
Level 3e: *know that the appearance of the Moon and the altitude of the Sun change in a regular and predictable manner*

d) Where has the water gone?

Factors that influence the temperature of an environment include: time of day; season; wind speed; aspect and altitude; solar radiation. While these are clearly too complex for young children to grasp, some interesting early experience can be linked to this. Explorations could include:

- What clothes do we wear when it's hot? When it's cold?
- How do animals behave in the sunshine? In the shade?
- What happens to a puddle on a warm day?

Help the children place a marker (chalk or string) either around a puddle or at its longest/widest points. Examine the puddle at regular intervals and repeat the markings. The children's comments could be recorded on tape at each stage.

NC coverage
AT4 Level 1d: *be able to describe the apparent movement of the Sun across the sky*
Level 2b: *understand the meaning of hot and cold relative to the temperature of their own bodies*

e) The moving shadow

A rounders post and base (or any other long, straight piece of wood with a base) can provide the basis for a variety of sun/shadow experiments. (NOTE: Warn the children that they must on no account look directly into the sun.)

Place the post in a clear, sunny space in the playground. Draw a chalk line along its first shadow. Continue to draw chalk lines at significant times – playtime, dinner time, home time. The 'movement' of the shadow indicates the movement of the earth around the sun, ie if the shadow is in front of the pole the sun must be behind it. If the same weather conditions prevail the next day and the chalk marks are examined, they will tell when it is playtime, dinner time etc. This topic could be extended in a number of directions:

- Work on the history and use of sundials (the National Maritime Museum, Greenwich, London has a very good collection).
- *Would the shadow stick be any use in the dark? How could we measure time in the dark?* (One ancient idea was to mark off a slow-burning candle in hour-long intervals.)
- Human shadows – *Can you make your shadow do what you do? Can you be each other's 'shadows'? Can you escape from your shadow? When is your shadow biggest/smallest?*
- Some children might like to find out more about the sun. The sun is a star, but it looks much brighter and bigger than other stars because it is nearer the earth. The sun is 150 million km from earth. It has a surface temperature of 6000 degrees centigrade. Light travels at 300 000 km per second, and light from the sun takes 8.3 minutes to reach earth.

NC coverage
AT4 Level 1d: *be able to describe the apparent movement of the Sun across the sky*
　　　Level 2d: *know that light passes through some materials and that when it does not shadows may be formed*
　　　Level 3e: *know that the appearance of the Moon and the altitude of the Sun change in a regular and predictable manner*

f) How far?

Enormous distances are beyond the comprehension of very young children but a scale/paper construction can involve them practically and give them some understanding of the relative sizes and distances in the universe.

1. Draw a circle 4 millimetres across on a small piece of paper (earth).
2. Put a dot on another piece of paper (moon).
3. Draw a circle with a radius of 16.5 centimetres (sun).
4. Take these into the playground (or large hall) place the 'moon' 9.5 centimetres from the 'earth' and the 'sun' a further 26 metres away. This will give the children

some idea of how far away the sun is, and how big it is compared with the earth and the moon. Further discussion could lead on to consider night, and the movement of the earth and moon round the sun. (I have seen this type of presentation suspended aloft in a school dining hall. It was both dramatic and informative!)

NC coverage
AT4 Level 2e: *know that the Earth, Sun and Moon are separate spherical bodies*
Level 3e: *know that the appearance of the Moon and the altitude of the Sun change in a regular and predictable manner*

g) Soil

Soil is made up of particles of rock; humus; water; nutrient ions; air; organisms. The following experiments help demonstrate the composition of soil:

1 Sieving

a Collect a range of sieves, graded from a large mesh to a very fine mesh.
b Get the children to sieve a sample of soil through each mesh in turn, starting with the largest. Collect the results of each sieving.
c Encourage the children to examine and compare the sieved particles. Useful words include: sharp, gritty, pebbly, smooth, soft, damp.
d Remind the children to examine anything left in the sieve.

2 Settling

a Put some soil in a jar with a lid.
b Add water and shake hard.
c Allow the jar to stand undisturbed for two or three days.
d Invite the children to examine the layers shown in the jar when everything has settled down, and discuss what they see. They could draw the different layers.
e Any material floating on the top could be taken out and examined through a magnifying glass. This is humus.

NC coverage
AT3 Level 2a: *be able to group materials according to their observable features*
Level 3c: *understand some of the effects of weathering on buildings and on rocks*

h) Air, air everywhere

Talk and observations about air and its importance could be followed by a dramatic demonstration. This is based on the question: *Can we see what air does?*

Prepare a peeled boiled egg and a milk bottle. Place some newspaper in the bottom of the milk bottle and set it alight with a taper. As soon as the flames die, insert the egg in the mouth of the bottle. Because the burning paper has used up the air in the bottle more has to be sucked in to replace it. This suction draws the egg into the bottle too.

NC coverage
AT4 Level 3c: *understand that forces can affect the position, movement and shape of an object*

Useful Addresses

Information and resources:

Animal Information Bureau   c/o Chris Henwood, 179 Pavilion Road, Worthing, West Sussex BN14 7EP
AVP   School Hill Centre, Chepstow, Gwent NP6 5PH
BP Educational Services   PO Box 5, Wetherby, West Yorkshire LS23 7EH
British Rabbit Council   Purefoy House, 7 Kirkgate, Newark, Notts NG24 1AD
British Telecom Education Service   PO Box 10, Wetherby, West Yorks LS23 7EL
Cat Action Trust   PO Box 1639, London N8 4RY
CLEAPSS School Science Service   Brunel University, Uxbridge UB8 3PH
Countryside Commission   John Dower House, Crescent Place, Cheltenham, Glos GL50 3RA
Dogs' Home, Battersea   4 Battersea Park Road, London SW8 4AA
Domestos Hygiene Advisory Service   50 Upper Brook Street, London W1Y 1PG
Electricity Council   Public Relations Department, 30 Millbank, London SW1P 4RD; Film and Video Library 15 Beaconsfield Road, London NW10 2LG
Ford Motor Company   Public Relations Department, Eagle Way, Brentwood, Essex CM13 3BW
Friends of the Earth   26–28 Underwood Street, London N1 7JQ
Galt Educational   Brookfield Road, Cheadle, Cheshire SK8 2PN
GSN Software Ltd   50 Stamford Street, Ashton-under-Lyme, Lancashire OL6 6QH
Harbutts' Educational Services   Freepost, Bretton Way, Bretton, Peterborough PE3 8BR
Keep Britain Tidy Group   Bostel House, 37 West Side, Brighton, Sussex BN1 2RE
LDA   Department F, Duke Street, Wisbech, Cambs PE13 2AE
MESU   Unit 6, Sir William Lyons Road, Science Park, University of Warwick, Coventry C14 7EL
National Dog Owners' Association   39–41 North Road, Islington, London N7 9DP
National Society for Clean Air   136 North Street, Brighton, Sussex BN1 1RG
Noise Abatement Society   PO Box 8, Bromley, Kent BR2 0UH
Pedigree Petfoods   c/o Denise Reed, Education Liaison Officer, Pedigree Petfoods Education Centre, National Office, Freeby Lane, Waltham-on-the-Wolds, Melton Mowbray, Leics LE14 4RS
Philip Green Educational Ltd   112a Alcester Road, Studley, Warwickshire B80 7NR
Philip and Tacey   North Way, Andover, Hants SP10 5BA
Pictorial Charts Educational Trust   27 Kirchen Road, London W13 0UD

Reckitt Household and Toiletry Products Reckitt House, Stoneferry Road, Hull HU8 8DD
Rickitt Educational Media Ilton, Ilminster, Somerset TA19 9HS
RoSPA (Royal Society for the Prevention of Accidents) Cannon House, The Priory, Queensway, Birmingham B4 6BS
RSPB (Royal Society for the Protection of Birds) The Lodge, Sandy, Beds SG19 2DL
RSPCA (Royal Society for the Prevention of Cruelty to Animals) Education Department, Causeway, Horsham, West Sussex RH12 1HG
SAPS c/o Maggie Bolt, Homerton College, Hills Road, Cambridge CB2 2PH (Tel: 0223 411141)
Technology Teaching Systems Ltd Penmore House, Hasland Road, Chesterfield S41 0SJ
The Slide Centre Ilton, Ilminster, Somerset TA19 9HS
Viewtech Audio Visual Media 161 Winchester Road, Brislington, Bristol BS4 3NJ
WATCH 22 The Green, Witham Park, Waterside South, Lincoln LN5 7JR

Places to visit:
Dinosaur Museum Icen Way, Dorchester, Dorset DT1 1EW
Ffestiniog Railway Museum Harbour Station, Porthmadog, Gwynedd
Lakeland Motor Museum Holker Hall, Cark-in-Cartmel, Cumbria
London Transport Museum Covent Garden, London WC2E 7BB
National Maritime Museum Romney Road, Greenwich, London SE10 9NF
Natural History Museum Cromwell Road, South Kensington, London SW7 5BD
Science Museum Exhibition Road, London SW7 2DD
Thames Barrier Visitors' Centre Unity Way, Woolwich, London SE18 5NJ

Index

Addresses 176
air 174
air and water 103
air movement 18, 124, 130
air pollution 91
anatomy of a topic ix
animals 42–49
AT cover vi–vii
attractive classrooms 152

Battery power 27
behaviour 40
birds 49
birds' nests 153
bird table 48
bird warmth 58
blow football 130
body differences 33
bottle banks 92
bouncing balls 19
bricks 75
bridges 156
buildings 73–80
building houses 79
building materials 74
bulbs (electric) 28
burst pipes 61

Calendar location of topics vi–vii
camera 85
candles 70
carbohydrates 110
changing materials 135, 139
chimneys 75
Christmas crib 30, 31
circuits 28
cleanliness 160
clocks 3
clothes 57
class body surveys 34
codes 84
cold 56–64
    feeling 57
    testing, measuring, observing 57
colour 8–16
    experiments 9

colouring foods 11
making 11
profile 10
using 11
comparing materials 135
computers 85
conductors 28
cross-curricular activities 7, 15, 23, 31 41, 49, 55, 64, 72, 80, 86, 94, 104, 116, 122, 133, 142, 154, 161, 165, 169
cushions 166

Danger 27
decibels 92
deserts 66, 71
dinosaurs 121–122
disguise 157
distances 173
Diwali 30, 31, 156
dogs 44
drinking 99
dryness testing 74, 79

Earth 170
Easter 161
eating 33
echo 5
eggs 163, 164
electricity 24–31
electrical 'lucky dip' 31
electric plug 25, 27
energy 17–23
enlarging 162
environmental care 87–94
everyday movements 126
everyday smells 148
exercise 110
eyes 33

Fabric 140
family 33, 40, 43
fats 110
favourite foods 35
feeling things 144
festive occasions 155–168
fingerprints 34

Index 179

flashing lights 83
floating and sinking 96, 103
flowers 51
flower search 53
flower vocabulary 54
foghorns 83
food for energy 110
food preservation 109
food we eat 108
friction 125
frost 58

Glass 75, 135, 137, 139
gravity 125

Habitats 47
hands and feet 34
hats 163
heat 65–72
    and cooling 67
    and illness 67
    conductors 71
    electricity 26
    feeling 66
    keywords 66
    moving 66, 70
health precautions 107
home 143–154
how we breathe 39
how we eat 38, 39
how we feel 147
human/pet family size 48, 49
hygiene and health 105–116

Ice cube tests 61
icicles 60
improving environments 152
incubator 47
individual assessment record sheet viii
individual differences 118

Jobs/equipment at home/school 144, 150
journeys from home to school 144, 151

Kaleidoscope 15

Lamps 159
life cycles 43
life in water 92, 102
life long ago 118
lifting 125
light 8–16
light chart 172
lighthouses 83
light show 159
listening to classroom sounds 149
litter 88, 89
living creatures 118
living things (animals and birds) 42–49
living things (plants) 50–55
local environment projects 93

log piles 132
long distance communication 83
'look alikes' 44
looking 144
    at home 144
    at school 144
    in the playground 144
    'up and down' 74
lungs 39

Machines 74, 77
magnetic Santa Claus 31
magnetism 29–31
masks 157
materials 134–142
material strength test 167
May 1st 166
megaphones 4, 83
messages/storing information 81–86
metal 135, 137, 138
minerals 110
mini-beasts 132
mirrors 9, 13, 14
mortar 76
movement 124, 132
moving 123–133
    a chair 124
    creatures 124, 132
    ourselves 126
muscles 34
music 1–7
musical paper 3
musical sounds 5

Neglect 90
nesting 48
Noah's Ark 104
noises at home/school 144
noise in buildings 75
noise pollution 92
noise reduction 93
noise surveys 93
noise warnings 93
now and then 117–122

Old people 120
organisation of book iv
our bodies 33
ourselves 32–41

Passing messages 82
people 118
personal hygiene 160
perspex 75
pets 43, 45, 120
places to visit 177
planning and recording iv
plans 80
plant collection 51
plant growth 51

plaster 76
plastic 141
pollution 90
popular infant topics xii
power 18
powered movement 21
practical points iii
profile cards 36
Prometheus 72
proteins 110
pulleys 78
pulling 125
pulse 110
puppets 124
pushing 125

Radio 84
rainbows 12
record of a topic x
re-cycling waste 91
rest 111
rocks 136
rolls and wheels 124, 129
roots 52
route maps 151
rubber 75

St Catherine 72
school 143–154
science curriculum guide xi
season chart 170
seeds 52
see-saws 127
senses 33
shade 8–16
shadows 12, 173
shape 18, 43, 46
shiny surfaces 13
ships 104
shoes 168
size 161
skin 33
slates 75
smelling 37, 109, 144
smoke signals 83
snowballs 61
snowflakes 59
soap 160
soil 174
sorting food 38
sound 1–7
speaking tube 3
speed of human movement 40
spinner 128
'stained glass' 161
stones 136
stream visits 91
'streetometer' 168
strength 160

sun 9
surface work 20, 102, 127
swings 127
switches 29

Tape recorder 85
tasting 37, 149
teacher demonstration 22
teeth 113–115
telephone 84, 86
temperature 58
thermometer 62
'thinking cards' 25
tiles 75
timelines 119
tin can telephone 3
toilets 103
tools 74, 77
topics related to AT 1 v
touching 37
toys 128
tracks 43, 47
turnip lantern 158

Unusual homes 153
using materials 135

Vehicle movement 18
vibrations 2
video 85
vitamins 106

Warmth 62
washing 96, 98, 103
waste 90
water 95–104
waterproof 97
water sources 100
water vapour 100
weekly weather chart 171
wet or dry 96
wheels 21
windmills 131
windows 146
wires 25
winter 63
wood 75, 141, 166